D1237288

SATIRE

SATIRE

Spirit and Art

George A. Test

UNIVERSITY OF SOUTH FLORIDA PRESS
TAMPA

Library of Congress Cataloging in Publication Data

Test, George A. (George Austin)
    Satire : spirit and art / George A. Test.
      p.   cm.
    Includes bibliographical references and index.
    ISBN 0-8130-1087-X
    1. Satire—History and criticism.   I. Title.
PN6149.S2T4   1991
809.7—dc20

                                 91-464
                                 CIP

The University of Florida Press is a member of University Presses of Florida, the scholarly publishing agency of the State University System of Florida. Books are selected for publication by faculty editorial committees at each of Florida's nine public universities: Florida A&M University (Tallahassee), Florida Atlantic University (Boca Raton), Florida International University (Miami), Florida State University (Tallahassee), University of Central Florida (Orlando), University of Florida (Gainesville), University of North Florida (Jacksonville), University of South Florida (Tampa), University of West Florida (Pensacola).

Orders for books published by all member presses should be addressed to University Presses of Florida, 15 Northwest 15th Street, Gainesville, FL 32611.

The Lord who sits enthroned in heaven
    laughs [the rulers and kings of the
    earth] to scorn.

—Psalms 2:4

The world of fools has such a store,
    that he who would not see an ass,
    Must abide at home, and bolt his door,
    And even break his looking-glass.

—Unknown

CONTENTS

PREFACE

This book assumes that what is commonly referred to as satire is merely the aesthetic manifestation of a universal urge so varied as to elude definition. Expressions of the urge are found in myths and rituals of many cultures at various stages of existence. Expressions are found in informal and utilitarian representations as well as in serious nonliterary artistic forms. This assumption and the attempt to accommodate its multiform expressions have led me to a concept of satire that is not tied exclusively to literary terminology as a way of discussing its nature. This in turn releases me from relying solely on the work of literary scholars and critics as the source for understanding the phenomenon. I have gladly accepted the contributions of anthropologists, psychologists, folklorists, and others not directly concerned with literary satire. I hope I can demonstrate that their research and interpretations contribute to an understanding of satire whatever form its expression takes. The major antecedent for this approach is Robert Elliott's *The Power of Satire*, although Alvin Kernan's article "Aggression and Satire: Art Considered as a Form of Biological Adaptation" encouraged me to be receptive to extraliterary sources. Elliott's and Kernan's willingness to use concepts from outside traditional literary criticism provides insights that have not yet been exploited.

Given my eclecticism, it would not do to adopt a particular psychological or critical theory as a controlling frame or guiding motif. Neither Freud, Fish, nor Frye will be found to dominate the approach of this book. There is nothing from Paris, Prague, or Geneva, no Bloom or Eco or Marx of some contemporary critical scheme. Rather this book attempts to establish some roots of the presumed universal urge in myths and rituals, analogues and parallels. This context provides a more useful basis for defining the nature of satire than an exclusively literary approach. So the first four chapters attempt a definition of satire as well as a description of its roots in myth, ritual, and folk behavior.

The final four chapters deal with the artifice of satire, but without restricting coverage to literature. These chapters address such questions as: What is the nature and place of verbal aggression in satire? What can replace such vague and ambiguous terms as *parody, burlesque,* and *travesty* commonly linked to satire? Is the irony of satire special and what does it contribute?

The emphasis throughout is on four elements basic to satire—attack or aggression, laughter or humor, play, and judgment. This emphasis is as close to a theory of satire as the book will come. I argue neither for a single cause, effect, function, or purpose to account for satire, nor for correction, catharsis, or revelation.

Since the concept of satire has not in my view ever been successfully fused into a unitary theory, I have expanded the approach hoping that a satellite dish may capture what a microscope has failed to. This approach then proceeds under the assumption that satire occurs in a variety of cultures, in various forms of development, in various periods of history, at various levels of society, and in disparate manners of presentation, hence the resistance of the material to a unitary theory.

Introduction

The emotions that are thought to give rise to satire are generally acknowledged to be the least admirable human emotions—anger, malice, hatred, indignation. The emotions that satire is said to evoke are likewise emotions that make most people uncomfortable—shame, anger, guilt, anxiety. The view of humanity in satire is a negative one—tumultuous, crowded, aggressive, cynical, pessimistic. This is because the characters in satiric novels and plays are universally unattractive, the kind we would not want to get stuck next to on an airplane trip—greedy, stupid, self-centered, arrogant, self-righteous.

It is not surprising, then, that satirists have been the most persecuted of artists—exiled, silenced, sued, physically attacked. And yet satirists and persons who study satire have never been able to agree about what it is that satire is supposed to accomplish. Perhaps that is because satire in the minds of many people is misunderstood. And why not? There is no accepted definition of what satire is, only general dictionary descriptions. Students of satire cannot always agree on which works are or are not satiric or whether some forms (parody, invective) are or are not satiric. Satire may appear in a work as one of several attitudes present, sometimes dominant, sometimes subordinate, a source of further confusion. Confronted with satire, people may accuse the satirist of being unfair, of not presenting a positive alternative, of being cynical, of being pessimistic.

The lukewarm or unfavorable reactions to satire and the confusion about it are easy to explain. Who wants to read about or see more wickedness and foolishness? Newspapers and television news supply enough. It may be that just as humans have a physical pain threshold, they have as well a psychological pain threshold. Confronted with examples of folly and evil, we can take only so much. Or the view of humanity that satire presents may not square with what we believe or want the world to be. Or it may be that confronting the foolishness and immorality that humans are capable of causes us, like the human eye that shrinks from too much light, to turn aside. It is as if such behavior reminds us of the potential for similar behavior in ourselves. Its subject matter then may be unsettling, baffling, upsetting. All this is complicated by one element of satire not yet mentioned, yet essential to it: laughter. Satire often laughs at very serious things and that is not acceptable to many people. What people think is funny is not simply idiosyncratic but determined by varied and complex conditions. Satire may combine slapstick humor, wordplay, and subtle irony in such a way that an audience will have trouble keeping up with the changes. That satire may make fun of people or events in the news or may ridicule other types of literature, art, or mass media means that to understand some satire, the audience has to bring certain kinds of information or knowledge, a demand that cannot or may not always be met. Because of this often close tie to matters outside itself, satire tends to go out of date very quickly and become as dead as last month's news. So what satire is about and the way it goes about presenting it makes it a strange and confusing thing at times.

And yet devotees of the *Doonesbury* comic strip and Nicole Hollander cartoons, fans of George Carlin, readers of Art Buch- wald, or Mike Royko, admirers of the novels of Ishmael Reed, Peter DeVries, or David Lodge, while they may not necessarily share each other's tastes in satire, testify to the fact that satire is alive and well. It is alive and thriving because it springs from feelings and behavior that are shared by many people. As with any other kind of expression it may become at times esoteric and obscure, but that does not change the fact that at its core satire speaks for and to human beings of diverse backgrounds.

The core of satire can be understood by approaching it on an everyday level. Everybody at some time or other becomes angry at or indignant with people or events. When that happens, we may grin and bear it, or we may let our feelings out—immediately or later, at the person or event or at a substitute. One form of letting out our feelings is to attack verbally the conditions so as to change them or at least to get rid of the anger and frustration. We call people names, we insult them, we are sarcastic, we mock them, we ridicule them. Few people go through an entire day without at some point doing verbal damage to someone or some group or some event, another driver on the freeway, rock musicians, tax cheaters, shyster lawyers, politicians, Communists, fundamentalists, high taxes, high prices, stupid TV commercials (a pleonasm?), graffiti on the subways. When people misbehave or break rules that go against what we accept and share, we may become aggressive. When our personal wishes and expectations are violated, even though they may not be generally shared by others, we may become aggressive. And finally if an event, action, or attitude threatens our self-esteem, we may become aggressive (Marcovitz). A common and basic way to express aggression is verbal.

We have a variety of ways that we can be verbally aggressive against others and the events around us. A sarcastic letter to the editor about poor community services, to a business concern about a product falsely advertised, to a political representative whose vote on an important issue we disagree with—such letters if strongly worded and richly sarcastic are a form of verbal aggression. We wish to upset and disturb certain people and perhaps make them see the error of their ways. Or we may tell a person to his or her face that we dislike something that person said or did. But since we like the person or have to continue to work or live with the person, we say our piece kiddingly, half-seriously, jokingly. That way the person may not become as annoyed as if we had attacked point-blank and directly. We put into practice the cliché that many a true word is spoken in jest. But perhaps the person who angered us is too powerful—a boss, a teacher, a parent—to be attacked even kiddingly. In that case when they are out of sight we may mimic with slight exaggeration the manner of speaking, the tone of voice, what was said: Get to work on time from now on. Spit out that chewing gum. Clean up your room this minute. The most violent kind of verbal aggression is of course name-calling. Anything about the person or group that will insult or degrade is spewed out: racial or ethnic epithet, family background, appearance, character, politics, religion. But people are not the only things that we vent our aggressions on. We may find a piece of music, a TV commercial, a book, a film, a slogan silly or stupid. To make it even sillier or more stupid we put new words to the song, we change events or characters, anything to make fun of the original. As we mock the way our boss talks, so we may mock the way something is written, exaggerating, changing in order to make the thing ridiculous.

Verbal aggression can be a harmful act, perhaps more harmful than some acts of physical aggression, since contrary to the childish chant, sticks and stones may break bones—but they mend. Words said in anger, however, may produce lifelong hurt. But sometimes a strange thing happens to verbal aggression on its way to the target: it picks up laughter and turns playful. Kidding, sarcasm, exaggeration, mimicry may be humorous and involve a kind of playfulness. They may of course be as baleful as verbal aggression itself, but depending on how they are confected, they can produce a diverting kind of instruction. Persons with verbal facility and imagination can compose a take-off on an office memo, mimic the company president at an office party, think up funny but true names and descriptions, all the while making a point without offending anybody—too much. Verbal aggression can therefore be very simple and direct (and perhaps harmful), but it can also be complicated, indirect, entertaining, and useful. In any case, by observing the behavior of those around us and of ourselves, we can conclude that verbal aggression, sometimes with elements of humor and playfulness in it, is extremely widespread.

When the behavior that has been described above as spontaneous, commonplace, perhaps almost instinctive, becomes formal, thoughtful, and artful, it is called satire. The creator of the satire may be reacting to the same kind of events, actions, and attitudes that stimulate the ordinary, nonsatiric person, but he or she will do so in a more elaborate and skillful manner, producing what may be called a kind of aesthetic aggression, an artful attack, a creative assault.

Satire, whether literary or oral, whether expressed through ceremony or in art forms, seems to occur in all societies and conditions of humanity, in all periods and stages of history, at all levels of society. While it may seem reckless to assert that satire is universal, there is much evidence of the extremely widespread existence of various forms of housebroken, usually verbal, aggression. Satire in its various guises seems to be one way in which aggression is domesticated, a potentially divisive and chaotic impulse turned into a useful and artistic expression.

But to describe satire as merely housebroken, cowed, or restrained verbal aggression is to sell satire short. Satire allows opportunities for creative verbal and formal gyrations that transform aggression into a social and artistic expression that satisfies peoples' need for play and humor. Satire then is in part an expression of playful aggression, a sportive assault.

A final and crucial element in this arrangement, and the most troublesome, is that of censure or disapproval. Satire ultimately judges, it asserts that some person, group, or attitude is not what it should be. However restrained, muted, or disguised a playful judgment may be, whatever form it takes, such an act undermines, threatens, and perhaps violates the target, making the act an attack. The infinite ways in which these elements—attack, judgment, play, and humor—are blended make satire the fascinating subject that it is.

It is most fascinating, of course, if we see satire as a legitimate aesthetic expression of basic human emotions—anger, shame, indignation, disgust, contempt—emotions that are aroused by universal human behavior—stupidity, greed, injustice, selfishness—(need we go on?). Even though in the hierarchy of most human value systems these emotions and such behavior are frowned upon, the emotions that generate satire will be expressed willy-nilly, and its subject matter shows little tendency to disappear from human activities. Love, honor, compassion, joy, grief, and other widely admired and acceptable emotions are given voice in all forms of art, but expressions of equally widespread emotions—anger, contempt, for example—tended to be shunted to the periphery, ignored and even denigrated. In literature the epic and tragic drama are traditionally viewed with greater favor than satiric comedy or the mock epic. The general attitude toward satire is comparable to that of members of a family toward a slightly disreputable relative, who though popular with the children makes some of the adults a bit uncomfortable (cf. the critical evaluation of *Gulliver's Travels*). Shunning is out of the question as is full acceptance. What to do?

Surely there is some metasignificance here. If Emerson's idea in "Worship" that "people seem not to see that their opinion of the world is a confession also of character. We can only see what we are . . ." is true, then the existence of satire creates a bind. We may not agree with the world according to the satirist—we can accept or reject any artistic expression on that basis—but to denigrate the satiric urge and its expressions as somehow inferior is to reveal something about who and what we are. What works and satirists are valuable, what the canon of satire is, even eventually what literature is, is a construct based on time, place, ideology, critical system, even "the whirligig of taste." The point is not to invert any literary or aesthetic value system but to argue that satire deserves as much of a break as any other artistic expression. Unruly, wayward, frolicsome, critical, parasitic, at times perverse, malicious, cynical, scornful, unstable—it is at once pervasive yet recalcitrant, basic yet impenetrable. Satire is the stranger that lives in the basement.

1

Elliott's Bind; or,
What Is Satire, Anyway?

More than a quarter of a century has passed since a leading scholar of satire came to the conclusion that attempts to define literary satire had come to an impasse. Robert C. Elliott, having surveyed the history of the meaning of the word and the "staggering diversity of forms, tones and materials" of satire, concluded that no single definition covered such diversity. Several years after Elliott's article Leonard Feinberg in an article, "Satire: The Inadequacy of Recent Definitions," fastened down the lid on the coffin constructed by Elliott.[1]

Noting that the word *satire* had been used to "designate a form of art and a spirit, a purpose and a tone," Elliott suggested that an approach that attempted to extract "family resemblances" from works of satire that were widely accepted as such might provide concepts and criteria for deciding on borderline examples and new cases. Despite the conclusions by Elliott and Feinberg the most prestigious collection of essays on the subject, *Satire: Modern Essays in Criticism*, edited by Ronald Paulson in 1971, proceeded as though neither Elliott nor Feinberg had ever raised the question. Even though articles and books on satire continue to appear, none has confronted the problem raised decades ago.

Why has there been no attempt to determine the nature of satire? Certainly one deterrent is the "staggering diversity" of forms, tones, and materials that a critic faces in European literature from Martial to Wyndham Lewis, to use Elliott's examples. Isolating common properties, even agreeing on a canon, was in Elliott's estimation "impossible." He was looking, as a good literary scholar, only at literature. But there has been increasing recognition that satire is by no means confined to written forms. It is found in other art forms from the graphic arts to music to sculpture and even dance. Therefore, works by Gillray, Daumier, Gilbert and Sullivan, Erik Satie, Moussorgsky, sculpture out of the Dada and Pop Art movements, and the dances of the late Myra Kinch and much else must be assimilated into the concept of satire. The mass media teems with satire from such stand-up comics of the 1950s as Mort Sahl and Lenny Bruce (Hendra) to newspaper columnists Art Buchwald and Art Hoppe, from rock music to cartoon strips, and films from around the world too numerous to mention. Despite their ephemeral nature, folk expressions in graffiti, almanacs, office memoranda, and mock festivals ought not be excluded from consideration. In many preliterate cultures satire occurs in trickster tales and oral poetry. Satire cannot therefore be restricted to the multifarious literary forms that baffled Elliott, nor to any media, nor to any culture at whatever stage, even though literary satire constitutes the most highly regarded and most fully examined segment of the phenomenon. Elliott's and Feinberg's conclusions about the lack of a satisfactory definition of the term was unknowingly an admission of the inadequacy of an exclusively literary approach, an unintended indictment, in effect, of a method. If their conclusions are valid, we have what we can call Elliott's bind: the attempt to erect a structure (that is, a definition or description of satire) with the wrong tools. Intention, affect, content, form, rhetoric—all literary concepts—have not done the job. What is needed is a broadening of the concept of satire itself and the use of ideas that are not exclusively literary.

Elliott himself had already taken a step toward broadening the concept of satire, thereby providing a way out of his bind. In his study *The Power of Satire: Magic, Ritual, Art,* he isolated the ritual curse behind direct attack satire and other satiric diatribes, thereby opening up an area of ritual and folk manifestations on which one "tradition" of satire rests. This tradition is related to other ritual forms which include satiric duels such as Eskimo drum matches (mentioned by Elliott), calypso exchanges, the black American "dozens," Scottish and English flyting matches, and others uncovered by anthropologists in Africa, India, Indonesia, and elsewhere. The satiric impulse is also basic to the "joking relationships" first noted in Africa but since revealed as part of the cultures of native

American groups, youths in Turkish cities, rural communities in Spain and Italy, and workplaces of England and the United States. These ritualized exchanges based on status are interpreted as resolving tension and potentially debilitating differences through sarcasm, jokes, and other forms of humorous aural aggression.

Other ritual forms can be discovered in symposia of ancient Greece and the courts of medieval Europe, in the behavior of court fools, and the ceremonial buffoons of native American tribes of the southwest United States. A surprising variety of societies have allowed certain persons the freedom to mock other individuals and social institutions in rituals. From earliest times the same freedom has been claimed by and granted to social groups at certain times of the year, as can be seen in such festivals as the Saturnalia, the Feast of Fools, Carnival, and similar folk festivals in India, nineteenth-century Newfoundland, and the ancient Mediterranean world.

Thus, satire, whether literary or media-induced, rests on a substratum of ritual and folk behavior that continues to the present. Celebrity roasts, mock festivals, and the performances of comics in nightclubs and in concert bear witness to ritual contexts in which satire still occurs. These and other folk and ritual manifestations can lead to a greater understanding of satire in general, as Elliott's investigation of the curse led to insights into the tradition of direct-attack satire. Restricting the study of satire to its literary manifestations has in effect cut off satire from its roots. Literary forms have not been able to confine or define satire, nor can satire be restricted by or to any other medium. Satire for better or worse is beyond any medium in which it occurs.

Since the first attempt to define satire by Quintilian down to the present, scholars and critics have been hobbled by restrictions, some self-imposed, others imposed by the nature of things. Quintilian had in mind in his definition only the hexameter medley of the sort "invented" by Lucilius and continued by Horace and in Quintilian's own time by Persius, even though he acknowledged the existence of the prose and verse mixture usually referred to as Menippean satire and had read Aristophanes' plays. He could not have known about, and if he had would probably not have admitted to the canon, Sumerian wisdom literature and beast fables, later including Aesopian fables, parts of the biblical *Book of Proverbs,* the early Greek invective-laden drama disliked by Aristotle, and the poetry of Hipponax and Archilochus. An even

fuller catalogue would include such examples of antiliterature as
the mock epics *Margites* and the *Batrachomyomachia,* and the mock
tragedies, the satyr plays. Satire, from the beginning of recorded
literature, existed in its own right as a spirit expressed through
other forms (poetry, drama, fables) as well as a reaction to literary
forms (epic, drama). No classification by genre or kind has ever
succeeded in fully integrating these diverse forms into a system.
Aristotle and Cicero did not include satire in their systems. Horace
included it as a special kind of poetry, a concept continued by
Quintilian, Philip Sidney, and John Dryden.

Other approaches have fared no better. Expressive criticism (the
term is M. H. Abrams's), which attempts to get at a literary work
through its creator, runs into serious problems with satire. The
understandable willingness to identify the satirist with his or her
persona and his or her characters has plagued satire since, in all
probability, the original curse itself. Thus Juvenal, Swift, Philip
Wylie, H. L. Mencken, and numerous Elizabethan satirists have
been viewed as moral monsters, their attacks interpreted as direct
clues to their persons. Because of the passionate and partisan nature
of their attacks, satirists have long been forced to seek refuge
behind anonymity and allegory, further complicating the problem
of getting to and at the creator. Satire has in fact served all kinds of
masters, good, bad, and indifferent. It served anti-imperialism in
Twain's "To the Person Sitting in Darkness," anti-Protestantism
in Mencken's "The Hills of Zion," and an anti-British attitude in
Ireland in Swift's "A Modest Proposal." In the Communist
magazine *Krokodil* satire serves the Russian state; in the poems of
Roy Campbell and Ezra Pound it cohabits with fascism. Attempts
to explain satire through the motivation, personality, or influence
of the satirist have produced insight into and understanding of
works and their creators but little in the way of widely accepted
understanding of satire itself.

Pragmatic criticism—interpreting and evaluating a work by its
effect—has been another pervasive way in which satire has been
approached. Satirists themselves have been the most persistent
advocates of this approach. Seeking to justify the unpleasant task of
dealing unpleasantly with the seamy or foolish side of life, they
have tended to claim that they are only telling the truth, thereby
redeeming their audience, punishing fools and sinners, and
generally setting the world right. In short, satire reforms. Unfortu-

nately, such a change, if it occurs at all, doesn't last long, and satirists are sometimes forced to back away from remedial claims for their art. Swift mocks such claims when he has Gulliver lament that the account of his travels has failed to mend the world. Pope in a letter to John Arbuthnot (2 August 1734) admits the ineffectiveness of "General Satire in Times of General Vice." He asks, "If a man writ all his Life against the Collective Body of the Banditti, or against Lawyers, would it do the least Good, or lessen the Body?" The other recourse, "some . . . hung up, or pilloried, . . . *may* prevent others" (italics added) and so he concludes, "I hope to deter, if not to reform." The same reservation is echoed in the career of Jules Feiffer. Starting as a satirist bent on reform, he has admitted that in the face of dramatic nonreformation he has come to enjoy his work more but expects less of it. A cautionary note remains, he admits, but the urge to reform is no longer the primary force. Despite the lack of evidence to support the claim of reform through satire, both the justification and convention persist, as a short tour through articles and reviews in scholarly journals and popular magazines and newspapers will show.

But no critical approach is adequate when some members of an audience do not "get" what the satirist is doing, as has sometimes been the case with columns by Art Buchwald, which have been taken quite literally by readers, some even being sent to Moscow as reports on conditions in the United States (Murphy, 52). This reaction is similar to that of the man who after reading *Gulliver's Travels* attempted to find Lilliput on a map. Mencken's "history" of the bathtub, a take-off on the little-known-facts news article once beloved by editors on slow news days, was a satiric hoax that no one got. Mencken eventually confessed to the hoax in order to keep his "factual" account from getting into record and history books. Mencken was himself not immune to the failure to "get" satire, missing the ironic humor in Thorstein Veblen's *The Theory of the Leisure Class.* Thus may intertextual astigmatism make fools of us all. These examples are benign compared to the fate of Daniel Defoe, whose ironic *Shortest Way with the Dissenters* (1702) landed him in the pillory and bankruptcy when dissenters and churchmen alike were offended by his seeming to advocate violent measures against those outside the Anglican Church. A recent extreme case was that of Naji al-Ali, a Palestinian cartoonist, condemned by various countries and political groups in the Middle East, deported by Lebanon and Kuwait, who died in London 29 July 1987, a month after he was shot in an assassination attempt. Naji al-Ali attacked religious fanaticism and the absence of human rights in the region, among other excesses, no matter where they occurred. The satirist in some cases then not only subverts the idea that art is a representation or reflection of life but sometimes reduces to absurdity attempts to understand it on those terms. Furthermore, neither the persons nor groups represented in satire, their behavior nor their ideas are unique to satire, nor is the manner of representation. The relation of satire to literature is both parasitic and symbiotic, as it is to life itself. Thus attempts to deal with it only as a literary phenomenon with intention and effect will wonder what to do with those who, like the owl in Mark Twain's "Blue-Jay Yarn," don't see the point of it.

Satire, then, is a phenomenon more extensive than its literary manifestations, even though they are among its most memorable examples. It can neither be fully understood nor explained by the tools and approaches of literary criticism. (This may account for the marginal status accorded to satire in most literary theories, since they are unable to accommodate the multifarious kinds of satire, even when their theorists overcome their aversions to the aggressive and sometimes unconventional nature of the stuff.) So the satirist and his or her purpose, satire and its affect, and the content and form of satire may be put aside as ways to understand and explain satire.

Satire may more easily be explained and understood as a bent possessed by many human beings but more highly developed in some individuals and expressing itself in an almost endless variety of ways. The aptitude may reveal itself in a mock nursery rhyme or a mock office memo, in a take-off on a film genre, in graffiti, in poetry or fiction, in mock opera, in newspaper cartoons, in a seemingly endless number of ways. The faculty, if that is the best word for it, will in its essence manifest itself in an expression or act that in various ways combines aggression, play, laughter, and judgment. Each of these acts or expressions is a complicated form of behavior particular to an individual but also influenced by a person's social environment and ultimately by that person's culture. What triggers aggression? What causes laughter? How does one play and why? And what values determine judgments? These questions are answered by a person's culture, which teaches what is permitted and what is not. In addition to determining what may cause emotions, a culture also determines how people may behave when experiencing a particular emotion. Violent physical aggression may be expressed in football, boxing, and hockey but not in family relationships. A person may laugh at the twitches of Rodney Dangerfield but not at someone suffering from Parkinson's disease. But no one is obliged to enjoy the physical violence of sports or laugh at the twitches of Mr. Dangerfield. Hence each individual defines more specifically how he or she will act within the range allowed by the culture. The same is true from culture to culture, none identical despite some overlapping in causes and reactions. If all of this seems obvious from observing various cultures and eras, it should also be true of how aggression, play, laughter, and judgment manifest themselves in satire. In fact, such cultural differences from age to age, from social class to social class, account for some of the basic problems in defining satire.

What can be satirized? Can real persons be attacked as Aristophanes attacked Socrates and Philip Roth attacked Richard Nixon? Or is lampoon distinct from satire as argued by Samuel Johnson in his *Dictionary* and Gilbert Highet in his *Anatomy?* Personal venom and malice are generally frowned upon as motives for satire, probably because such emotions don't have a place in the society of gentle folk. But if the victim deserves the censure, does it matter what the satirist's motive is? Similarly, name-calling and other direct expressions of verbal aggression are and have been inadmissible in certain social circles, but in some societies verbal aggression is a form of entertainment and a viable means of testing one's ability to control one's temper. If satire is meant to reform persons, can there be such a thing as "cosmic satire," which probes the nature of humans rather than ridiculing the behavior of individuals? Is satire conservative, looking back at a better time from a decadent era as Juvenal's does, or is it liberal, attacking what is entrenched and stifling and calling for a change for the better as Twain's sometimes does? Can satire be a "civilizing agent," as Edgar Johnson maintains (36), if it strikes fear in others as Bacon and Hazlitt claim? And so it goes. Given the diverse ways in which aggression, play, laughter, and judgment can manifest themselves and the multifarious ways in which they reveal themselves in satire, it is little wonder that attempting to define satire has been like trying to put a shadow in a sack.

Just as each of these elements can be found in other aspects of human activity, so each can be found in various expressions of art. These elements can be found especially in those literary expressions closely related to and sometimes confused with satire, namely, humor, comedy, social criticism, parody, burlesque, farce, and travesty. Are these expressions part of a nuclear family or of an extended family, and how differentiate among them? Isolating the elements of aggression, play, laughter, and judgment in satire is by no means an innovation. Satire has long been recognized as an expression of attack. Laughter has commonly been associated with satire, although not all critics agree that it is an essential component. Wordplay, to use an obvious example, constitutes an important element of satire, although the concept of play which this study will develop draws on the work stimulated by Johan Huizinga's *Homo Ludens* and is therefore richer than wordplay alone. That satire is judgmental is hardly news either. Robert Scholes has pointed out that "fictional worlds . . . are charged with values" (105), and although values vary in importance from one kind of fiction to another, they are central to satire. No one of these elements is more important than another, although each expression of satire will combine the elements with varying emphases.

Even combining various aspects of satire to define its essence is not new. Having admitted that satire is too varied to be called a genre or a form, Samuel M. Tucker in 1908 and Frances T. Russell in 1920 opted for defining satire as a spirit. For them however the satiric spirit was essentially the point of view of the satirist, a person who in Tucker's words projected "a sense of superiority," "a tendency toward exaggeration," and various other qualities. Russell, on the other hand, collected the statements made by satirists in their works and observations of critics up until her time, and on the basis of consensus by testimonials established the characteristics of the satirist and nature of the satirist's mission. However understandable their attempts to find some unity beyond the mishmash of forms, they continued to cast their observations in the vocabulary of those they were attempting to supersede. Tucker and Russell hoped to move the discussion to another part of the equation —the satirist, and his or her role and spirit—but ended by being reductive and subjective.

Students of satire since World War II have argued that literary satire is art and ought to be treated as an aesthetic object and not a biographical or sociological document, or worse, a Rorschach test revealing its creator as sadistic, malicious, or mad. With satire "reclaimed once and for all as art," in William Kinsley's words, it is possible to put aside irrelevancies and distractions and proceed directly to the satire. The work or expression of satire is observable, its techniques, diction, form, devices discussable. And yet from the "staggering diversity of forms and tones and materials" it is possible to isolate four elements that those works and expression of satire generally agreed to be satire have in common. Each element, comprehensive yet focused, will be present to some degree but combined in different ways from work to work, from expression to expression. Not only will the four elements be combined in different ways, they will have differing and varying importance and will manifest themselves in different ways. The varying patterns and combinations will be kaleido-scopic in effect, composed of the same but ever-changing and changeable elements.

Aggression. That satire is an attack is probably the least debatable claim that one can make about it. Ben Jonson speaks for a tradition of satire as aggression in the "Epistle Dedicatory to the Universities of Oxford and Cambridge" prefixed to the quarto edition of *Volpone* in 1607 when he says he will spout corrosive ink into the faces of his adversaries so that they will be branded until the day they die. The Earl of Rochester, according to an early biographer, Gilbert Burnet, believed that a man could not write good satire "unless he be heated by Revenge." Dryden taunts Thomas Shadwell in *Mac Flecknoe* for failing to be aggressive:

> With whate'er gall thou sett'st thyself to write
> Thy offensive satires never bite. (199–200)

Satirists have been described as biting, snarling, railing, and carping, reviled as dogs, vipers and other serpent-like creatures, beasts (of prey, of course) and (all-purpose) monsters. See Joshua Poole's forty-one word list in *The English Parnassus: or, a Helpe to English Poesie* (1657) (176), under *Satyre*. Descriptions of satire bristle with the weaponry of violence: "a polished razor keen" (Mary Wortley Montagu); "I wear my pen as others do their Swords" (John Oldham); "a scourge of rough and knotted cords" (James Russell Lowell); "sharp quills" (Joseph Hall); "a whip"

(V. C. Clinton-Baddeley); "a whip of steel" (Ben Jonson). Despite the intention to inflict pain or discomfort on another implied by these weapons, the aggression can take only symbolic form. Thus whatever the nature or degree of attack in satire, it is aggression by verbal, visual, aural, or other aesthetic means. The aggression may be direct or indirect. It may be as obvious as name-calling or epithet-slinging; it may be as subtle as a beast fable or other allegory. The question of where to draw the line between direct satire and something that is a direct attack but not satire has sometimes been a sticking point in discussions of satire. Direct attack that lacks some of the elements of play and laughter would seem least likely to qualify as satire, being unadulterated verbal aggression without any redeeming verbal play or humor. Direct satire that involves a persona would immediately indicate an element of play and, depending on the nature of the language, some humor or wit as well. But despite such ameliorating elements, such satire remains clearly and obviously aggressive. When the persona of Juvenal speaks out against the Rome that has been overrun by Greeks, the personae of Pope or Rochester against humans as rational creatures, of Wylie against "momism," no doubt exists about who or what is under the gun.

As the elements of fictionality increase so also the degree of indirectness. As characters and plots become more prominent in the works, the presence of the satirist becomes less obvious. Thus direct and indirect satire are not opposites and certainly not mutually exclusive. Characters become distinguishable from the satirist in ways that personae may not always be. Characters become involved with other characters, they travel, they act, and are acted upon. They do ridiculous things, are subjected to reprehensible acts. In short, the characters and their actions come to stand for what the satirist is attacking. The ways in which this is accomplished are almost limitless, but however it is done, the aim is to derogate, disparage. Whether this is done by associating the target with lower forms of life, by making the target an animal or animal-like, or by making the target subhuman by having him or her behave in an automatic or mechanical way, the satirist is carrying out a form of symbolic aggression. To picture the target as mad, foul, or someone in the grip of one of the seven deadly sins or some other antisocial or inhuman quality or characteristic is to attack by demeaning the target. Such characters are rarely presented as fully developed fictional characters but as caricatures, or allegorical figures, again, less than human.

The scene and plot of satire, as Alvin Kernan has described them, are also forms of symbolic aggression. The scene is "always disorderly and crowded," producing the effect of "disorderly profusion" *(Cankered Muse,* 7–8). It is a "picture of a dense and grotesque world of decaying matter moving without form in response only to physical forces and denying the humane ideal which once molded a crowd into a society and the collection of buildings into a city" (14). The plot of satire may not resolve itself into a satisfying conclusion, unlike tragedy or comedy. Rather than metamorphosis, recognition, or epiphany, satire proceeds by intensification, ends with irresolution, "constant movement without change" (33). Given the multifarious forms of satire, it would be too much to expect Kernan's descriptions to apply to all satires in all forms, but they have validity as tendencies and as such project implicitly an unattractive and undesirable reality. By these means the satirist objectifies his aggression indirectly. Northrop Frye has called satire "militant irony," thereby affirming the aggression that is distinctive to it as well as isolating satire's most potent and widely used weapon. From its uses of wit, charactonyms, and other verbal devices to its comprehensive animal worlds, and preoccupation with "truth" and "reality," satire exploits the ability of irony to expose, undercut, ridicule, and otherwise attack indirectly, playfully, wittily, profoundly, artfully.

The symbolic aggression of satire, however expressed, is probably the main reason why satire is either misunderstood or denigrated. By acting out those emotions that are potentially socially disruptive and therefore often strongly frowned upon, satire risks being rejected, causing retaliation, misunderstanding or bewilderment. In such attacks we have on public display some of the least socially acceptable emotions: anger, indignation, frustration, righteousness, hatred, and malice. As in actual social relationships, the venting of such emotions, or the pose of venting these emotions, as in satire, tends to generate more of the emotion being vented, and, what is more obvious, creates an adverse reaction in the audience. The more obvious the emotion, and it need not be displayed directly, the more likelihood of an adverse reaction. The works of Aldous Huxley, for example, have consistently generated in reviewers and critics charges of cynicism, hatred, misanthropy, and puritanism. The works of Rochester, Saki, Ring Lardner, and Juvenal have on occasion evoked similar reactions.

Psychologists who have studied the emotion of anger, for example, do not believe, despite the possible adverse consequences of expressing it, that anger should always be suppressed. Rather they suggest limiting it to expressions when there is a legitimate plea for justice and when it may result in the correction of misbehavior. Clark Glymour in a symposium on obscenity in the *Times Literary Supplement* (12–19 February 1988:159) argues that "giving offence may be the best way to some benign and more urgent goal, whether broadening tastes or inducing tolerance or simply saying what is true. And an offence can be so excused because it is so witty, so clever, so ingenuous, so courageous, or even so *artful*." Even repugnant emotions may be justified if they attack or illuminate injustice or other morally reprehensible behavior. And this, of course, has been the traditional justification for satire, another apparent case of psychology catching up with art, or perhaps life imitating art. Still the more overt the expression in satiric form the more trouble it has had being admitted to the canon. The "tradition" of first-person verbal attack or diatribe has in any case been an isolated phenomenon in Western culture, both in its literature and in bourgeois society, so that it is possible that those critics of satire who place it outside the pale may be rejecting it not for aesthetic reasons but for socially induced standards.

That the various guises and degrees of fictionality often employed (at times for reasons that have nothing to do with aesthetics) make allusive or indirect works of satire somehow superior is a matter of taste and definition. Such indirection is on occasion a necessary part of discretion, a protective device that may save the satirist from persecution, prosecution, even death. Making people unhappy is a risk for most satirists, and if the enemy is powerful, the risk can be dangerous. Voltaire went into a kind of exile, Daumier went to prison, and *Private Eye* and *Hustler* have gone into the courts for practicing satire. So the aggression of satire comes with the territory. The target must be diminished in importance, made to look foolish, stupid, or vicious. Just as the direct-attack satirist assumes a position of superiority by adopting a pose of honesty, plainness, or intelligence and implying standards that are being abandoned or subverted, the indirect satirist puts the target on the defensive by making it appear inferior, since the indirect satirist is limited in the devices available for attack from a position of superiority. Whatever the case, where there is a discernible target whose worth is being questioned, there is an attack in progress.

Play.   To yoke the symbolic aggression of satire with a spirit of play is to commit barefaced paradox. And yet the games people play, from put-downs to polo, from "chicken" to war games, combine varying degrees of aggression with forms of play. Satire is not unique in uniting seemingly incompatible elements. Leaving aside aggression and looking only at the play elements, we find it permeating satire, from its presence as imagery and wordplay to its animating the very essence of the satiric act or expression. Sarah Cleghorn's "Quatrain" provides a good example of play as satiric imagery:

> The golf links lie so near the mill
> > That almost every day
> The laboring children can look out
> > And see the men at play.

With the conventional concept of play as an activity of children, Cleghorn sets up a reversal to criticize an economic system that deprives children of the opportunity to play while allowing adult men to do so. Mark Twain in "To the Person Sitting in Darkness," his mock encomium against European and American imperialism in the early twentieth century, accuses political leaders of playing "The Game." In this case the game is a confidence game in the guise of claims of progress and advancement of "civilization." Alexander Pope uses two kinds of games in his *Rape of the Lock,* an actual card game which symbolizes the sex game that is the central action of the poem. In Pope's poem as well as in Books I and II of *Gulliver's Travels,* imagery moves in the direction of being an overarching myth, that life is in fact a game. The Lilliputians in Book I and Gulliver himself in Book II can be conceived of by virtue of their size as toys, which is in fact what Gulliver is for Glumdalclitch, the Queen of Brobdingnag and others. In Book I Gulliver had exhibited a similar playfulness toward the Lilliputians. The gamelike qualities of life are for Swift and Pope confined to the world of the belles and beaux and to the society of Lilliput, but in those contexts they are all-encompassing.

Such is also the case with Stephen Potter's series of variations on gamesmanship, which satirize the ploys, deceptions, and chicanery rampant in a competitive society. Life, in Potter's projection, is a series of games of do or be done to, "the moral equivalent of assault and battery," as he once described it (quoted in Alden). If people play games as Potter shows (and Swift and Pope as well), it does not follow for them that life is a game or that play is anything but childish (or at least nonserious), frivolous, even immoral.

Play for certain twentieth-century satirists becomes on the other hand a positive element which in fact cuts the other way. In Jean Giraudoux's *The Madwoman of Chaillot* the Countess and her friends represent a playful attitude that allows them to cope with the ugliness and materialism of politicians and businessmen. The world of illusion, imagination, freedom, and joy in which the countesses live is more real than the plastic world hawked by the entrepreneurs. The con game of the imperialist in Twain becomes the con game of the industrialists in Giraudoux. That the life of the mind could indeed become the game of life had been anticipated in Alfred Jarry's " 'Pataphysics . . . the science of imaginary solutions," which became a kind of cult in France organized around a College de 'Pataphysics with a hierarchy of chairs for such subjects as "Dialectics of Useless Knowledge," "Crocodilology," and "Pornosophy." The "believers," including Raymond Queneau, René Clair, Eugene Ionesco, and others in French literary circles, count years from the date of Jarry's birth, 8 September 1873. The statutes of the college include the statement that

> All mankind consists of 'pataphysicians, but the College
> of Pataphysique separates those who are not ignorant of
> this fact from those who are. (Qtd. in Esslin, 549)

In short, life is a game; some know it and some don't. Those who don't have lost the ability to be like a child, caught up in the world of work, science, progress, and utility.

In a nice instance of having it both ways, satirists have used the concept of playfulness to indict those who are too much like children and those who are not enough like them. George Santayana in his essay "The Comic Mask" also endorses what he calls "innocent make-believe." He asks,

> What could be more splendidly sincere than the impulse
> to play in real life, to rise on the rising wave of every

feeling and let it burst, if it will, into the foam of exaggeration? Life is not a means, the mind is not a slave nor a photograph: it has a right to enact a pose, to assume a *panache,* and to create what prodigious allegories it will for the mere sport and glory of it. . . . Fancy is playful and may be misleading to those who try to take it for literal fact; but literalness is impossible in any utterance of the spirit, and if it were possible it would be deadly. Why should we quarrel with human nature, with metaphor, with myth, with impersonation? The foolishness of the simple is delightful; only the foolishness of the wise is exasperating.

Play as a weapon for attacking elements of society which are foolish or evil is not confined to satirists, as Santayana shows. Santayana speaks disparagingly of "Bible-reading Anglo-Saxondom," in his eyes the antithesis of "innocent make-believe." Others before and since would agree. Schiller argued for a play instinct and said that "man is only whole when he plays." And Nietzsche says in *Ecce Homo:* "I know of no other way of coping with great tasks than as play." Both Johan Huizinga and Roger Caillois, leading scholars and advocates of play, present it as a missing component in twentieth-century life, bodying out, so to speak, an element in the philosophies of Schiller and Nietzsche.

Despite using the imagery of play as childish, satirists have practiced the ideas advanced by Schiller, Nietzsche, Santayana and others. Even as the satirist claims to be setting forth the truth, he or she is manipulating the language, be it the "disabling adjectives" of Philip Wylie or the complex play of words in La Rochefoucauld's maxims. The personae, caricatures, stereotypes, and fable figures that dominate works of satire put make-believe at the center of the spirit. Maynard Mack once said that "all good satire . . . exhibits an appreciable degree of fictionality" (84). But Peter Hutchinson in *Games Authors Play* (1983) does not include satire among the games played although he does discuss travesty, parody, burlesque, and other techniques used by satirists, satire being complex play rather than simple play as these techniques tend to be. The "prodigious allegories" invoked by Santayana, fantasies, fables, and imaginary worlds, are examples of imaginary play of the highest kind. Such playfulness may not satisfy the pure and ideal concepts of play advanced by some "play-ologists," for example, Huizinga and later Fink and Ehrmann, serving as it does a master other than itself, a means and not an end in itself. Concepts of play, however, vary from academic discipline to academic discipline, from culture to culture, age to age, from Piaget to Derrida. One concept sees play as an acting out in a "framed" context "frustrations, or subjective worlds, not permitted expression within the more conventional norms of society." The cues of play involve communication by "repetition, exaggeration, miniaturization, changed register [i.e., range of instrument], stock characters, special location and guaranteed illusion," in various combinations. That satire fits this concept of play is obvious (Sutton-Smith, 318–19).

Play is in fact indigenous to the spirit of satire and its source and analogues in myth and ritual. The trickster figure of mythology, the closest thing to a mythic source that satire can claim, is a figure of deception, roguishness, and illusion. He is a prankster, a jokester; he is unreliable, enormously libidinous, a hell-raiser. In short, the trickster is someone in whom the need to play has been raised virtually to a way of life. Such a life can be ridiculous, even chaotic, but is also satirizes religious rites, people's gullibility, the unwise use of power, the hypocrisy of the gods. This does not exempt him from also being the butt of satire by showing his stupidity, greed, and other folly. Although a rich and unsettling figure, the trickster serves as a mythic projection of the satiric impulse incorporating the element of play. Moreover, satire often has been associated with the "dionysian consciousness"—the phrase is Norman O. Brown's—which sees life as a festival, a kind of ritual of play. Greek drama grew out of the Dionysian festivals in which clowns were allowed the freedom to spew invective at bystanders, and out of "beast mummeries" (Norwood, 6) in which persons dressed as animals entertained the crowd. From the weddings and harvest festivals of Etruria emerged Fescennine verses, abusive and obscene exchanges of banter between rustics, preserved in miniature in Horace's Satire 1,5 (51–70), or against persons of wealth and power. The same freedom was allowed during Saturnalia as can be seen in Horace's Satire 2,7 in which Davus points out some of the same faults in Horace that Horace has criticized in others. In the medieval Feast of Fools, in the fiestas of highland Chiapas in southern Mexico, in the Holi festival in northern India, and the celebrity roasts that have grown up in the last hundred years in the United States we find the juxtaposition of satire and play, the freedom to attack in jest in a ritual context of eating, drinking, merrymaking, and a departure from the routines of normal living. Adult forms of play then are often rituals in which the aggression of satire is expressed in a socially countenanced way. This is in accordance with the concept of *paidzeim spoude,* that is, playing seriously or seriously playing, as exemplified in Socrates. Although he scarcely had satire in mind, what Plato said about the right way of living could describe much satire and its antecedents:

> Life must be lived as play, playing certain games, making sacrifices, singing and dancing, and then a man will be able to propitiate the gods, and defend himself against his enemies, and win in the contest. (*Laws* 7, 796)

Laughter.   Byron in *Don Juan* says "Cervantes smiled Spain's chivalry away" (13, 11). Pope in his imitation of Horace's Satire II says,

> Whoe'er offends, at some unlucky time
> Slides into verse, and hitches in a rhyme,
> Sacred to ridicule his whole life long,
> And the sad burthen of some merry song. (77–80)

Swift says in an "Epistle to a Lady,"

> All their Madness makes me merry:
> Like the every-laughing Sage,
> In a jest I spend my Rage:
> (Tho' it must be understood
> I would hang them if I cou'd). (174–80)

British film director Lindsay Anderson said, "In making *Britannia Hospital,* I thought, people are going to laugh and be amused and be made better by it" (quoted in Kakutani, "Satirist"). And in the beginning there is Horace's "There's no law against telling the truth with a smile." Even a limited and cursory collection of quotations about satire or works of satire reveals that laughter is commonly associated with satire and that the laughter it generates takes various forms. For Horace the smile is a sugarcoating that makes the truth more palatable than the naked truth. For Swift the jest of satire is a metaphorical substitute for hanging. The others quoted above, however, imply that laughter has been an agent of change for the better in those who have shared the laughter. The laughter of ridicule or the truth coated with laughter shames the fool into changing his ways. Such a concept is at the heart of the belief in satire's ability to reform those who have fallen into vice or folly.

Certainly it is true that being laughed at can be a trying experience, and the shame that results can be a powerful social deterrent or punishment. But in its simplest form this view assumes that satire functions the same way that placing criminals in the stocks functioned in Puritan New England. Only if a society is small and homogeneous can such punishment have much likelihood of success. Such is the case described by David Gilmore in his *Aggression and Community: Paradoxes in Andalusian Culture,* where we see how the "subsurface hostility in the form of satire, parody, or sardonic wit, . . . murder by language" that occurs during Carnival "enhances the unity of the group" (117–18). Satire in ritual contexts may sometimes have worked this way in other times and places, especially in tribal communities, neighborhoods in medieval cities, and European university communities, but only when the shame and the magical power of the word prevailed. All we know is that ritual satire has taken place in a variety of social settings, but there were no Harris polls to follow up and determine the effectiveness of the proceedings.

A modern counterpart, the celebrity roast, provides no indication that the fear of being roasted or actually being roasted has ever changed anyone's behavior, although some invited guests have been known to stay away rather than be subjected to laughter at their expense. That deep-seated changes in behavior can be accomplished by laughter, even the laughter of ridicule, whatever its relevance in preliterate societies, has long been a convention, a pious hope, and little more. Lindsay Anderson added to his notion that laughter would make people better: "It's a very naive idea, but I think if I didn't believe it somehow I wouldn't be able to go on making films. I strive to remain skeptical rather than cynical, but sometimes it's a hard struggle."

Swift's use of the jest also suggests another widely held concept of laughter, catharsis in this case, for Swift and perhaps for the audience. Undoubtedly laughter may produce an engaging communal experience, especially if the audience joins in laughter directed against a worthy victim. But there is no clear-cut evidence that catharsis, communal or individual, is anything but a subjective and unproved concept. Laughter can be an exhilarating experience, and if Norman Cousins's experiment has any relevance for others besides himself, a healthy one as well. But there is no necessary connection between that kind of humor and comedy and the laughter generated by satire.

To think that the laughter of satire is transforming or cathartic and that it will produce those effects in all individuals fails to recognize the complexity of what causes laughter. Laughter after all is both personal and social. Society may define and determine what may or may not be laughed at, but no individual will laugh at all the things that society allows that individual to laugh at, nor will that person necessarily refrain from laughing at what is socially unacceptable. In fact, laughter is determined not only by society but is more narrowly defined by social class, influence of parents, siblings and peers, educational background, ethnic or racial roots, and by community and geographical region. Moreover what causes a person to laugh may change according to one's period of life and as interests, tastes, and values change. Ultimately these influences are incorporated into a personality and temperament whose laughter profile is unique. In short, a person's sense of humor is as unique as his or her fingerprints. Theories of laughter that attempt to account for it by a single source or cause must not only take into consideration the manifold influences mentioned above but must also deal with the social context that prompted Lord Chesterfield to point out that laughter is not a socially acceptable emotion and that which allowed Elizabethans to tour Bedlam for laughs.

Laughter itself is richly ambivalent. It can be the expression of derision, fear, triumph, eroticism, or holy union. Laughter can reflect total immersion in a particular moment or it can indicate separation from a moment and the standing apart as an observer. In the "Legend of the Holy Rood," when Adam learns that he is at last released from death—he laughs. On the other hand, the mystic Meister Eckhart expressed divine joy at his own soul laughing together with God. The Magical Papyri and the Zohar speak of the "great laughter" which is the creative energy. The fool of the Tarot cards is the "embodiment of laughter," touching "all the elements of laughter, from being an amused bystander to being taken up by the divine, from being scorned to being loved" (Sexson, 33).

The laughter evoked by satire is rarely simple, sometimes strained, occasionally strange, capable of cutting both ways. Gilbert Highet notes that "a degree of amusement . . . may range anywhere between a sour grin at the incongruity of the human condition and a delighted roar of laughter at the exposure of an absurd fraud" (150).[2] If the presence of aggression were not enough to provide a strong reaction, aggression coupled with laughter has resulted in satire and satirists becoming themselves the targets of those in power who are attacked, as Byron learned when the early cantos of Don Juan were published. If the power to reform or to purge remains questionable, there is little doubt about its power to stimulate political leaders to send out the gendarmes and private citizens into the courts. Satiric magazines have been especially successful in this respect, including Britain's Private Eye and France's Le Canard Enchaîné but also Tia Vincenta in Argentina in 1968, and classic cases against Simplicissimus in Germany and La Caricature in France in the 1830s when Daumier was jailed for his cartoons—all sued, harassed, or closed down to thwart their spreading laughter. Philip Roth's Our Gang, Barbara Garson's MacBird, Thomas Nast's cartoons of Boss Tweed in Harper's, certain works of Swift, and the controversial Marprelate Tracts—all illustrate the ability of satire to generate laughter and scandalous reactions. Horace's dictum may have worked for him, but it is not an infallible prescription, as many satirists have found to their chagrin. Laughter as an element in the satiric mix may provoke as easily as it mollifies.

And yet the presence of laughter-inducing devices and techniques is virtually a certainty in satire. Every device known to humor and comedy can be found in satire. From anticlimax to zeugma they all turn up in satire somewhere. Moreover satire incorporates into itself such modes as farce, parody, black humor, burlesque, travesty, dadaism, the grotesque, and surrealism, all of which are either inherently comic or contain strong tendencies in that direction. Devices or techniques that are peculiar to satire tend to be associated with their creators and not be transferable to closely related types of expressions. Hudibrastic verse, for example, has never been successfully imitated, and the disabling adjectives of Philip Wylie and the imagery of literalness favored by Swift have not been widely copied. Satire tends to appropriate its laughter-provoking devices and techniques rather than originate them.

And satire's piracy has known no limits. From the guffaw of coarse laughter evoked by farce and slapstick to the titter of embarrassment elicited by scatological allusions to the smirk of self-satisfaction at the inanity of foolishness, satire draws upon the multifarious ways in which humans can be induced or counted upon to laugh. Even the excesses of Juvenal's Satire VI, the horrifying catalogues of human stupidity in *Gulliver's Travels,* or the blasphemies of Lenny Bruce may extract an embarrassed smile as they shock and dismay. This kind of laughter is a long way from Horace's telling the truth laughing, and there is no way of knowing whether Swift or Juvenal or Bruce meant to evoke laughter or that it would be forthcoming if they wanted to evoke it. Such extreme examples as these are more often than not isolated moments in the works of which they are a part. Even if there is only embarrassed silence at such times, laughter will dominate elsewhere, so that reactions more commonly associated with tragedy or pathos will be departures from the norm. This is only to say that satire is no different from other aesthetic expressions in that consistency or purity of tone cannot be insisted upon. Satire may lapse into farce or parody as well as into tragedy or pathos. So long as the laughter continues, such lapses are not so noticeable, and are troublesome perhaps only when the departures are such that in another context besides satire they would be thought tragic or pathetic. Edgar Johnson in the introduction to his *Treasury of Satire* argues that melodrama and burlesque are opposite sides of the coin of exaggeration. Melodrama takes itself seriously, burlesque does not. But, and Johnson does not say this, both may evoke laughter although melodrama does not intend to do so. Witness Oscar Wilde's reaction to the death of Little Nell in Dickens's "Old Curiosity Shop." Since satire trades extensively with the coin of exaggeration, it is not surprising that it will on occasion cohabit with such exaggerated expressions as the grotesque, tragedy, melodrama, pathos, and sentimentality as well as with farce, comedy, and other normally laughter-inducing modes. If they induce laughter of whatever kind and combine with aggression, play, and judgment, then the pedigree of the beast is established.

Judgment. Satire as an artistic expression is neutral. It is aggression waiting for a target; it is laughter waiting for a stimulant; it is play waiting for a game. The ingredient that activates and directs the elements comes alive itself with a satirist making a judgment, turning satire into a weapon, blunt or penetrating, combining judgment with the other elements in a unique mix. As a weapon it has been used for the worst of motives; it has been used for the best of reasons. It has been used by malicious, envious, and spiteful persons, and it has been used by idealistic and moral persons. It has been used by persons in all walks of life, all kinds of cultures and systems of government, in countries all over the world. It has been used to attack governments and to bolster governments, it has been used to attack religion and to defend religion. It has been called the "reprehencion of foulysshness" (Barclay in *The Ship of Fools*) at one extreme, and at the other used by Dryden in *The Medal* against sedition and in *Absalom and Achitophel* against treason. Charles Churchill said that "satire is always virtue's friend," and Chesterton claimed that "the essence of satire is that it perceives some absurdity inherent in the logic of some position, and . . . draws the absurdity out and isolates it, so that all can see it" (8). Whether the target is vice or folly, absurdity or enemies of the state, the satirist is concerned with passing judgment. We may not approve of the motive for the judgment, the judgment, or the way it is presented, but those are matters that are separate from the nature of satire itself. *Censure* is a common synonym for *satirize* (see Samuel Johnson's definition); *criticize* is another common equivalent. But *censure* carries a heavy connotation that is not appropriate to all satire. Horatian satire, for example, is distinguished by a gentility and urbanity that is almost the antithesis of censure. But there is little doubt what Horace's sentiments are when his satires put down sycophants, conspicuous consumers, and adulterers. As with all satirists Horace shows disapproval, passes judgment.

Horace's judgments are moral judgments, and many, perhaps most, satirists have based their judgments on the "truth" as Horace did. Dryden even went so far as to classify satire as an expression of moral philosophy. Charles Churchill says,

> When satire flies abroad on falsehood's wing
> Short is her life, and impotent her sting;
> But when to truth allied, the wound she gives
> Sinks deep, and to remotest ages lives.
>   ("The Author," 217–22)

A twentieth-century spokesman for the moral function of satire is W. H. Auden, who states that "the comic butt of satire is a person, who, though in possession of normal faculties, transgresses the moral law beyond the normal call of temptation" (*Dyer's Hand* 383). Alastair Fowler claims that "a radical moral stance is perhaps the most striking feature of the satiric repertoire" (110). But the satirist's "truth" may be not only moral but also ethical, political, aesthetic, common sense, or shared prejudices. The standards by which political cartoonists measure presidents and prime ministers, for example, may have more to do with political reality than with morality. The standards of Ring Lardner were often the prejudices of the average American male of the 1920s, the standards of Jane Austen those of a woman in a male-dominated society ruled by economic concerns. The presence of dirty linen on a character was for Pope and Swift a telling condition. The trenchant manner in which satirists often advance their judgments, especially those just mentioned, tends to impart to the judgments a moral quality even when the judgments are idiosyncratic. Thus the way in which judgments are advanced may count more than the judgments, or rather the basis for the judgments, since Swift's standards in Book IV of *Gulliver's Travels,* for example, and Petronius's standards in the *Satyricon* have provoked a good deal of debate over the years. Few would deny that conditions in these works are not as they should be, even though there is not full agreement about what the source of the trouble is.

In most satires what the satirist disapproves of tends to be clear-cut because the satirist has succeeded in keeping the target in focus and in the foreground. There cannot therefore be unintentional satire. The view that life in the last half of the twentieth century cannot be satirized because it is already a form of satire is merely another way of saying that one disapproves of certain aspects of twentieth-century life. Examples of grotesqueness, decadence, or folly in life are departures from norms or standards or values that exist in the mind of the beholder. Forest Lawn cemetery, presidential press conferences, the salaries of professional athletes, the multimillion dollar "sex industry," and nuclear war strategy each elicit varying reactions and judgments, but finding them reprehensible is only the start. Satire exists when that judgment is combined with the other three elements. The satirist must judge in order to be judged.

Every satirist presents judgment in his or her own way, the techniques many and varied. At the simplest and most direct, the satirist may speak to the audience through a voice or a persona who indicates what is wrong wlth society. This approach is seen best in formal verse satire, but it can also appear in other forms, for example, in characters who epitomize a kind of norm, as in the "noble savage" in *Brave New World* and Celia and Bonario in *Volpone*. Judgments may be implied by standards embodied in images such as the Great Chain of Being, Christian myth, or values presented in works of literature, such as *The Aeneid* or *Paradise Lost*. Thus Pope's *Dunciad* draws on Milton, Virgil, and Christian myth to denigrate the pretensions of the dunces. Jonson uses the Great Chain in *Volpone* in the same way. Another technique seeks merely to present the targets at their most ludicrous, stupid, hypocritical, or disgusting. Holy Willie, the "lady" in Westminster Abbey, the modest Projector, the targets of Gillray and Rowlandson, and Jack D. Ripper are so grotesque that the separation between them and the audience is to be expected. Ultimately the kinds of worlds and the creatures in them which are typical of satire present a judgment. Reducing characters to animals, machines, or madness or creating worlds that are dominated by such values removes actions and values from the "normal" world and places a stigma on them. To these techniques must be added all the verbal devices that can be used to undercut, exaggerate, and intensify the judgment, the richest being irony in its many guises.

Satire then can be seen as a complex metaphorical act, whether it be ritual, folk expression, or art form. It is at once an act of judgment, aggression, play, and laughter. The satirist melds the roles of judge, castigator, jester, and trickster, a richer mix of roles by far than John Oldham's claim that the satirist is 'Both Witness, Judge, and Executioner' (*Works*, 1, 141); his instruments thus become the gavel, the whip, the bauble, and the mirror. In ordinary experience these roles are not only kept separate but are thought of as mutually exclusive. A judge may hand out a sentence, but he does not administer the punishment. And a courtroom is no place for a jester or a trickster, whose roles are in another dimension of life entirely. And yet the satirist combines these roles into a prototypical expression of satire. It is not possible to say that such an expression should have equal parts of the four elements but only that they be present in some combination. Some satirists will play one or more roles more readily or more comfortably than the other roles, may perhaps downplay or virtually ignore one of the roles. Thus some satire will be more aggressive, some funnier, others more playful, others more judgmental. Any particular combination may also be influenced by the cultural context and traditions in force during an era and how the satirist relates to such influences. But the disparate roles will be combined in some way, Hermes in black robe, black mask, and motley, truly an odd figure.

Aggression, play, laughter, and judgment are all social forms of behavior. They originate in an individual; they manifest themselves in acts or expressions; and they ordinarily need an audience to be completed. It is possible for a person to do all of them while alone, but such instances would probably not occur very often and would in any case not be very satisfying or fulfilling. All may also exist in the imagination as forms of fantasy and other internal expression, but not until they exist in a social context do they have relevance to satire. As described here the four elements serve a double purpose. In the first place they provide a way to differentiate satire from similar forms of expression, forms that are sometimes confused with satire. This approach to satire also isolates the expression of the spirit from questions regarding the satirist's intention, the reaction and influence on the audience, and the cultural context out of which the work of satire comes. This approach does not deal with the relation of one work of satire to another nor with the question of what good satire is. The question of what is good satire would involve, according to this scheme, evaluating the variety and efficiency in the mix of elements. All of these matters have, of course, been the subject of numerous discussions concerning both the nature of satire and the value of individual works. Without in any way discounting the interest in and usefulness of these approaches, none has provided a way out of Elliott's bind. Attempts to know the intentions and motives of a satirist tend very often to be exercises in futility, and when the motives of a satirist are reduced to a single intention, the results have been questionable. Satirists are as varied and complex as other human beings, and they concoct their works for varied and complex reasons.

On the other side of the question—the audience—there are similar difficulties. As with any other work of art, a work of satire may not be said to have completed its mission until an audience has had a go at it. For satire there are immediate problems, namely the failure of some to understand or correctly interpret the work. While such problems exist for any piece of art, because of the special nature of satire and its relationship to the world outside, the possibilities for a breakdown in communication between the satirist and the audience are greater than with most works of art. Satire by its very nature asks an audience to make a connection between the work and the context in which it occurs, be it social, political, religious, aesthetic, or one of the other contexts in which satire can spring up. Because satire usually has a vital connection with a specific cultural context, in fact, can hardly exist without such a context, it remains the most primitive of arts. While some art may aim for self-sufficiency, satire remains bound to its communal origins and social function. Whether the satirist is attacking a person, an institution, a group, a work of art, a kind of behavior, a way of life, a value, or a belief, the satire makes most sense and takes on life when the audience plugs into the external connections. Satire in effect asks—demands—that its audience engage in a dialogue of a special kind. In addition to making associations, the audience is expected to assimilate the special mixture of aggression, play, laughter, and judgment that is set before it. Each of these alone can create difficulties. Aggression may cause resentment or other unfavorable reactions. Differences of opinion concerning the judgments are potential sources of contention. The playfulness of satire, especially when yoked with serious questions, may disconcert some. The complicated nature of laughter provides another dimension of difficulty. Together the possibilities for problems are compounded moment by moment. By its nature satire usually causes trouble, not merely because it is an attack and a judgment, but also because satire, at its most complex, demands its audience be sophisticated, sensitive, and sympathetic: sophisticated about the audience context in which the satire transpires, sensitive to the means at work, and sympathetic in sharing the aggression and judgment (unless the audience is itself being attacked). Recognizing the special mix of elements that constitutes satire does not preclude discussion of some of the traditional concerns about satirists and their works. But under-standing these elements provides a way to focus on the nature of satire itself.

Isolating these elements offers a way to understand what is happening when satire emerges in works that are not predominantly satiric and when predominantly satiric works occasionally lapse out of the spirit. Such lapses and inconsistencies may be disconcerting since they violate expectations based on knowledge of what is presumed to be a genre as well as expectations based on unity of tone and so on. Applying the four elements to "impure" works furnishes an approach that helps determine to what extent and in what ways such works are satiric. Similar in ideas, Johnson's *Rasselas, Prince of Abissinia* and Voltaire's *Candide* demonstrate how the combination of elements can account for important differences. Voltaire attacks more sharply, more playfully, hilariously so, while Johnson is judgmental to the point of being didactic, thereby reducing the other elements to being only nominal. Despite a dark strain that runs through both works, Voltaire incorporates a greater number of laughter-inducing elements and a greater amount of playfulness in his work without compromising the attack and the sharply presented judgment.

The same approach can also help to distinguish satire from related forms of expression that share some but not all the elements of satire:

—*Humor* can be seen as an expression in which the play and laughter elements dominate, aggression is minimal, and judgment is lacking. The verse of A. P. Herbert and Ogden Nash and many stories by James Thurber are examples.

—*Farce* also dispenses with judgment, but it contains large amounts of aggression, play, and laughter. In serious drama farce occurs mixed with serious matter, as in Shakespeare's *Comedy of Errors* or Jonson's *Silent Woman*. It occurs more frequently in the film and television in the silent Keystone Cops routines, Laurel and Hardy shorts, and such TV sitcoms as *I Love Lucy* and *The Honeymooners*.

—*Invective* occurs when the aggressive element is uppermost, judgment is prominent, the play and laughter elements are minimal. X. J. Kennedy's anthology *Tygers of Wrath: Poems of Hate, Anger, and Invective* contains many examples.

—*Fables, apologues,* and other allegorical forms are dominated by the play element, which masks and mutes the aggression and judgmental elements. Chaucer's "The Nun's Priest's Tale," Krylov's fables, and Orwell's *Animal Farm* are satiric versions. If aggression and judgment are lacking, as in animated film cartoon shorts and exempla such as how the elephant got its trunk, there is no satire.

—*Social criticism* shares with satire the elements of judgment and attack but lacks the elements of laughter and play. Richard Wright's *Native Son* is social criticism, but Ralph Ellison's *Invisible Man* is satire.

The quadripartite approach to satire also allows for distinctions among closely related forms and expressions such as parody, travesty, spoof, comedy, and burlesque. Without a judgment and lacking an attack, parody, burlesque, and travesty are forms of humor. Rich Little's imitations of film stars and political figures are humorous parodies since there is no attack or judgment in his presen tations. Spoof is a term used to refer to nonsatiric burlesque and travesty, since the elements of play and laughter leave no room for attack and judgment. Comedy also emphasizes play and laughter, contains some judgment but very little if any aggression. When ag gression appears in comedy, it is often present in isolated characters and scenes, which turns comedy into satiric comedy, depending on how much emphasis is placed on aggression and judgment.

Various other shadings are possible with this scheme. Satiric invective, for example, without laughter and play becomes abuse and billingsgate, nonmetaphorical, unrhythmical, unwitting, unal-literative. Certain modern writers show satiric tendencies, but the tendencies become blurred when the elements of judgment and aggression do not emerge clearly. In works by Nathanael West and Franz Kafka, for example, clear-cut judgments are sometimes undermined, aggression muted. The elements of play and laughter remain, although they show up as blackly and bleakly humorous and grotesquely and surrealistically playful. But satire remains an important spirit in their works. Their idiosyncratic handling of judgment and eschewing aggression makes them interesting exam-ples of the special nature of some twentieth-century satire. A similar strain can be detected in the so-called "cosmic satire" of works by Anthony Burgess, John Barth, and Kurt Vonnegut (Tilton, chap. 1). Aggression and judgment are so muted that it has been claimed that "compassion is the attitude of cosmic satire" (20).

Such generalities need elaboration on the nature of the laughter, the techniques used to develop playfulness, descriptions of the aggression, and the ways in which judgment is couched. Such elaborations can use standard literary concepts and terminology. They would spell out in more detail how the elements merge into one another and how important each is. Satirists do not use the four elements like the ingredients in a recipe, nor do they create their works to satisfy schemes of analysis and systems of classification dreamed up by critics and scholars. And since such schemes and classification cannot anticipate the seemingly infinite number of ways in which the devices and techniques of rhetoric and literature can be blended and ordered, it is unlikely that this approach will be without cracks and faults.

In any case, satire will not tumble into bed with any scheme. Just as the mythic trickster figure continues to puzzle anthropologists and other social scientists, so satire keeps literary scholars and critics at odds. They advance their schemes after looking back down a long narrow corridor of literature decorated with busts and scrolls and other critical schemes. In a sense this backward view denies the very nature of satire. For satire is mainly about a time and a place and people. It is the Gridiron Club of Washington, D.C., journalists roasting the President of the United States and other political figures. It is the Do-dah Parade in Pasadena, California, which precedes but takes off from the annual Rose Bowl Parade. It is columnists Mike Royko of the *Chicago Tribune* and Calvin Trillin of *Nation* magazine. It is graphic cartoonists Jules Feiffer and Don Wright. It is Doug Marlette and Veronica Geng. Peter Schickele annually resurrecting "P. D. Q. Bach." The half-time shows at football games by the Princeton University Band in the 1980s. Peter DeVries. Rainer Fassbinder. Ralph Steadman. Stanislas Lem. Vladimir Voinovich. *S.O.B.* and *O What A Lovely War.*

What does all this satire accomplish? A modern aesthetic Pilate might ask, what does art accomplish? For whatever else it is, satire is art, however peculiar and baffling it may be. It provides occasions for laughter, playfulness, judgment, and aggression, a peculiar combination that is often bewildering. On such occasions we are dealing with folly and evil according to the way in which they are presented to us. We may be called upon to laugh, to be indignant, to wonder, to be repelled, to become involved through these and other emotions in a variety of mixes. The reactions evoked by satire are by no means the only reactions to the depravity, injustice, and stupidity of the world. One may try to ignore them, one may try to explain them away, or one may try to change them, among other reactions. And then there is satire. No final answer to foolishness and wickedness, nor is it a reaction that everyone is attracted to. But were the disposition for satire somehow to disappear from the make-up of human beings, and the variegated expressions of it were to vanish, the dance of life would be diminished by the absence of a strange and vital gesture.

2

The Trickster
and the Spirit of Satire

Will the Real Trickster Please Stand Up?

The trickster figure of world mythology is at once one of the most pervasive of mythological characters, one of the most complicated, and one of the least understood. Or such is one possible inference, since about the meaning of the trickster there is little agreement. The pervasiveness of the trickster figure is in fact one cause for the lack of agreement. Best known perhaps from Paul Radin's study of the Winnebago (Wisconsin) Indian myth cycle, the trickster also occurs in tales of the Algonquin and Santee of eastern North America, and in the stories of tribes in the Plains area, the Pacific coast, and the Southwest region. But the trickster is by no means confined to American Indian cultures or to the North American continent. In Africa the trickster is found in the tales of the Ashanti, the Dahomey, Yoruba, Nganasan, and many other groups. Native cultures in Polynesia and Australia once told stories with trickster heroes. Hindu myths contain tricksters. Germanic and Greek myths contain figures that are analogous to the tricksters of preliterate peoples. Such a list is by no means complete, but it illustrates how widespread the trickster is in world mythologies. The idea of the trickster has also been applied to folk figures such as Till Eulenspiegel and Reynard the Fox and to an array of literary characters from Panurge and Falstaff to Sut Lovingood and various characters in black American fiction. Such extensions, while suggestive, only complicate an already confusing subject, so the emphasis here will be on the figures from the myths of traditional tribal peoples from around the world. The pervasiveness of such mythological figures is undisputed, but the meaning and significance of the trickster are far from agreed upon. As Paul Radin has noted:

> This symbol which Trickster embodies is not a static one. It contains within itself the promise of differentiation, of god and man. For this reason every generation occupies itself with interpreting the Trickster anew. No generation understands him fully, but no generation can do without him. Each had to include him in all its theologies, in all its cosmogonies, despite the fact that it realized that he did not fit properly into any of them, for he represents not only the undifferentiated and distant past, but likewise the undifferentiated present within every individual. This constitutes his universal and persistent attraction. And so he became and remained everything to every man—god, animal, human being, hero, buffoon, he was before good and evil, denier, affirmer, destroyer and creator. If we laugh at him he grins at us. What happens to him, happens to us. (*The Trickster,* 168–69)

One problem in coming to grips with the trickster is that no trickster, no particular story or set of stories epitomizes the typical trickster. The figures and the stories of his adventures contain common elements, but from culture to culture there are differing emphases. The amount of and emphasis on scatological and sexual subject matter, the kinds of trickery, and the degree to which the trickster is victim or hero or both in the same story or set of stories—all complicate the problem of trying to introduce some coherence into such a variety of material. Cycles involving Raven, Mink, and Bluejay were part of the lore of native American tribes of the Pacific Northwest, yet each cycle emphasizes a different aspect in the trickster: the Raven preoccupied with satisfying his greedy hunger, the Mink his sexual appetites, the Bluejay with outdoing his betters in the hunt or war. Coyote, whose stories were told from the Mississippi River to the Pacific Ocean, except for the Northwest, has something of the Raven and the Mink in him and a great deal of the Bluejay (Boas, 473; Pelton). Tricksters in European mythology are no less baffling. The variety of roles performed by Hermes—thief, shepherd, craftsman, herald, musician, athlete, merchant—forced Norman O. Brown to educe an evolutionary theory to account for them. Loki, the Norse trickster, although not so multifaceted as Hermes, apparently underwent an evolutionary change (DeVries; Rooth; Davidson, *Gods,* 176–82). Cultural variations in the trickster and differences in what is known about the development of cultures and their tricksters help make the trickster an elusive figure.

Attempts to generalize about such variable material immediately collide with the contradictions displayed by a character who combines deceit and stupidity with heroism, who can be not only obnoxiously selfish but also unselfishly heroic, that idealized mythical figure who brings fire or water or other benefits to the human race. Explanations for this paradoxical figure[1] have ranged from Franz Boas's theory that the trickster is a degenerate version of an original and ideal figure of the hero to C. G. Jung's interpretation that the trickster corresponds to a "psyche . . . that has hardly left the animal level" (200). Maui, the trickster of the Maori and Polynesian people, illustrates the contradictory nature of this figure. An inveterate breaker of taboos and seducer of young maidens (he was known as Maui-of-the-thousand-tricks), he also stole fire from the gods, lassoed the sun to put it on a regular course, but died attempting to re-enter his mother's womb, thereby determining that rebirth would never be available to mankind. As cultural hero, the trickster is a changer, a transformer, or arranger (as opposed to the creator or maker hero) (Bynum, 162, 331–32). His service as cultural hero is not distinct from his behavior as trickster, since his benefits result from thievery, bravado, and general all-around hell-raising. Such performances often find the trickster out-maneuvering the gods. In the society of humans the trickster is shown as the breaker of taboos and the mocker of sacred things; sometimes he gets away with it, sometimes he is the victim of his own stupidity, greed, and ineptness.

Apart from the contradiction of the trickster and cultural hero combined in one figure, some trickster stories are characterized by what seems to be a preoccupation with scatological material and sexual license that further complicate the search for a comprehensive interpretation. In the Ashanti story of how jealousy came to the world, Ananse puts a purgative into the pot causing a husband to vacate his bed nine times during the night, allowing Ananse to have his way with the wife each time. The Winnebago laxative bulb story ends with trickster awash in a sea of his own excrement, an odious but presumably for the Winnebagos farcical scene. Phallic symbols were part of the cult of Hermes, the Greek trickster, an indication of his role as magician and marker of boundaries, since stone amulets in the shape of phalluses were used to bring good luck and dispel evil.

Despite these earthy proclivities the trickster is usually associated with the gods in some way. Often he is a messenger, as with Hermes, in other instances agent or antagonist of the gods, sometimes doing their bidding and sometimes thwarting them. Coyote the Navajo trickster takes a position near the door of the assembly of the gods so that he may ally himself with either side of the assembly, the good represented by the south side, the evil by the north side. Legba, trickster of the Fon of West Africa, is above all a mediator, although the role comes inadvertently. Legba had once been a doer of good deeds, but credit for his deeds went to Mawu, the female element of the Fon God. She, however, blamed him when anything evil happened. He objected to never receiving any credit and always bearing the blame, but Mawu insisted that since she was the master and Legba the servant the arrangement was as it should be. In retaliation Legba schemed against Mawu. He told her that thieves were planning to steal yams from her garden, so she warned that any such thievery would bring death. Legba stole her sandals one night, entered the garden, stole the yams, leaving her sandal prints in the garden. Legba gathered the people in order to match their sandals with the marks left in the garden, but none could be found. Legba's suggestion that Mawu set her sandal in the print annoyed her by its insolence, but when her sandal matched the marks in the garden, she was humiliated and accused Legba of tricking her. Finally she swore to leave the earth for the sky. In those days the sky was only six or seven feet above the earth, so Mawu was able to keep track of Legba, and when he committed a fault, she scolded him. Since Legba was still not out from under Mawu's thumb, he encouraged an old woman to throw her dirty dishwater at Mawu's resting place. This so angered Mawu that she moved further away, leaving Legba on earth. The removal of Mawu to heaven did not sever the connection between Legba and her but only allowed Legba to have some independence. For the Fon he remains the dominant agent which all beings, humans and gods, must use in order to address God. Despite their connections with the gods, Legba and other tricksters remain earthbound, neither fully of the earth nor wholly of the realm of the gods.

The trickster is thus an outsider, either by accident, as with Legba, or by choice as with Coyote, yet in no sense a pariah. On his own terms and in his own way, he serves both humans and the gods, and both have a place for him in their schemes of things. The trickster's marginality is also emphasized by his being protean in the extreme. He may be human, animal, divine, male (but capable of becoming female). Eshu of the Yoruba and Legba of the Fon are always given human form, but their neighbors, the Ashanti, have Ananse the spider as their trickster. Among North American Indians the trickster may take various animal forms, coyote among the Plains Indians, rabbit among the Algonquins, or raven or bluejay among the Pacific Northwest groups. As a human he may appear as a child, an old man, or simply ageless. Loki in Scandinavian mythology normally took the human shape but was capable of transforming himself into creatures belonging to the three realms of nature: salmon or seal, mare or falcon, fly or flea.

In some ways the most disconcerting trait of the trickster is his being the cause of laughter. His stupid, childlike, or obscene behavior often makes him the object of laughter. Wakjunkaga the Winnebago trickster instructed his anus to keep watch while he slept by the fire, but despite incessant flatulence it is unable to repel the foxes who come to steal meat. In another Winnebago story, trickster gets caught inside an old elk skull, falls into the river, and while floundering in the water is mistaken by the Indians for a supernatural being. Hermes is for the most part a singularly unhumorous trickster, although even he has a story in which he steals his mother's clothing while she is bathing. Thus the trickster plays tricks on others, breaks taboos, and ridicules the sacred, thereby making others the objects of laughter. The Fon proverb, Legba everywhere dances in the manner of a man copulating, suggests that Legba and other tricksters may themselves be the objects of laughter. The trickster's insatiable sexual appetites, his gluttony and greed, often place him in jeopardy and result in chaos.

The humor of bizarre behavior and contradictory traits juxtaposed with adventures as cultural hero are so disparate that the humorous element may at times be neglected or ignored. It is imperiled in part because some theories of the trickster focus on too limited material (for example, Jung's comments are based mainly on Radin's collection of Winnebago stories) or because the trickster is being fitted into some grand design (Jung again, but also Levi-Strauss). (The extent to which nonindigenous values are imposed by outsiders is an open question.) But to ignore or play down the humor in trickster stories is to do violence to the material and skew whatever meaning is ascribed to the figure. The humor is often broad, scatological, blasphemous, obscene, but also subtle, indirect, and satiric, the two kinds not necessarily unrelated, since farce and satire are by no means foreign to each other. It is the satiric element in the trickster material that suggests the trickster as a mythical source of satire, the trickster as a kind of inadvertent "archetype" through which and into which preliterate people and traditional cultures projected their mockery and ridicule of behavior that undermined social cohesiveness and allowed for socially approved ritual for disarming hostility and aggression.

The connection between satire and the trickster has not escaped the attention of the commentators, taking its place for some as one aspect among several. Mac Linscott Ricketts, for example, sees the trickster as "the world's greatest clown," the "embodiment of . . . all kinds of humor" (Ricketts, 347), satire being, of course, one kind. Jung saw a connection between the trickster and the Saturnalian rites celebrated in the medieval Feast of Fools and its variations, in picaresque tales, Italian low comedy, and the humor of Rabelais. But a more direct and less hypothetical connection was discussed by Radin himself when he noted that the Winnebago cycle was intended as a "satire on man and on Winnebago society" (*The Trickster,* 151). Satire was a telling element in the Rabbit trickster tales of African slaves in the southern United States. One of a number of tricksters carried to the eastern shore of the Americas, including Brazil, the Caribbean, and Virginia, the Rabbit trickster functioned not only as it did in its former environment, that is, as a way to mock socially undesirable behavior in the immediate culture, but also as a way for slaves to mock white culture, a world filled with "violence, injustice, cruelty" (Lawrence Levine; Edwards). R. S. Rattray believed that

Ashanti trickster tales originated as animal fables disguised as attacks on persons with undesirable character traits or whose conduct was antisocial, priests who cheated or tricked others, chiefs who were unjust, neighbors who were deceitful or greedy, masters who were oppressive. Storytellers were free to satirize in stories so long as they did not name names and so passed off their tales as make-believe (*Akan-Ashanti Folk Tales,* x–xl). If Rattray's account has any validity, the trickster figure was to some extent a device through which certain attitudes could be expressed.[2] This use of the trickster could therefore account for the antithetical and many-faceted image that the trickster projects, the varying material and functions determining the character rather than a pre-conceived character gathering about himself disparate and unassimilable material.[3]

But even as a guise for satiric strategy, the trickster is far from a simple figure. But then it is as difficult to generalize about "the satirist" and the nature of satire as it is to generalize about the trickster himself. What, for example, do Horace and Juvenal have in common? Aristophanes and Jane Austen? Byron, Bierce, and Blake? Heine, Hogarth, and Huxley? The manners, the forms, the techniques of satirists have been so rich and varied that analyses of satire tend to categorize in order to encompass the variety and complexity of the subject, to anatomize rather than to synthesize. Similarly the trickster presents several different satiric faces. Loki of Nordic mythology attacked the scandalous behavior of the gods, functioning as a direct-attack satirist, as did Juvenal. No one could stand up to Loki's repartee and mockery of sacred things. The Spider (Ananse) of West African folktales and the Rabbit of East African folktales attack indirectly the irrational authority symbolized in predatory beasts which they humiliate or punish.

Like many a protagonist of literary satire, the trickster is not only the attacker, he is also the butt or object of satire. Nanabozho, Algonquin culture hero, becomes at times the victim of his own stupidity and greed. Bamapama, trickster hero of the Murngin tribe of Australia, broke numerous taboos including incest, and for these acts, like the Coyote of North American Indian mythology, he became an object of disapproving laughter. The roles played by the trickster figure vary from the *alazon* who is outwitted by his animal companion (for example, 'Ti Malice in Haitian folklore) to the fool whose stupidity causes him to dive-attack his own reflection in the water, to the rogue whose adventures are a series of exposures of misused power and stultifying tradition. Eshu, the Yoruba trickster, has been assigned the role of satirist by Joan Wescott, who points out that Eshu "dramatizes the dangers which face men and the follies to which they are prone, and as such he serves as a red light warning" (345).

The trickster as "archetypal" satirist evokes the same kind of ambivalent reaction that satire and satirists evoke. The satirist, and an antecedent the magician, according to the argument developed by Robert C. Elliott, is feared and respected (*Power*, chap. 6). The creative powers of the satirist can be used to maintain order in society by enforcing the values and behavior needed to keep the community stable and peaceful. But the same powers can be used selfishly, vindictively, maliciously, tending to, if not anarchy, at least unsociability, even unsociality. The creative playfulness of a Swift, a Voltaire, or a Rabelais beguile us even as they make us uncomfortable with hard questions about human nature. Audiences laughed and marveled at the dialect wizardry and manic playfulness of Lenny Bruce but decried his breaking linguistic taboos and his depressing exposure of institutional hypocrisy.

As the trickster's position in myth is a mirror image of the satirist's position in society, so interpretation of the trickster is bedeviled by the same kind of contradictions and ambivalences. The very name trickster provides one clue to the anarchic and repugnant side of this mythological figure. His behavior is marked by deceit, even malice, as in the case of Loki's incessant gossiping about the gods. But beyond that there is a trickery with words, Hermes, for example, invoked by cursing tablets, leaden slabs buried in the ground with curses inscribed on them. Hermes, whose trickery in words and deed, caused Pandora to open that fateful box; Hermes whose way with words was later to make him god of rhetoric (Brown, 13–14); the art of communication to which satire is so indebted. Legba's nickname, *Aflakete,* or "I have tricked you," sets forth his primary quality, but Legba also served because of his mastery of languages as the mediator; among the gods, between gods and humans, and among humans (Pelton, 72). Although the trickster is a markedly erotic figure, his sexuality is not unreservedly procreative. The mischief of Eshu is illustrated by the song performed by his cult at a festival in 1957:

> We are singing for the sake of Eshu
> He used his penis to make a bridge
> Penis broke in two!
> Travellers fell into the river. (Qtd. in Wescott, 344)

But other trickster stories show him as stupid and capable of being easily duped. Afloat on the ocean in sight of land, he has to ask how to reach the shore. The Fox trickster prominent in several South American Indian tales is invariably undone by his own boastful and lewd nature. Such behavior, which is common in trickster tales from a variety of cultures, is hardly endearing. Hermes, in fact, became in the plays of Aristophanes the butt of satire as the self-seeking, fast-talking con artist, portrayed in the Sausage-Seller in the *Knights,* Unjust Reason of the *Clouds,* and the litigious type in the *Wasps.* Hermes appears as himself in *Wealth,* a down-at-the-heels god forced to threaten retribution door to door because no one troubles to sacrifice to the gods any longer. Even earlier Hipponax (second half of the sixth century B.C.), a savage and uninhibited railer, whose attacks are alleged to have driven some to suicide, took Hermes as his patron god, identifying presumably with the malicious outsider. And so the classicist Karl Kerenyi was moved to describe the trickster as the "spirit of disorder, the enemy of boundaries" ("The Trickster . . . ," 185). He is at once the breaker of taboos, the buffoon, the anarchist, the fool, the masochist, and the sensualist.[4] Although he may never be redeemed, he is not all bad.

Over against the hell-raiser, there is the rebel, the iconoclast, the enemy of unbridled power, and the teller of truth, which is not to make the trickster a moralist or do-gooder. Loki, whose wicked tongue caused him to be excluded from a banquet of the gods and goddesses, became gate-crasher and then party pooper by reciting in detail the infidelities and faults, including his own, of those present. No one denied the truth of his charges, but his audacity in telling them earned him the enmity of Thor and imprisonment until the end of the world.

Eshu, by an elaborate disguise, destroys the friendship of two men who were always seen together and who dressed alike to express their feelings for each other. Their quarrel over Eshu's disguise revealed that the friendship was superficial and that they were fools, as Eshu claimed. The adventures of some North American Indian tricksters imply a parody of religious myths, as with the "excrement advisors" who counsel Coyote (Ricketts, 336–37), as spirits and sacred objects counsel the warriors and priests of other myths. The story of the Plains Indians trickster who got his head stuck inside an elk skull and falls into the river, where he is mistaken by Indians for a supernatural being as he flounders about, implies a mockery of credulity about supernatural occurrences by a standard satiric device of showing that things are not always what they appear to be. Legba's trick against Mawu is not only a story of how she is eventually obliged to leave the earth, as all gods should, but also a satiric attack on injustice and pride. So, by nature, sometimes maliciously, sometimes not, the trickster mocks the mighty, the fools, and their behavior. Such irreverence is an important attribute of many tricksters, even though their motivation is rarely, if ever, altruistic or even moral. Like Kernan's description of the "satirist," the trickster portrays an ironic two-sidedness, one that serves justice, right, and social stability (in Kernan the public image), the other that is malicious, obscene, anarchic (the private side of Kernan's "satirist"). The description of Coyote tends to be largely derogatory, the object of suspicion even when he seems to be doing something worthwhile. Yet many of the adjectives applied to Coyote are also applicable to the satirist: "sneaking, skulking, wary, shrewd, tricky, mischievous, provoking, exasperating, contrary, undependable, amusing, disarming, persuasive, flattering, smug, undisciplined, cowardly, foolhardy, obstinate, disloyal, dishonest, licentious, lascivious, amoral, deceptive, sacrilegious, and, in a sense, persistent" (Reichard, 422–23). All of these have probably been applied to writers of satire at one time or another.

But beyond the characteristics of the trickster-satirist is the vision of the world inherent in satire itself. This is effectively captured by a mosaic of quotations from an account of the Yoruban trickster figure, the Tortoise, and the oral tales in which he is the central character. These quotations could as easily describe the verse satires of Juvenal, satiric works by Swift, the world and method of the picaresque novel, a Lenny Bruce monologue, or a Vonnegut novel. Or it can serve as a description of satire in general. Tortoise stories, we are told, occupy a "junior role in the literary family." They are told only at night, and children are warned against telling them in the daytime at the risk of losing their sight or at least their way home. Those in positions of influence, elders and priests who guard the order of society, refused to tell the tales of the Tortoise and his adventures.

These trickster tales present a "picture of society at its worst, . . . the world turned upside down by self-interest, passion, and contempt for social convention." The protagonist is a "figure who is the pure incarnation of chaos and disruption, the supreme agent who upsets the social order by fault of his personal excess. Greedy, intemperate, self-serving, he is also vain, impetuous, discontent, and rude. . . . Wholly self-obsessed, . . . the total affirmation of human will against the boundaries of social restraint." The other characters are "men-as-animals, animals-as-men, externally dehumanized so as to reveal the most human aspects of ourselves." The piece of satire attempts to "disarm reason, to lure the audience into an illogical frame in which nonsense becomes the basis for a new set of human action." It "knocks the props out from under narrative logic and collapses expectations," insinuating "a spirit of out-of-jointedness . . . into every facet of the mode," twisting "reality into conformity with its own distorted vision." Its chief aim appears temporarily "to disintegrate the bonds of social control and declare war on rules that hinder personal liberty," "to cast aside the everyday routine." It "makes a comic game of pomposity, power, and prestige"; "gods and kings are favorite targets for derision." The satirist "envelopes the audience in a tale of conflict to which it must respond, and the images it creates inspire tension that must be appeased at the story's end." "The principal function (of the satirist's tale) is to warn against the repetition of crimes and thoughtless acts that might engender chaos in people's lives" (La Pin, passim).

By no means an exact overlay or perfect analogue for satire in all places and all times, this descriptive mosaic still manages to capture the essence of satire, its vision of the world and some of the ways it works its wicked magic. That tales of the trickster should be the inspiration for such a description underscores the pervasive, protean, primeval presence of satire.

Thus the trickster and his stories portray to a significant extent the critical spirit, laughingly pointing out human vagaries, vices, and follies, bringing people nose to nose with their limitations, often by invoking the anarchy and chaos they so fear. His humor may be cruel and stupid, it may be mocking and irreverent. But it is a mark of the trickster and satirist as giant killers, slayers of the enemies of the community, those whose behavior ill serves society. The trickster may also become what he attacks. As an object of ridicule he becomes the victim, the scapegoat whose stupidity, greed, and pride must be exorcised by society. The trickster is disposable and indispensable, hero and scapegoat, feared and respected. By being or becoming what he attacks, the trickster-satirist reduces the distance between the folly and vice out there among others and the folly and vice in here in ourselves. Identification with the trickster-satirist becomes a trap by which we are able to see ourselves as the objects of satire, the ultimate satiric and ironic trick of the trickster.

What Good Is a Fool?

The mythological trickster is a creation of human imagination as is the concept of the archetype itself. That people in different cultures should create characters that share similar traits and exhibit similar behavior suggests either a large element of coincidence or else a common reaction to similar experiences and common needs. The failure to agree about what the trickster represents need not be a sticking point if it is agreed that the trickster at least in part served as a device that evoked laughter to criticize by indirection certain individuals and social behavior that deviated from community norms. It is probably impossible at this point to determine when and how this aspect of the trickster figure took shape. Whether the satiric elements were accretions by storytellers with what we would call a satiric bent, or whether such elements were solely laughter-evoking incidents cannot be determined, given the distance of time and the differences of cultures.

When the characteristics of the trickster are transferred to social reality and incorporated into human societies as a part of their rituals, we are on somewhat firmer ground. Clowns and fools do exist, and in certain societies the connection between such persons and the mythical trickster is quite explicit. Among the Dakota a person became a ritual clown (Heyoka) by having a vision of the god Iktomi, a trickster, or one of animals associated with him. The Koyemshi clowns of the Zuni were regarded as sons of the mythical figure who served also as a cultural hero and creator for the Zuni, that being one of varied roles played by a trickster figure.

Bamapama, the trickster figure among the Murngin of Australia, was the founder of the ceremonies in which the clown became the trickster figure behaving in crazy and obscene ways. Both Eshu and Elegba were imitated in ceremonies or festivals, the festival dedicated to Eshu falling in late December and early January, approximately the same time as the Roman Saturnalia.

The connection between the trickster figure, the clown or fool, and satire in European cultures is more difficult to establish. In preliterate societies the connection and justification are explicit, in European cultures circumstantial and tantalizing, but in the light of the explicit connections in other cultures, highly suggestive. There seems to be good reason to assume that trickster Loki, and perhaps other trickster-like figures of Scandinavian mythology, contributed to the *eiron*-like figure of Amleth, the antecedent of Shakespeare's Hamlet. Amleth, whose story is told three times in the *Danish History* of Saxo, the twelfth-century chronicler, survived his uncle's plot against him by playing the fool and using trickery. The connection between Loki and other Scandinavian trickster-like figures and Amleth is supposition, although that between Amleth and Hamlet is not. It is difficult if not impossible to sort out the connections among and development of trickster figures in Scandinavian myths, according to H. R. Ellis Davidson, but the powerful influence of Loki on Old Norse myths and legends and on Icelandic sagas is undeniable. The trickster and his eventual counterpart, the fool, are in Davidson's view "irrevocably linked to one another" (Davidson, "Loki," 16–17).

In Greek mythology Hermes, "a shape-changer, a liar, cheat and thief, a great lover and full of trickery and laughter," has long been recognized as a trickster figure (Burland, 70). Son of Zeus and Maia of the Peides, he was no creator or conqueror but a messenger and traveler, a dabbler in magic and adventures that often had unfortunate consequences. Like some tricksters of preliterate cultures, Hermes was the subject of cult worship, the phallus his sacred object, a sexual association common among trickster figures. In Crete the Hermaea involved role-reversal, a practice common in the Roman Saturnalia and later festivals in which satiric rituals occurred. *The Homeric Hymn to Hermes,* the authoritative text on Hermes as the thief, uses him as a source of sexual humor and the occasion for satiric imitations of Homer and Hesiod, the poem being performed in a court setting that implies a ritual presentation (Brown, 131–36). Concurrently with the *Hymn*, which is generally dated in the second half of the sixth century B.C., Hipponax found Hermes a congenial spirit to invoke in support of his savage and obscene satiric attacks. But a century later in Aristophanes' plays Hermes had become the butt of satire, a not unusual status since trickster figures (and Gulliver and Folly and many others) have allowed satiric writers to have it both ways. Many centuries later Thomas Mann equates Felix Krull, his picaresque hero, with Hermes and has Krull serve as both the object of satire and its (albeit unconscious) practitioner. Only in Aristophanes and indirectly in Hipponax and the *Homeric Hymn* may Hermes be seen as an actual clown as they follow in the spiritual footsteps of their trickster father.

Suggestive connections between the trickster and satiric clowning occur in Hermes' sons (whether by Iphthima or the Naiades is not certain). Hermes' sons are the Satyrs whose features—pointed ears, small horns and goat- or horselike tails—and behavior definitely associated them with animal antecedents. (Hermes is never seen as an animal, but he has animal characteristics—guile, stealth, trickiness—and is closely associated with several animals, as cattle thief, as inventor of the lyre from a tortoise shell.) The Satyrs dress in the skins of animals and wreaths of evergreens and are shunned because they steal, drink, and live sensual lives in the forest. Elderly versions of Satyrs are Sileni (they begin to show up in Greek art as a separate generation about the early sixth century B.C.) and although they have many of the characteristics of Satyrs, they also have intellectual abilities. Both Satyrs and Sileni were connected with the worship of Dionysus. The connection between the festivals of Dionysus and the origin of Greek comedy was noted briefly by Aristotle and has been argued persuasively by twentieth-century classical scholars, especially H. Herter and A. W. Pickard-Cambridge. The role of the Satyrs and Sileni in the ceremonies out of which the old lampooning and invective-spewing comedy came is not known but that they had no role is hard to believe.

Their role in that tantalizing Attic form known as Satyric drama is better known. Here they serve as a chorus (in the only extant play, Euripides' *Cyclops*), dress according to popular notions, and add mockery to Euripides' satiric imitation of a tragic theme. A final connection between the Satyrs and Sileni and satire is that between the Sileni and Socrates who shared not only an acknowledged ugliness but also the use of irony in the search for wisdom and truth. Socrates and popular Greek philosophers are credited with the invention of the diatribe (although its literary forms are attributed to Bion), the influence of Socrates showing up in the persona, irony, and spirit of Horace's *Sermones* (Anderson, 23). Given the animal-like features and behavior of the Satyrs and Sileni and their proclivity for comic hell-raising, one can easily imagine their being at home with the Koyemshi and the ritual clowns of other cultures. Unfortunately, on the basis of one short Satyr play one cannot assume too much about their function as satirists nor on the basis of similarities make too much of their connection with Socrates. But long ago the word *satire* was thought to have been derived from *satyr,* a theory long since discredited. Despite the faulty etymology, the connection in spirit may have contained a truth that ought not to have been discarded when the etymological connection went by the boards.

Satirists show up in early Celtic literature and in Arabic literature, but their special powers seem not to be attributed to any connection with tricksters or similar figures. But the magic of the curse and other forces of language with which they are endowed, are not far removed from the powers that tricksters are gifted with, Hermes associated with cursing tablets, Loki the railing trickster, Elegba the master of languages, Coyote and Rabbit forked-tongued comics. So, since the source of the power of the Celtic and Arabic satirists is never specified, it is not hard to imagine a trickster lurking in the dim mythological background. The special powers ascribed to clowns, fools, and satirists whose antecedents are tricksters lingers on in various guises. In medieval and later times it was often assumed that the "natural" fool, that is, one whose mental powers were somehow limited, was "touched" in such a way as to make him exempt from the ordinary claims of normal behavior, thereby bestowing a freedom to act and speak in a way denied normal persons.

A kind of reverse version of this power can be seen in the retroactive influence once attributed to Swift's "madness," the combination of infirmities that oppressed his last years. Even today the manic routines of a Robin Williams or a Richard Pryor can so amaze an audience as to leave it wondering, "Where does he get his material?" thereby implying a talent and imagination that is not quite comprehensible. In an age with different superstitions such bedazzled reaction might imagine a mythological trickster source for their zany and raunchy routines. Apart from imaginary or designated connections with mythical or extraordinary powers, the fool/clown and the trickster had and have many traits in common. Laura Makarius in her study of ritual clowns and tricksters lists the following that are relevant here: "Excentricity [*sic*] in dress and demeanor; systematic trampling over rules and norms; full license to ignore prohibitions and break them; ambivalence; magical power; . . . individualism; asocial characteristics, insolence, buffoonery, phallicism, vulgarity, a sort of madness" (66). Although Makarius's study is concerned only with ritual clowns in primitive societies, her list applies to many modern counterparts as well as to figures found in folklore and myth.

Given the role and power of such figures, it is not surprising that all societies have provided means to contain and control their behavior. When the fool/clown was believed to have magical powers, it was understandable that a community or society found ways to channel the powers that could be misused but that were so necessary for some not clearly understood reason. Although such magical resources are no longer associated with their modern versions, anyone who has seen an audience roar its approval of the anti-establishment or antisocial jokes of a stand-up comedian, or individuals leaping to their feet with clenched fists waving in the air in support and agreement, can still sense a strong rapport between the performer and the audience that suggests communication at a very basic level. The reactions of presidents and politicians to cartoonist Herblock and humor columnist Art Buchwald and reaction of certain groups to comedian Lenny Bruce suggest that such figures exert a residual power to disturb and amuse that ties them to a tradition that goes back to the trickster figure however attenuated it may appear today.

Although his guises have been as varied as the societies in which he has appeared, the fool is the human version of the mythical trickster. According to the taste of the time, the relationship to his audience, and the manner of performance, the fool has appeared as dwarf, clown, juggler, acrobat, buffoon, court jester, wise fool, fool of the Tarots, country bumpkin, Jack Pudding, mountebank, *sot,* macaroni, merry-Andrew, *zanni,* knave, "holy fool," innocent, joke teller, wit, merrymaker, Punch, Harlequin, comic actor, newspaper columnist, nightclub or cabaret comedian, vaudeville joker, cartoonist, radio, film, or television comic. Such persons may cause laughter by their grotesqueness (dwarfs), facial or bodily contortions (clowns), or their inherent stupidity or ignorance (bumpkins). They may tell jests or jokes or purvey other forms of verbal contortions (the comic, the columnist, or the wit). One person may combine several ways of causing laughter, as for example, Triboulet, the famous court fool of Louis XII and Francis I, who was a simpleton with a talent for mimicry, music, and dancing, or Will Rogers, who combined rope twirling with joke telling and satiric comment, or Richard Tarleton, famous English comic actor. The laugh-invoking behavior of the fool may be natural as in the case of Triboulet, as conscious as that of George Carlin ("Occupation: Foole"), or as feigned as that of Will Rogers ("All I know is what I read in the newspapers"). Feigning stupidity or ignorance or naïveté to cause laughter is a small step away from pointing out such traits in others, thereby inducing laughter.

The various guises in which the fool has appeared, the differences in taste from nation to nation, age to age, and culture to culture, and the ephemeral nature of the "occupation" have tended to obscure the fact that one important function performed by the fool was and continues to be satiric (Gluckman, 102–4; Caillois, *Man and the Sacred,* 141). It was not until the advent of the technology to record images and sounds that the fare of the fool could be preserved to any extent. No jesters of the courts of royalty, houses of the wealthy, or chambers of churchmen from ancient Greece to eighteenth-century England have had their Boswells. Even less is known about the clowns of primitive cultures. Of the 136 representative cultures in the Cross-Cultural Survey of the Institute of Human Relations at Yale University, only fifty-six contain relevant material, partly because such information is incidental to the main purpose of the investigation, understandable since few anthropologists have seriously engaged in the study of humor in primitive culture (Apte, "Humor Research," 194). Some fools of European societies such as Tarleton, Scogan, and Claus Narr became the persona around which collections of jests were gathered, but more often than not such collections were commercial ventures and may or may not have had anything to do with the actual person. Moreover the office of fool was a precarious one, especially if the fool attempted to be satiric. He ran a double risk, the risk of entertainer not pleasing the audience and the risk of the satirist offending the audience.

The natural fool or simpleton was protected in part by the superstition that such persons were in some way divinely inspired and therefore spoke the truth. The freedom to speak forbidden truths was incorporated into the roles of the jester and the stage fool so that at various times they function satirically as wise fools. As one seventeenth-century play had it, the fool therefore "hath a patent of immunities / Confirmed by costume, seald by pollicie, / As large as spatious thought" (*Antonio's Revenge,* IV, 1). The court fool and other jesters of the early Renaissance, as Enid Welsford has noted, sometimes actively involved themselves in controversies, as those who mocked religious ceremonies in the spirit of reform or those who in support of their masters attacked the reformers. Still others such as the "chaouls" of the Tartar princes reported by John Doran amused their masters with satirical songs. Philip of Macedonia occasionally allowed his fool to make satiric remarks about his royal person. But any fool who insists too strongly on being satiric may suffer the fate of Lenny Bruce, whose encounters with the laws of England and the United States stemmed at least in part from his breaking social taboos.

The satiric function of the fool emerges with greater intensity in the fool as literary character and in ritualized satire than it does in the person of the fool. In ritualized satire social customs allow and even institutionalize the behavior of the fool. The legendary or quasi-legendary Si-Djoha and Buhlul the Madman from Arabian literature, and Marcolf and Till Eulenspiegel from the literatures of Western Europe had attached to them stories and anecdotes in which they put down kings, the rich and the wise, satirized women (Marcolf), religion (Buhlul), and tradesmen (Eulenspiegel). Even though the character of Marcolf changed during the evolution of the legend, the use of the persona for satire is constant. Marcolf and Eulenspiegel thrived amid the great manifestation in art of the ritual world of the fool which flourished between the mid-fifteenth and mid-seventeenth centuries. During that period fool societies abounded throughout Europe, especially in France, presenting during festival and other holidays *sotties,* that is, skits and revues performed by members dressed as fools, which viewed humans as endlessly foolish. Writings in which fools are characters or which portray humans as fools were so numerous during these centuries that they can be designated as a body of work known as "fool literature." Sebastian Brant's *The Ship of Fools* and Erasmus's *Praise of Folly* are the best known works of literature to come out of this tradition, both important works of satire of their kind. This preoccupation with the fool also manifests itself in the art of Holbein, Bruegel, and Dürer, among others. At another level it occurs in the fly sheets, the illustrated broadsheets, and other manifestations of the popular printer's art devoted to the theme of "the topsy-turvy world" (*die verkehrte velt*). The fool figures prominently in the work of Rabelais and Shakespeare, after which the fool as a character in literature pretty much disappears.

The appearance of the fool was most conventionalized during the period of his greatest popularity and importance. Little about the fool's appearance, however, was exclusively the fool's nor did the guise stay the same for a long period. A shaved head, a hood, frequently with ass's ears, a coat or jacket of motley, sometimes with bells attached, and a bauble or marotte became the conventional signs of the fool in the court, on the stage, and in art. Although the animal symbolism of the ass's ears seems clear enough, the use of foxtail and coxcomb is less so, although both have traditional connections with satire. The fox and various kinds of birds were also forms in which the trickster appeared. The fool's bauble, which varied in form from an imitation phallus to a bladder to a replica of the fool himself, was a mock scepter marking the fool as ruler of all fools, a means of mock castigation, and perhaps an abased imitation of primitive fertility rites. Although the idea of a costume for the fool has long since disappeared, latter-day fools often have objects which have come to be associated with them, as the violins of Jack Benny and Henny Youngman, the cigar of Groucho Marx, the long cigarette holder of Phyllis Diller, the cane of Charlie Chaplin, the auto horn of Harpo Marx, and the rubber mallet of Pigmeat Markham ("Here come da Judge!"). Despite the similarity during the Middle Ages between the shaved heads and hooded figures of the fools and monks, no case has been made for the fool mocking the monks, since shaved and hooded fools can also be found in Greek and Roman art and drama.

The person of the court jester, the supposedly traditional appearance of the fool, and prominence of the fool figure in medieval art and life have combined to obscure the fact that cultures and societies as varied as the Eskimo, Aztec, Arabian, Pueblo, Mexican, Zulu, Xhosa, Roman, Hebrew, Chinese, North and South American Indian, the United States, and Western Europe have or have had persons whose function was to entertain others by engendering laughter in some way. The complexity of this function and the fool's relationship to the culture in which he or she operated has been described in various ways through the ages. Robert Armin in his *Nest of Ninnies* (1608) noted that fools occurred in three forms: sinner, social critic, and merrymaker. The fool in *Wit Without Money* (1639), however, is described as "an innocent, a knave-fool, a fool politic" (II, ii, 15). Enid Welsford and William Willeford have attempted to refine the fool into an archetypal figure, for the former that of "spiritual freedom," for the latter a psychological phenomenon which allows humans to glimpse the void behind chaos from a position of order and structure. Mary Olive Busby and Barbara Swain have seen the fool as a scapegoat figure, a metaphorical safety valve or lightning rod for expressing or attracting socially unacceptable truths, behavior, or views. For Anton Zijderveld the fool created a looking-glass world in which reality was reversed and loosed from its moorings. The implied chaos was "regressive," an implied warning to society of what could happen. But such a reality was also "progressive" in what possibilities for change inhered in it. The fool's message was thus both anarchic and prophetic. Unfortunately, the urge for a unitary view or interpretation of the meaning of the fool figure ends in needless oversimplification, generally emphasizing one aspect of the fool while sometimes overplaying or ignoring others. One of these aspects has been the rich association with satire in the fool, whether it be as instrument or object, natural or artificial, conscious or unconscious, in the court or in the marketplace.

The Fool Lives: Ritual and Satire

The stand-up comedian and the newspaper humor columnist are such familiar figures in contemporary life that we fail to see the ritual, muted in an open and diffuse modern society, in their role. They are in fact contemporary institutionalized versions of the fool figure of legend and literature, their audience often remote and scattered, their impact diluted or roundabout. It has not always been so. From Archilochus to the present, a variety of individuals, in motley and out, have served satire in a ritualized form. Performing before often small but sophisticated audiences, their function as satiric artists was encouraged and even rewarded.

Greek verse in the iambic measure was largely satiric, recited at banquets or symposia, probably by the poet himself. Eduard Fraenkel points out that symposia were not merely the occasions for reciting poetry (sometimes accompanied or sung) but were by their existence an incentive for composing poetry (36–41; Humphreys, 219; Murray, 1308). Speeches in the iambic meter had been part of the byplay of fertility celebrations, and bearers of the phallus were free to shout abusive and obscene speeches at anyone they chose. The word *iamb* came to mean the same as to abuse or to revile, in effect, what is today called invective. The Greek tradition of lampoon, personal attack, in the iambic meter existed before Homer and was associated with comic invective whose subject, vocabulary, and form were distinct from elegy and epic poetry. The tradition of Greek literature and the institutions of the banquet and the symposia combined to make iambic poetry a type of ritual satire.

The first and greatest of the iambic poets was Archilochus (c. 680–c. 640 B.C.), whose work expresses the iambic spirit in its most compelling form. Lampoon, especially of someone who had broken a promise to him, is central to his most effective satiric poetry. Legendary is the attack on Lycambes who earned Archilochus's ire by promising his daughter in marriage and then withdrawing the promise. Archilochus's invective was said to have driven Lycambes and his daughter to suicide.

Performing before the sophisticated audiences of the age of Antonines, Lucian (A.D. c. 115?–c. 180) developed the dialogue into a satiric tool of great lightness and brilliance. The special dramatic element of his dialogues made them virtually a new art form. The novelty of his dialogue of the dead, dialogues of the gods, and dialogues of the courtesans and the irreverent attitude toward mythical heroes and the gods made Lucian one of the most sought-after of performers. The satiric dialogue, a long-lived and widely used form, was born out of the ritual of performance (Baldwin, chap. 6; Bellinger, 3–29).

The *sirventes* of the troubadours are ritually similar to the poems of the iambist of Greece. Satiric *sirventes* comprise a substantial subgroup of poems written by troubadours as part of the court life of southern France and nearby Italy and Spain. *Sirventes* took their poetic and musical form from the *canso,* whose technical complexity mattered most to the troubadour since it was the quality of the *cansos* that determined a troubadour's reputation. No *sirventes* has its own form. It was as though a composer of modern popular love songs put satiric lyrics to his own songs or to the love songs of another composer, becoming a combination of Burt Bacharach and Martin Mull. *Sirventes* comprise a sizable and varied body of satiric verse, varying in tone from the gentlest of spoofs to personal invective. Their subject matter runs from the cowardliness of kings to the immorality of women of the court. Two *sirventes* bear a remarkable similarity to the spirit of the American "roast," one by Peire d'Alverne (or de Aubergne) (fl. 1145–80) and another by a troubadour known as the Monk of Montaudon (fl. 1180–1212). Montaudon says,

> Since Peire d'Alverne has sung
> of those troubadours now past,
> I will sing, as best I can, of those
> who have appeared most recently;
> and let them not be angry
> if I criticize their failings.

He then spoofs nearly a dozen and a half of his contemporaries in a spirit of lighthearted mockery. Satire thus had a recognized and accepted place in the court life of southern Europe from about 1100 to 1350, the era of the troubadours (Bonner; Wilhelm; Hueffer).

The posting of pasquinades, which began in Italy around the turn of the sixteenth century, became a form of ritual satire that lasted for nearly three centuries. The legendary beginning of the pasquinade has it that a battered statue (perhaps of Hercules) was uncovered in Rome and set up in a square of the city. Nicknamed Pasquino in honor of a scathing-tongued schoolmaster or perhaps cobbler, innkeeper, tailor, or barber (versions of the legend tend not to be very firm on this detail), the disfigured trunk became the place to attach satirical verse in Latin commenting on the Pope, his government, and prominent persons of the times. The "Feast of Pasquino" occurred on April 25 when the statue was dressed up to represent some pagan deity or classical personage, although the dressing of Pasquino in satiric squibs went on as events demanded. A subordinate part of the legend of Pasquino was the introduction of another statue, found in the Campus Martinus and said to have represented a river god, dubbed therefore Marforio (*a foro Martis*). A pasquinade could thus also be a question-and-answer dialogue with a Marforio asking leading questions of his progenitor (Disraeli; Puttenham, 1, 27).

The tradition of satirical antipapal commentary continued in Rome until the 1870s. Stendhal in the early nineteenth century in *Rome, Naples,* and *Florence* said that he doubted that "there be any race in Europe with a greater fondness for the bite and ingenuity of satire than the worthy citizens of Rome," who "desire above all else . . . to show their strong contempt for the powers that control their destiny, and to laugh at their expense: hence the dialogue between *Pasquino* and *Marforio*" (472–73). In 1860 Charles Eliot Norton reported that Pasquino "still pursues his ancient avocation" (395–405). Fernando and Renato Silenzi, chroniclers of three centuries of Pasquino satire, date the demise of Pasquino as 18 July 1870 when Italy was unified and papal political power reduced (224). The Church, of course, had never approved of Pasquino, and Pope Adrian in the sixteenth century ordered the statue thrown in the Tiber in retaliation for the pasquinades which opposed his election (he was Flemish), some composed by Pietro Aretino, known in his time as the "scourge of princes." Legend reports that Adrian was dissuaded from doing so for fear that the frogs would croak pasquinades (Alexander; Cleugh, 46–53).

But in its time the *terrae filius* speech seems to have been regarded as perhaps the most pestiferous form of ritual satire by an individual discussed so far. Originally a serious part of the Oxford University commencement ceremony, the *terrae filius* speech (its counterpart at Cambridge was known as the "prevaricator") gradually became so distasteful to some that attempts were made to banish it from the ceremony. Some *terrae filius* were expelled, some beaten, one had his speech burned publicly. Returning after a twenty-year hiatus in the early eighteenth century (it isn't clear whether the performances of the *terrae filius* caused the cancellation), the *terrae filius* never attained the notoriety that it formerly had (Buxton and Gibson; Smith and Ethninger). For well over a hundred years the *terrae filius* had poked fun at the university and those connected with it. In Thomas Baker's play *An Act of Oxford* (1704) the *terrae filius* is described by one character as

> ". . . the Universal Jester, the
> Terrour of fuddling Doctors, and fornicating
> Commoners, a Serviter of Scandal, an Harlequin
> of Sciences," his speech and "Antipanegyrick . . .".
> Grimace, and Front, a sort of Law-Oratory
> without Truth of Modesty.

The fool of course had not disappeared from European life with the decline of "fool literature" following Shakespeare's day. In England fool literature continued in folk culture and in the popular theater, in rural fairgrounds with traveling troupes and on the London stage with the recognized playwrights. Of the many guises in which the fool appeared, the "fairground Fool" persisted from the fourteenth to the eighteenth century, mainly as "satirical mouthpiece and butt" (Billington, x, chap. 5 passim), during the latter period. John Arbuthnot and others transformed the Jack Pudding figure into a metaphor for persons who lined their pockets by gaining power or associating with those in power. Articles in *The Craftsman, The Gentleman's Magazine,* and elsewhere used the fool imagery to attack Whigs and Tories. But the rustic fool was ridiculed by John Gay and Henry Fielding for his slapstick and witless laughter, and Samuel Butler in his *Characters* describes the fool as "a centaur, a Mixture of Man and Beast, like a Monster engendered by unnatural copulation, a Crab grafted on an Apple . . . neither made by Art, nor Nature, but in Spight of both, by evil custom."

By the end of the eighteenth century the Fool figure was beginning to trifurcate into prototypes recognizable in comedy since that time: the folk-Fool continued in England down to the present century; respectable comedians who played comic roles on the stage; the satirist comic who put aside the rustic Fool and created a new kind of clown, closer in appearance to the present-day circus clown but still retaining the freedom of the Fool to criticize those in power. Such was Joseph Grimaldi (1778–1837). During the first three decades of the nineteenth century Grimaldi spoke to those who were crowding into the city slums of England with memories of the rustic Fool. According to Richard Findlater,

Grimaldi became the spokesman for the average person by attacking the fads and fancies of fashionable society, the conduct of the Napoleonic war and Georgian greed (157). He mocked the Prince Regent's admiration for the red-coated Hussars by appearing on stage wearing black coal scuttles (for boots), horseshoes (for heels), a muff (cap), and so on. Because Covent Garden where Grimaldi appeared was threatened with withdrawal of royal patronage for Grimaldi's antimilitaristic satire, he was forced to desist. After Grimaldi's retirement in 1827 satire by the Fool figure receded from the British popular stage.

Later in the nineteenth century in the United States satire and humor were purveyed in a ritual context by such platform performers as Artemus Ward, Josh Billings, Petroleum V. Nasby, and, of course, Mark Twain. Following in the lyceum tradition of education and culture via lecturer, humorists after the Civil War mocked the tradition by delivering lectures that were spoofs of those beloved by middle-class audiences eager for moral and cultural uplift. An appearance by Billings contained a dozen or more mini-"lectures" on various subjects, including the busybody, the dog, hotels, ants, the shade tree, rats, patience, hornets, flirts, and so on. His advice to lecture committees mocks the entire ritual from arrival to departure. Twain introduced the self-introduction in which he mocked that stilted and embarrassing prologue. His lectures, however, tended to steer clear of subjects that would offend his audiences, especially as he became better known. In general, religion and politics were avoided by Billings, Ward, and Twain. Nasby, on the other hand, confronted the issues of race, equality for women, and the morality of what Twain would christen the Gilded Age. Unlike the others who tended to pose as innocents and whose delivery was determinedly informal and deadpan, Nasby lectured with an ironic wit that drove home his points, billing himself as "The Crossroads Politician."

The performance of the satiric fool since the nineteenth century is clearly less ritual than commercial performance. No longer tied to seasonal or institutional contexts, the fool is also divorced from various forms of religious and political patronage. The freedom gained thereby is, however, compromised by the growing dominance of commercial considerations. If a latter-day Grimaldi is no longer beholden to royal patronage, twentieth-century literary comedians had to be careful not to alienate their audiences by trampling on their sensibilities and treasured beliefs. Nevertheless they continue to speak their piece however attenuated the ritual contexts. Minstrel shows, lecture stage, and circuses in the United States, music halls and vaudeville in England, and the theater, cabaret, and circus in Europe have provided the scene for ritual satire by fools in the nineteenth and twentieth centuries. These have been supplemented by the rise of the mass media. Since the 1960s virtually no place is safe from satire. Night clubs, factories, public squares, auditoriums, arenas as well as theaters and circus rings have served as scenes for ritual satire, which is not to be confused with the commercialized comedy that has become a commodity dispensed in franchised comedy clubs, TV sitcoms, and spoof films.

Although the humor industry has expanded into a vast enterprise, especially in the United States, it has not eliminated the satiric fool. He perseveres, although rarely at the center of things. Whether in the guise of stand-up comic or one-person revue, he persists in the form of Mort Sahl in San Francisco, Pieter-Dirk Uys in South Africa, Dario Fo in Italy, Arkady Raikin in Moscow. Satiric clowns and fools are featured in the works of political theater groups such as the El Teatro Campesino, the Theatre du Soleil, and the San Francisco Mime Troupe (Schecter, viii). The manic monologues of Robin Williams, *The Great Dictator* of Charlie Chaplin, *The General* of Buster Keaton, and occasional columns by Royko, Trillin, and Buchwald show that the fool persists even in the midst of rampant commercialism. From the Cracow, Poland, cabaret, Under the Ram, which had its thirtieth anniversary in 1986, to the touring Montana Logging and Ballet Company, the fool lives to practice his age-old role of puncturing the pretensions of humanity in contexts which society tolerates.

At other times and in other places, *flytings,* dialogues, *sirventes,* iambic poems, pasquinades, *sotties,* raillery, and *hijas* have passed from ritual into literature. In short, the line between ritual satire and literary satire is at times virtually nonexistent. They share the same targets, techniques, imagery, and verbal devices. But to suggest that literary satire and ritual satire are analogous would do violence to the concept of ritual. The separation of the literary satirist from his or her audience, especially in contemporary life, precludes the formal conditions and patterned circumstances necessary to ritual. In Victor Turner's terms, literary satire exemplifies the *liminoid,* ritual satire the *liminal.* The former is secular, fragmentary, and marginal to central social processes, subversive; whereas ritual satire is religious, integrated into natural and social processes with a common meaning for the community ("Variations").

But literary satire is beholden to ritual satire as precursor in spirit and as a source of a rich variety of forms. Literary satire, as William Kinsley has argued, is unlike any other literary form in the relation between its audience, its victims, its form, and its creator. It involves, in Kinsley's words, an "energetic interaction of fact and fiction." Although the piece of literary satire is a fictional projection, it succeeds most fully when its audience relates that fiction to the world outside the fiction. The satirist attempts to persuade the audience to join (or at least enjoy) the attack, which requires the audience to relate the work to a person, event, group, or other real entity from the world shared by the satirist and the audience. This unique characteristic of satire is readily understood and accounted for by reference to satire's mythic and ritual antecedents in which the sharing is immediate, explicit, and communal, unlike the sharing in literary satire.

But the "interaction" that Kinsley speaks of can be extended to the forms and genres on which satire feeds. Satire is the most cannibalistic of art forms. It hardly exists apart from other genres, forms, and modes. Satire occurs in the novel and in poetry, in painting, music, and architecture, but no example can be called "a satire." Satire takes on the form of burlesque, dialogue, obituary, recipe, and numerous other forms, literary and folk, but none can be called "a satire." It will be a mock-encomium, a mock almanac, mock-heroic, a send-up, a take-off, a put-down, always derivative, never a thing itself. But this characteristic illustrates another kind of interaction. Satire's usurping of other forms creates a kind of microritual involving the satirist, the audience, and a form. The reader (to use literature as an example), seeing something that looks like a novel, a poem, a series of dictionary entries, or a recipe, will on the basis of previous experience with such forms have certain expectations, in short, the constituents of a ritual. The satirist of course violates the expectations. The reader will normally grant the satirist the freedom to do so, just as the viewer grants the fool or the comic the freedom to say outrageous things in certain contexts and circumstances. For the literary satirist, however, the ceremonial and communal aspects of ritual satire have become so attenuated as to exist only residually and psychologically.

Ritual satire and literary satire have coexisted and interacted for a long time and will probably continue to do so. Less widespread than it once was, ritual satire appears incipiently and abortively amid conditions that cannot sustain it for long. But that it continues to exercise its power can be illustrated by examples in which failure to recognize that power brought in one case embarrassment, in the other tragedy. One was Mark Twain's speech at John Greenleaf Whittier's seventieth birthday dinner, the other the career of Lenny Bruce.

The dinner for John Greenleaf Whittier's seventieth birthday given by the *Atlantic* magazine is remembered mainly because Mark Twain put his foot in his mouth. William Dean Howells served as toastmaster, and among the guests were Emerson, Longfellow, Holmes, and Twain. Twain's comments for the evening consisted of a story in which Emerson, Longfellow, and Holmes are presented as overnight visitors in the cabin of a miner in the Sierras where they arrive tipsy, spend the evening playing euchre, and steal the host's boots when they leave in the morning. The miner is not convinced by Twain's assurance that the three are impostors, especially since Twain has informed the miner who he is. The miner's response is, "Impostors, were they? are you?"

Newspapers across the country reported the event, many finding Twain's story insulting to the nearly legendary literary figures from New England, according to Henry Nash Smith. Some enjoyed Twain's audacity, but on the whole Twain's performance was looked upon as one of those lapses in taste best forgotten as quickly as possible. Twain's reaction was ambivalent, apologetic at first, later finding his speech "just as good as good can be," concluding that perhaps his delivery had been faulty. Like some bungling trickster, Twain had wrought well but had overestimated his ability to carry it off. Three decades later he considered delivering the speech again, this time at the annual "roast" of the Gridiron Club of Washington, D.C., newspapermen. His tale would have been appropriate as part of the Gridiron Club proceedings, but he chose instead to reminisce about his days as a newspaperman. In Twain's good-natured mocking of his literary elders, we have an inadvertent, miniature version of what has since become an American institution, the ritual roast. The testimonial birthday dinner is a ritual with its own ground rules obviously different from those of the roast. Twain's benighted attempt to mix the two caused all the trouble.

A more tragic example of the violation of the ritual is the career of Lenny Bruce. During the last five years of his life he underwent trials for obscene performances in San Francisco, Chicago, Philadelphia, and New York City, and was twice denied entry into England. Bruce's outspokenness so incensed a person in one audience that afterward he threw Bruce through a plate glass window. Like the Dakota and Koyemshi ritual clowns and the legendary trickster, Bruce toyed with taboos, defining and exploring the limits of what was acceptable, more often than not by breaking the taboos. Thus he played with then such taboo subjects as snot, venereal disease, homosexuality, and race. He mocked the Pope and other religious leaders and joked about racial and ethnic hostilities and stereotypes. Although he was acquitted in two trials, and the decision in one trial was reversed in his favor, his career slowly declined. The causes were complex and probably deep-rooted in his past, but certainly the time and energy consumed by his desire to act as his own lawyer at the New York trial, his increasing use of drugs, and the difficulty in finding places that would allow him to perform all contributed to his downfall and death. As "ritual clown," a seeming throwback to another time and place, he could not be accommodated in a society that had no forum or ceremony for such a figure. In addition, he finally became less and less a clown and performer and more and more an advocate for a cause, less artist, more fanatic (Goldman). Kenneth Tynan described Bruce as a "nightclub Cassandra bringing news of impending chaos, a tightrope walker between morality and nihilism" (qtd. in Kakutani, "Drama Critic"). Like a latter-day Loki, Bruce's license to satire was revoked because he violated the ritual. His anger and hostility overwhelmed the satire. Breaking the ground rules became an end in itself as he became more important than the ritual. In Bruce's act, the anarchic tendency, always a threat in ritual satire and in satire in general, dominated the ritual which it is designed to control.

Ritual satire ultimately serves the purposes of some community. It can suggest ethical or moral norms by mocking behavior that is detrimental to social cohesion or which deviate from group standards. It can promote social communion through laughter. It encourages self-control in the face of ridicule. Conversely it may promote individual and social health by allowing for the release of anger, frustration, and hostility, and by permitting relaxation of routine and discipline. But since too much release and relaxation may lead to anarchy, ritual satire sets boundaries that emphasize communal values over individual desires. "Ritual," anthropologist Max Gluckman has pointed out, "is effective because it exhibits all the tensions and strife inherent in social life itself" (265; see also Babcock). Ritual satire uses the sound of laughter and the glory of humor and verbal energy as forces whereby humans control and channel aggression and criticism in order to re-create and transcend themselves and society.

To suggest similarities between trickster characters from primitive folk tales and contemporary stand-up comics, between Legba and Lenny Bruce, seems on the surface ludicrous. Can vast cultural differences between so-called primitive and highly technologized societies be put aside so easily? Without in the least suggesting that such differences are negligible, the evidence strongly implies that the roles, functions, and behavior of certain characters and individuals throughout history and in various cultures have a great deal in common. Whether imbedded in folk tales, folk rituals, institutional traditions, or commercial endeavors, groups and society have allowed, even encouraged, certain types to flourish in a special context and relationship with those around them. Such individuals have sometimes produced literary satire, sometimes satire without literary or artistic trappings. Whatever the result, they provide archetypal antecedents and ritual underpinnings that enhance our understanding of satire as a literary expression.

3

Satire and Ritual

> There is no doubt that all human art primarily developed in the service of ritual and that the autonomy of "art for art's sake" was achieved only by another secondary step in cultural progress.
>
> Konrad Lorenz, *On Aggression*

Satire, What Is Thy Sting?

In ancient Sumeria and in twentieth-century United States, in American Indian tribes and professional clubs of women, in Newfoundland and India, cultures in great numbers and forms have allowed or encouraged groups of individuals to perform or express themselves satirically in a communal context. Such persons or groups have or have had in effect a license for satire. Using various direct and indirect means, they deride, mock, and ridicule individuals, groups, and institutions of their communities. Because their satire takes place under special circumstances, it can be considered ritual satire. Holidays, feasts, festivals are often the occasions for such satire; courts, clubs, processions, ceremonies (or burlesque versions thereof) are often the setting; costumes, disguises, music, and special props are often pressed into use. In some cases individuals acting alone may be allowed the freedom to behave satirically, but more often groups are allowed this freedom. Depending on the society in which such occasions occur, the groups may be clubs, guilds, professional organizations, youth groups, religious orders, whole towns or villages, or informal and impromptu groups. Their activities range from highly formal and traditional to spontaneous and ephemeral. Whatever the form and circumstances, normal day-to-day routines are breached, an unusual degree of freedom is available, playfulness abounds, a special spirit is abroad. Such communal activities, here called "ritual satire," share all the characteristics of literary satire and in some cases may even be antecedent to it. Generally, however, ritual satire co-exists with satire in literary or oral tradition.

Ritual satire is clearly a more public and more social expression than much literary satire is, that is to say, whatever form it takes, it acts more directly and more immediately than most literary satire. It is possible therefore to observe more easily the reasons, or the social rationale, for ritual satire. Unfortunately, it is not always clear whether the rationale is being provided by an anthropologist or folklorist observer or reporter or whether the rationale comes from the participants themselves. Whatever the source, it seems safe to infer that both individual and social purposes are served, that psychologically and communally some benefit is assumed by the participants. What is good for individuals may also serve the welfare of the community. Individuals may air grievances, directly or indirectly, hoping for rectification or adjustments.

For the community, potential sources of breakdown or disruption may be removed or alleviated. In some cases ritual satire allows taboos and traditions to be broken or at least mocked and laughed at. This kind of psychic loosening presumably provides a concomitant reduction of tension in the social group, or at least a willingness to abide by the taboos when they are reimposed, so to speak. But ritual satire also controls and channels aggression. It can be seen to divert physical aggression into verbal aggression, perhaps a more manageable force than physical aggression. In any case, it allows verbal aggression a legitimate day in the sun, focusing, limiting, and channeling it. But even while the community allows such behavior, it may also be putting individuals in the position of teaching them to control their responses to the aggression. An individual may be unleashing frustration and anger, but the person is urged to maintain control, even if he or she is a target. The aggression that is unleashed is usually directed against other individuals or groups who have violated or transgressed fundamental social acts or behavior, displayed greed, arrogance, or other shameful antisocial conduct. Ritual satire may be carried on as a part of some other more inclusive ritual or it may be a special ceremony all its own. In either case it provides a break or pause in the ordinary routine of everyday life, probably a welcome change no matter the culture or community. But more than that there is an increased sense of community. Since differences in status and positions tend to be erased, restrictions on behavior removed, and in some cases roles reversed, the kind of spirit called *communitas* by anthropologist Victor Turner may be thought to prevail.

The use of ritual as a substitute for violent and socially destructive behavior has often been remarked. Karl Menninger, and Freud (Kernan, "Aggression and Satire," 128) before him, has stated that "civilization consists, in large part, in finding and using alternatives to the physical violence which was once—except for flight—man's chief defensive weapon" (Kernan, 143). Ritual, according to René Girard, is "nothing more than the regular exercise of 'good' violence" (37). Although in most so-called developed or complex societies, a judicial system is the most effective mechanism for controlling violence, preliterate and simple organized societies have used sacrificial rites and compensatory measures (20–21) as ways to canalize potentially destructive behavior and acts. In a symbolic sense ritual satire can be seen as both sacrificial and compensatory, a substitute for physical violence in the absence of a judicial system or other institutional means for dealing with a vast body of behavior that may be antithetical to the psychological and social health of individuals as well as to the successful functioning of the community itself. The individual attacked in ritual satire becomes the symbolic surrogate victim sacrificed for the harmony of the community. Even in a society with laws, much antisocial behavior is untouched by the legal system, so that Alexander Pope in his imitation of the First Satire of the Second Book of Horace declares his intention to write satire against

> . . . you who 'scape the laws. Yes, while I live, no rich or noble knave Shall walk the world, in credit, to his grave. (118–20)

The social control of unsocial behavior is given a modern statement in Henri Bergson's *Laughter,* in which the circumstances are far removed from the tribe and the folk but the process however delicate is analogous. Inability to adjust adequately to the demands and consequences of living, Bergson notes, results in "every degree of mental deficiency, every variety of insanity," . . . and at times crime. On the other hand, too mechanical an adjustment, "*inelasticity* [Bergson's emphasis] of character, of mind, even of body, . . . the possible sign of slumbering activity as well as an activity with separatist tendencies, that inclines to swerve from the common centre round which society gravitates," is equally as unacceptable to society. Laughter is the *social gesture,* the corrective, used by society to achieve the "greatest degree of elasticity and sociability" (18–20). Anthropologists, observing societies much different from Bergson's, have come to use the phrase "institutional humor" to describe humor that serves as a means of social release and regulation (Jacob Levine). In both cases it is behavior that is aggressive, critical, playful, and humorous, in short, satire. This is not to claim that the participants in the festivals and ceremonies of preliterate or medieval societies saw themselves as satirists. Unwittingly perhaps and to some degree, however, they carried on as satirists do.

Ritual satire no longer serves the important social function it once did. It continues to exist in isolated cultural eddies, but the social and economic conditions that made it once a widespread phenomenon have changed and with it the folk culture that was for the most part the main nurturing agent of ritual satire, at least in many Western societies. A curious feature of this change was that very often conflicts between satirizing groups and the authorities, religious or secular, became more numerous. Certain kinds of ritual satire became in effect victims of the power centralized in the nation and other political entities, and of the conflict between Catholicism and Protestantism. Conflicts between literary satirists and the powers that be are nothing new, the history of satire being rich with examples: Pietro Aretino forced to flee from Rome by a vengeful Pope Adrian, Voltaire forced to live in Switzerland and to disavow some of his works for fear of persecution, Gogol living abroad voluntarily in reaction to the attacks on *The Inspector General,* Mark Twain's critical reputation stunted by the suppression or downgrading of his later (satiric) works, Lenny Bruce and George Carlin in court for their satiric use of taboo words. But the displacement of ritual satire by literary satire and the disappearance of the conditions that nourished ritual satire have left society with few mechanisms for the organized social control that was the function of ritual satire. The need for nonlegal recourse remains, however, and such contemporary phenomena as satiric "awards" and the recurring outbreak among literary folk and other intellectuals since the seventeenth century of clubs of wit such as the Scriblerus Club and the Algonquin Wits may perhaps be explained by the lack of ritualized forms for expressing satiric feelings and ideas. Whatever the status of the satirist, and it is widely admitted that satire is the leper of literature, the satirist and society cannot exist without each other. The satirist needs the vices and follies of individuals alone or in the aggregate, and societies or its groups need the satirist as an agent for sacrificing, however symbolically, the embodiments of vice and folly so as, in Girard's words, to "restore harmony to the community, to reinforce the social fabric."

Satire by Association

Ritual satire is most readily grasped when seen in its communal context. It is first of all often part of a larger occasion, a religious, seasonal, political, harvest, or victory celebration. Satiric groups are often set apart from the mainstream of social life by age, profession, or special status. Youth groups, guilds, and secret societies take upon themselves the role of satirists or are permitted to mock individuals or groups or events that are socially disjointing. In Girard's terms corporate groups satirically reenact the mock sacrificial rites that divert potentially dangerous or at least undesirable social behavior into other channels.

In small self-contained communities such as tribes, rural villages, and small cities all kinds of rituals provided the occasion for satiric protest. Such communal satire was deeply imbedded in society through the Middle Ages and into the early modern period in Western Europe and its colonial outposts as well as in Eastern Europe and Russia. The gradual decline of such practices as the charivari, carnival, and the feasts of fools, for example, is the result of complex social, cultural, economic, political, and religious trends and forces, although some features of communal ritual satire persisted well into the twentieth century. This is not to say that ritual satire in a communal setting no longer exists. Celebrity roasts and mock festivals in the twentieth century merely indicate that homogeneous communities needed for ritual satire have changed in composition and concept but that the need for and function of such satire persists. Whatever the era or place homogeneous groups sharing common presuppositions and a willingness to suspend taboos and ignore normal social, political, or economic hierarchies indicates that communal satire satisfies some basic need. Whether the occasion evokes the group or whether the group exists for the occasion, the community allows and even encourages satiric ritual that is somehow useful to the social health of the community, however it is defined.

Ritual sacrifice in a variety of forms occurred in many ancient and primitive societies. Ritual sacrifice was a part of the Roman Saturnalia, the Greek Cronia, and the Babylonian Sacaea, but in these festivals the person sacrificed was a slave who for one day had been elevated to ruler in the reversal of roles and behavior that characterized these celebrations (Caillois, *Sacred,* 122–23; Reinach 93–98). The conventional explanation for the reversal is that it marked a return to a "golden age" when all persons were equal. A simpler and perhaps more convincing explanation would acknowledge that the temporary bringing down of those regularly in power might give more satisfaction to social underlings than any illusion of equality. Slaves ate at the masters' table, ordered them about, and mocked them. We have a record of this in Horace's Satire 2, 7 in which he relates how his servant Davus tells him what he really thinks of him. The roles of priests and consuls were exercised by slaves in what was probably a burlesque of the exercise of power. The temporary departure from normal and perhaps stultifying routine, the release of bottled-up emotions, and the momentary exercise of power may have given the festivals a purgative function that contributed to the health of the community.

But ritual sacrifice by means of verbal abuse is what we have in the *Apo* ceremony of the Ashanti people of Africa. The *Apo* ceremony took place during the middle of April in the eight days "when the edges of the year have met," as the Ashanti say, and allowed for the discharge of all the accumulated ill feelings for the past year. The "lampooning liberty," according to an eighteenth-century observer, was religiously sanctioned as a purging of hatred and evil, which assured the health of the individual and presumably of society. Chiefs and nobles were conventionally standard targets since their power to harm could be redressed during the *Apo,* as illustrated by the following sample of invective from an *Apo* ceremony:

The god, Ta Kese, says if we have anything to speak: Let
   us speak it,
For by so doing we are removing misfortune from
   the nation.

Do you people know the child who is head of this town?
The child who is head of this town is called 'the
   helpful one.'
When he buys palm wine he helps himself to the pot
   as well.

Your head is very large,
And we are taking the victory from out your hands.
O King, you are a fool.
We are taking the victory from out your hands
O King, you are impotent.
We are taking the victory from out your hands.

All is well today.
We know that a Brong man eats rats,
But we never knew that one of the royal blood eats rats.
But today we have seen our Master, Ansah, eating rats.
Today all is well and we may say so, say so, say so.
At other times we may not say so, say so, say so.

The ceremony was first described by a Dutch explorer, William
Bosman, in 1705 and again in 1923 by R. S. Rattray (*Ashanti*, 151).

A similar ritual, called by Victor Turner the "role of the
humbled chief," is known to have taken place at the installation of
new rulers among the tribesmen of Ndembu and of Gaboon
(*Ritual,* 81, 100–102). In both cases, new kings were verbally
abused as part of the ceremony in which they were elevated to their
new positions. Those who had been wronged by the new rulers
used the occasion as their last opportunity to express resentment.
Paul Du Chaillu, who described the ceremony in Gaboon in 1861,
noted that the prospective king "kept his temper, and took all the
abuse with a smiling face" (19–20).

Julius Caesar's reaction to similar treatment is unknown, but
Suetonius tells that on the occasion of his return from his Gallic
victories his troops were allowed to assail him with ribald verses
and songs alluding to his being used by a well-known pederast as

well as to his own proclivities for cuckolding other men. His soldiers were even allowed to sing about his lack of hair, something which he was very touchy about. They chanted:

> Home we bring our bald whoremonger;
>> Romans, lock your wives away!
> All the bags of gold you lent him
>> Went his Gallic tarts to pay. (21–22)

A democratic society might be the last place to look for a rite of sacrifice, but the made-in-the-U.S.A. "roast" is a latter-day version of just such a ceremony. Most familiar in its television form in which guests take turns inflicting a series of "insults" upon the person being roasted, the television roast is a diluted version of the roasts held by the Friars Club, an organization founded in 1904 and made up of persons from all areas of show business. Although a Friars' roast is ostensibly a testimonial dinner with all the sentimentality that entertainment folk are capable of regarding their profession, it also functions as a test of the roastee's ability to smile while the truth is spoken laughingly. As a guest of the Gridiron Club, a notable roasting club made up of journalists in Washington, D.C., President William Howard Taft confessed that "after some training, both as secretary of war and as president, I was able to smile broadly at a caustic joke at my expense and seem to enjoy it, with the consolatory thought that every other guest of any prominence had to suffer the same penalty" (32). Ideally the guest of honor at a Friars' or Gridiron roast is at the pinnacle of his or her career and therefore most worthy of encomium but also most in need of deflating, so that the roast consists of a curious mixture of affection and hostility, institutionalized satire American-style.

Despite its notoriety, the face-to-face insulting format of the Friars' roast is less favored than the revue format used by dozens of organizations from the Clover Club of Boston to the Press Club of San Francisco, including the Bonehead Club of Dallas, the Court of the Nisi Prius of Cleveland lawyers, the Puget Sound [Washington] Sportswriters and Sportscasters, the Advertising Federation of St. Louis businesswomen, and the Clover Club of Philadelphia, composed of influential men in that metropolitan area, the latter the oldest of all such clubs (Deacon). These groups present dinners, at least annually, to which local political leaders and others of influence and power are invited, to see and hear themselves ridiculed in skits and pranks. Since it began in 1885 the Gridiron Club has been host to every president except Grover Cleveland, whose temperament apparently did not allow him to participate in the facetiousness fostered by a small group of Washington newspapermen. The entertainment of their dinners consists mainly of musical skits with humorous words put to songs in order to satirize the main guests, political matters, and other events of the past year (Brayman). Each group has a license to satirize (Test, "Roast").

Although the spirit of ritual sacrifice is more diffuse than in the American roast, the *Apo* ceremony and similar rituals, the same impetus can be detected in the mumming found in nineteenth-century Newfoundland and the *Holi* festival in twentieth-century northern India. Mumming, best known in England for its special folk plays, was not essentially an expression of ritual satire. But mumming as it emerged in early nineteenth-century Newfoundland was in fact ritual satire on a communal level (Sider; Szwed). During the twelve days between December 25 and January 6 (Old Christmas) men and women in disguise went from house to house in the isolated coastal villages. They took great care to cover all parts of the body, to change their shape, and to disguise their manner of walking and talking. Once inside the house the mummers were free to abuse the host verbally, and the host could not retaliate, for to do so would earn him a reputation of being a poor sport. If the host family was able to guess the identity of the mummers, they immediately unmasked and partook of food and drink and resumed normal social relations. In large towns and cities parades and processions took place in which participants dressed in costumes that emphasized role and sex reversal, working men dressing as ladies, for example, a form of mumming that expressed a fine balance between "deference and aggressive mockery," to use the words of Sider. His study of mumming on Newfoundland emphasizes that in addition to its being a ritual for reducing personal tension and stress, mumming also served as a device for integrating the community in social and economic terms as well. When the fishing industry on which the communities relied changed under the influence of industrialization and capitalism, relationships in the villages changed and with the change came the demise of mumming in the early twentieth century.

In 1966 anthropologist McKim Marriott described the *Holi*

festival in Kishan Garhi, a village in northern India, in which Saturnalia-like, the high and mighty were humbled by satiric acts and the low and powerless were exalted by the mock role playing of their victims. The village bully was made by his victims to ride backward on a donkey, a practice also found in medieval satiric festivals. The woman who brought repeated legal actions against neighbors had her household temple decorated with the bones of goats. The village moneylender received what Marriott described as a "burlesque dirge" from a professional ascetic. Marriott himself, decorated with a garland of old shoes, was made to dance in the streets like a "witless bumpkin" (210–12).

If in some societies the spirit of ritual sacrifice is closer to the Saturnalian practice, in others it is closer to the performance of the trickster. Among the Zuni there existed the cult of Kachina priests known as Koyemshi, who were sacred clowns (Farb, 4–10). The behavior of the Koyemshi operated as a running satiric comment on the serious dancers in a particular ceremony. One Koyemshi would continue to dance after the conventional dancers had stopped, isolated and single-mindedly unaware that he was overdoing his devotion to the ceremony. Another carried on an imaginary conversation with the gods. But the Zunis also encouraged mockery of outsiders. One performance presented caricatures of a Mexican priest and an American military officer. A travesty of a Catholic vespers service contained a Koyemshi bawling out a paternoster, another portraying a passionate padre, and a third mimicking old people reciting the rosary.

In the highland Chiapas area of southern Mexico fiestas of ritual satire have come to be associated with Christian holidays and patriotic events, but their antecedents go back to pre-Columbian times. The "entertainers" of the fiestas are specially chosen men who dress in elaborate costumes often emphasizing animal characteristics. Although practice and emphasis vary from group to group, they tend to have in common several targets: women who behave in an unbecoming manner, religious leaders who fail in their duties, persons who renounce their Indian heritage by adopting European dress and speaking Spanish, and outsiders in general, whether they be members of other ethnic groups or other communities. Humorous quatrains called *bombas* and related to the Spanish *copla* are recited for satiric comment. A widely used satiric technique is the impersonation of animals, mythical characters, or outsiders, a practice which has its roots in Mayan culture and allows the impersonator to satirize others while releasing his own inhibitions (Bricker, *Ritual Humor,* 167–224).

Anthropologists have observed similar rituals elsewhere among other native American groups, most notably the Pueblo and Mayo-Yaqui groups. Special groups of men function as "ceremonial buffoons." The buffoons who existed in Indian tribes in the southwestern United States, in the Plains area, and on the West Coast were licensed to ridicule sacred and important ceremonies, persons, and customs. They burlesqued ceremonial dances, parodied the speeches of the shaman, broke secular taboos in their gestures and language. Outsider observers of such behavior have sometimes remarked on what seemed to be the extreme freedom allowed to the clowns, thereby suggesting the relative and variable nature of limits set on ritual satire (Steward; Bandelier).

Observers as different as John Bourke and C. G. Jung have pointed out the similarity of certain Indian satiric rituals to the medieval carnival ceremonies, the best known of which is the Feast of Fools. On the other hand, the Feast of Fools exhibits many of the features and the spirit of the festival of Saturnalia, although any direct connection between the fool festivals and the Saturnalia is at best only circumstantial. The Feast of Fools, known to have existed as early as the ninth century, was a series of mock religious events held between Christmas and the middle of January when the lower clergy of the large cathedrals held mock elections of "officials," ridiculed holy ceremonies, profaned the sacraments, delivered mock sermons *(sermons joyeuses),* and behaved in a manner not normally allowed to them (E. K. Chambers, 2, 274–335).

The Feast of Fools was celebrated in Italy, Germany, England, and France, but since the fullest and most extensive records of the feast occur in France, it is assumed that it was the most widely practiced there. Although there was no typical Feast of Fools and the feasts varied in the intensity of their mockery, there was usually a mock election to set up a "Pope of Fools," or at least a "Bishop" or a "Patriarch." Some versions had a "boy-Bishop," and a specialized version known as the Asses Mass, an *asinorum dominus* (Walsh). Those who participated sometimes donned the clothing of their opposites with priests and clerks wearing the garments of the laity or of fools, the laity donning priestly or monastic robes. Clerics in some celebrations turned their robes inside out. Some wore masks or animal visages or dressed as women. The mocking of the ceremony was carried on by underlings who said a "fool's mass," delivered a "fool's sermon," danced in the choir loft, diced on the altar, sang off-key, or chanted meaningless words. The smoke in the censers came from the soles of old shoes. As with the American roast, eating and drinking were incorporated into the ceremony. The revels often spilled over into the community with processions of carts led by the *dominus festi* riding a donkey. Bystanders were entertained with dancing, scurrilous verse, and horseplay, reminiscent of the Dionysian festivals of Greece. Plays were sometimes presented with citizens and churchmen as targets of the satire. Despite its religious context, the Feast of Fools was mainly a folk celebration based on the reversal of roles as an expression of ritual satire.

By the late fifteenth century the function of the Feast of Fools was being taken over by laymen as cathedrals slowly banished the celebrations (Davis, "Reasons . . ."). The secular Feasts of Fools were put on without sanction of the church or local government by informal groups of friends and family, by craft or professional guilds, but most often by organizations which called themselves "abbeys of misrule." Such abbeys are known to have existed as early as the thirteenth century when they were made up of adolescent youths. In the cities the abbeys became highly formal organizations with youth and adult members. They kept extensive records and printed their programs. The French abbeys have left the most extensive records of their proceedings, but fool societies existed in Switzerland, Holland, Germany, Italy, Poland, Hungary, and Bulgaria.

But "abbeys of misrule" so flourished in France that in one particular year one hundred and fifty such groups assembled for a convention in Cambrai. French fool societies (sometimes called *sociétés joyeuses*) were often highly organized, legally chartered with rules and rituals for joining, governed by a Prince of Fools or a Mother Fool and various assistants. Their activities were confined apparently to religious and secular holidays when they engaged in a ritualized inversion of normal life. Their relations with the authorities were spotty, depending on the tolerance of city governments. Records show that some fool societies were outlawed, others operated within the limits set by the authorities, that is, they satirized what those in power wanted or allowed. But public beatings or imprisonment with bread and water were not unknown. Whatever their targets, whatever their collaborations or misadventures, they persisted in viewing society as an endless procession of fools whose activities they were merely portraying.

Part of the festivities was a ritual procession marked by bursts of satiric verse, horseplay, and obscene behavior. But the *sociétés joyeuses* are best known for their satiric plays, *sotties,* which form a significant body of material in the history of medieval French comic drama. The *sottie* was a simple satirical revue performed by semiprofessional actors in fool's costumes, who engaged in acrobatic clowning, uttered dialogues with patter-like delivery, and presented simply plotted farces reinforced with puns, songs, and obscenities, whose characters were all fools in one way or another. The *Infanterie Dijonnais* used the charivari (a ritual form to be discussed later) as an instrument for satiric comment. *Les Cornards* of Rouen sometimes awarded the "abbatial cross" to the person who had done the most foolish deed during the year. The fool society at Lyon made up largely of typographers called themselves Followers of Master Misprint *(Suppôts du Seigneur de la Coquille)*. The most famous of French fool societies was the *Enfant sans Souci* of Paris, a fool society within the Basoche, an organization of underlings in the legal profession, which functioned within the legal community in the spirit of fool societies without adopting the fool's costume (Swain; Arden).

The Basoche itself was an organization of bailiffs, scribes, and law clerks who banded together for mutual support. As underlings they were aware of the chicanery and misuse of power around them and so their presentations were aimed at nobles, clergy, and, to a lesser extent, judges. Their performances were sometimes censored or prohibited, their members imprisoned, although during the reign of Louis XII (1498–1515) the Basochiens operated without hindrance. Although the Basochiens were amateur playwrights and actors who wrote and presented a variety of plays, one of their most important satirical products was the *causes grasses,* mock trials performed at Carnival time. In some trials scandals were presented involving persons known to the actors and the audience. In others, trivial or ridiculous *causes* received the minute attention and extensive legal knowledge applied to actual cases (Harvey).

The Babinian Republic, a fool society founded in Poland in 1568, based its organization on the Polish Constitution and filled its membership by inviting all those to join who had been adjudged to have done something foolish. If a person refused to join, he was badgered until he did. He was then given an office appropriate to his folly and awarded a license with a large seal. A person, for example, who talked about things he did not understand might be made an archbishop. Eventually nearly every important person in the government and in the church held an office in the Babinian Republic. When the King of Poland, Sigismund August II, asked whether the Republic had a king, the group told him that as long as he was King of Poland it did not plan to elect one (Willeford 226–28).

In Rouen the abbeys used the Mardi Gras parade as a means of political criticism and commentary. One year they attacked the venality of certain local magistrates who had demanded large sums from a pleader, refusing the modest hare offered because they said their wives did not like game. In the parade of 1580 they held up a "Socratic mirror" to the world. Business was so bad that the procession began with an elaborate funeral for Merchandise, followed by a float bearing Hope, in a laughing mask. Another float carried a king, the pope, the emperor, and a fool playing catch with a globe of the world: "Tiens-cy; baille-ca; Ris-t'en, Moque-t'en." ("Hold this; give that; laugh at them, poke fun at them.") There was also a procession of Old Testament prophets uttering prophetic riddles containing references to those responsible for increasing pauperism and religious troubles (Davis, "Charivari . . . ," 68; Ladurie; Bezucha; Carroll; Dirks).

Another widely used device of the abbeys was the charivari, a mock serenade carried on by any kind of device that would make noise, including kettles, horns, and bells, and directed against persons who defied social custom in some way, widows or widowers who remarried too hastily, couples in which there was thought to be an unusual disparity in ages, unfaithful husbands or wives, wives who beat or henpecked their husbands (see lines 373–89 in Andrew Marvell's "The Last Instructions to a Painter," for one description), as well as newly married couples. The fool society of Dijon, the *Infanterie Dijonnais,* used the charivari in 1579 to punish a certain Parisian, M. du Tillet, a newly appointed master of forest and waters who was guilty of beating his wife in May, the month when wives were exempted from beatings. In several skits his "case" was argued, and he was finally carried around the city riding on an ass, a degradation usually reserved for prostitutes, prisoners, and other malefactors of justice. In Lyon the year before, all the men who had been beaten by their wives were displayed by the wagonload to the citizens of the city. M. du Tillet and the wife-beaters were of course "serenaded" with noise as they took their ride (Swain, 78–79).

In 1751 Parisian charcoal burners used the feast of St. Peter of Vinculis, the patron saint of cobblers, to mock two young cobblers who had married aged widows. To emphasize the fact that the cobblers in their new marriages were dealing in second-hand "leather," two donkeys adorned with old leather, old shoes, and ox feet ridden by mummers similarly decorated led a parade of charcoal burners through the streets to the doors of the offending cobblers. One took the joke in good spirit and provided beer for the paraders, but the other received the charivari as an insult to him and his fellow cobblers, causing a street fight that ended with the donkey riders being thrown in jail (Walsh; Davis, "Charivari"; Ingram).

Variations of this sort of thing went on throughout Europe and parts of the United States down to the end of the nineteenth century. In England it was known as "rough music" or "riding skimmington," in Germany as Katzenmusik, and in Scandinavia as "riding the Stange." In the Andalusian area of Spain charivari was known as the vito, "a traditional shaming ritual in which transgressors against village morality or ethics were persecuted by satiric serenade," according to David Gilmore in his study of Andalusian culture. The practice there survived into the 1930s. Despite attempts by church and state over the years to outlaw the charivari, it died finally only as the result of social and cultural changes.

The Fastnacht festival of Germany and Austria, a ritual of extreme longevity dating from pre-Christian times to the twentieth century, has kept its satiric intent despite changes in the forms of the festival (Rudwin; Taeuber). A feature of the medieval Fastnacht was satiric plays in which all social classes from nobles to peasants were ridiculed. Clowns mimicked the onlookers, burlesqued sacred acts, and mocked the priests (DuBruck, 61–64). Medieval guilds were the centers for such rituals. After the seventeenth century, the plays became less important, but the fool who mingled with the crowd, making fun of those who had misbehaved during the year, persisted down to the 1930s at least. The fool's guild (*Narrenzunft*) prepared banners, floats, and posters for the annual procession in which persons or groups were satirized. In one community the Fastnacht festival had its own Fastnacht newspaper, the *Narro Zeitung,* with humorous advertisements and cartoons. The Fastnacht festival takes place prior to Lent, corresponding to the Carnival of Mediterranean and Caribbean countries.

In England nothing so extensive as the abbeys of misrule of France or as long-lived as the Fastnacht of Germany has existed. From the fifteenth century on, colleges, inns of court, towns, and villages elected mock mayors, mock princes, or lords of misrule as a way of satirizing delinquent leaders. Ecclesiastical ceremonies were satirized with mock baptisms of pigs, cats, and calves, the singing of hymns to vulgar tunes, and the churching of horses and cows. On one occasion in 1637 a local lord of misrule dressed in a surplice read a mock wedding ceremony and put the couple to bed. Behavior such as this raised the ire of polemicist Philip Stubbes, whose *Anatomy of Abuses* (1583) attacked heathenish practices connected with the election of lords of misrule. But such practices penetrated even the court of James I, where courtiers, in an attempt to cheer up the king, once staged a mock christening with the Marquis of Buckingham as a godfather to a pig.

But such rituals are an anachronism in Western society of the twentieth century, when the communal folk cultures that support such rituals are inexorably subject to change. With the rise of nations and their centralized power, the growth of industry and the media, and the concomitant changes in basic social and economic relations, folk cultures which nourished ritual satire lost their foundations (Peter Burke, 207–86; G. I. Jones; Goonatilleka). Only the roasting "clubs," supported by homogeneous groups similar in some ways to the medieval guilds that sponsored the abbeys of misrule, continue the tradition, now isolated, largely unknown, and unappreciated. But university law school "libel shows," graduation ceremony mock wills and mock prophecies, April Fool's Day issues of college newspapers, the exchange of roles between the nuns and schoolgirls in the great convent of the

Congregation of Notre Dame of Paris on Holy Innocents Day, and the lampooning of high school and college faculty at Class Day exercises, however pallid compared with their medieval antecedents, suggest the persistent need to institutionalize cleansing laughter and verbal energy. How else explain the outbreak of such phenomena as the First Annual Armadillo Exposition and Confab, which has lasted nearly a decade as a spoofing of the town festivals that flourish across the United States; the annual Dubious Achievement Awards of *Esquire* and *Boston* magazines; the Noble [*sic*] Prize awarded for satiric solutions to international problems by the Association for the Promotion of Humor in International Affairs; the National Nothing Foundation; and the Procrastinators Club of America, the latter "organization" dedicated to "underthrowing" sanctified American values?

And how explain the presence of "clubs of wit" in various societies since the fifteenth century beginning with *Bugiale,* or Lie Factory, to which Bracciolini Poggio and other scribal underlings belonged and which devoted its spare moments to satirizing monks, priests, and church leaders up to the pope? His collection of stories, *Facetarium Liber,* based, he claims, on stories originally told in the *Bugiale,* quickly went through numerous editions and was placed on the *Index Purgatorius* for its irreverent and uninhibited attitude toward the rich and respectable in the Church. In England in the eighteenth century there was of course the best known of such groups, the Scriblerus Club made up of Pope, Swift, Gay, Arbuthnot, and Parnell. Still later in England there was the Nonsense Club, and in pre-Revolutionary America the little-known Tuesday Club of Annapolis, Maryland, and later the Salmagundi Group with Washington Irving as its leader. In Russia Alexis K. Tolstoy and the brothers Zhemchuznikov produced the life and works of the memorable and consummate bureaucrat Koz'ma Prutkov. The intellectuals and artists who gathered in *Le Chat Noir* and *Le Lapin Agile* in France and *Die Elf Scharfrichter* and the *Schall und Rauch* in Germany at various times between 1880 and 1920 would seem to represent some almost primordial impulse to band together to satirize society (Test, "Club"). Such impulses could not be satisfied, except in the most temporary and fragmentary way, given the lack of an intellectual culture comparable to that of a genuine folk culture and the growing power of the state.

(Several clubs of wit lived under the displeasure of political leaders or the police.) Even if the clubs of wit can be seen only as residually ritualistic, their existence can be considered a link between ritual satire and literature, as earlier the abbeys of misrule helped in developing the *sottie,* the *coq à l'âsne,* and *Fastnacht* plays.

4

Satiric Reciprocity as Ritual

One-on-One Verbal Aggression

Humor in which two people insult each other to the delight of the audience is a staple of modern American popular entertainment. George Jefferson and the maid Florence, Archie Bunker and his son-in-law, the hapless Momma and Eunice of the Carol Burnett Show are familiar examples from TV shows of the 1970s. Radio provided the famous "duels" between Jack Benny and Fred Allen, Charlie McCarthy and W. C. Fields, Fibber McGee and Mayor Gildersleeve, and between the couple with the appropriate name, the Bickersons. Examples from film and drama include exchanges between Spencer Tracy and Katharine Hepburn in some of their notable films as well as similar exchanges in George S. Kaufman and Moss Hart's *The Man Who Came to Dinner* and Edward Albee's *Who's Afraid of Virginia Woolf.* In these examples the humor comes from the series of double put-downs in which the audience participates vicariously in verbal aggression that in real life would probably draw blood instead of laughs.

Such verbal exchanges are not unique to American culture. They occur in various cultures under various circumstances, many of them as rituals that in some cases serve serious social purposes. Whereas the examples mentioned above serve mainly to generate laughter, some verbal exchanges serve as a way to express individual aggrievement and as means for settling disputes. Some exchanges also function as a way of testing individual self-control and as means of expressing one's verbal facility. Whatever the purpose or combination of purposes, the audience is entertained and instructed.

One basic form that ritualized aggression takes is the verbal duel, a kind of public trial by verbal combat. Such duels occur in societies as varied as Eskimo, Scottish, black American, and Arabian. Some serve a serious social purpose; others are closer to straight entertainment with little social significance. But those to be discussed all present verbal aggression duels in a ritual context. The best known of the verbal duels may be the "dozens,"[1] a form of ritual insult practiced mostly but not exclusively by male adolescents in black American culture, in which two individuals ridicule each other's character and family, often focusing on their mothers. Since similar kinds of verbal exchanges are still practiced by young people among the Igbos of Nigeria and in other West African societies, including Ghana, it seems likely that the "dozens" was brought to the Western hemisphere by slaves. Once thought to have been practiced only by members of lower socioeconomic groups of black Americans, the practice seems to have spread to lower income whites in the South, as Erskine Caldwell's *God's Little Acre* shows, and to white high school students in other parts of the United States. In all cases a premium is set on imaginativeness, good delivery, active memory, and verbal facility. The exchanges take place in the presence of others who goad the players to greater effort and by their jeers and laughter recognize a winner. To resort to physical violence during a verbal exchange is an admission of defeat.

The following is a good example of the tone and subject of an exchange of the dozens:

First male: Hey man! How's your mama? I saw her last night, her hair was kinky, her drawers were baggy, and she was drunk as a skunk. She looked so bad she would have scared a baboon to death.

Second male: Say man! That was your mama, who was looking so bad even you didn't recognize her.

F: You pap's in jail and your mother's around the corner shouting pussy for sale.

S: Your mother's like a doorknob, everybody gets a turn.

F: At least I have a father and not fifty suspects.

S: Your mother goes to church, puts in a
    penny and asks for change.
F: I did it to you mama
    on the railroad track
    And when her ass went up
    The trains went back
S: I don't play the Dozens
    I play the 6-½
    And the way I did it to you mama
    Made you grandpa laugh
F: Some like it hot
    Some like it cold
    Some who like your mama
    Like it pretty damn old.
S: Your mother is so ugly, when she cries tears
    run down her back.
F: Your mother is like a cake, everybody gets
    a piece.
                                        (Onwuckekwa, 32–33)

The drum match or insult singing found among certain Eskimo
groups also involves a duel before an audience that decides who is
the victor, a premium being set on verbal facility, originality, and
keeping one's temper.[2] A pair of Eskimo duelers accompany
themselves on a drum or compose a chantlike song as part of their
diatribes. In this culture drum matches function as a way of
resolving disputes between individuals, as a device for social
control through ridicule, and as therapy for participants and
audience. The best received matches may be incorporated into the
oral literature of the community and repeated later as entertainment, although it seems unlikely that the moral point of such
exchanges would be lost on the listeners.

Here is a sample of one exchange:

Marratse's Attack

Words let me split,
Small words, sharp words,
Like the splinters
Which, with my axe, I cut up.

A song I shall sing of old days,
A breath from the distant past,

A sad and a plaintive song,
Forgetfulness to bring to my wife,
She who was snatched from me
By a prattler, a liar.
Bitterly has she suffered from him,
The lover of human flesh,
Cannibal, miscreant.

Equerquo's Answer

Only amazement I feel
At your preposterous words.
Only anger they cause
And the urge to laugh,
You with your mocking song,
Placing on me that guilt.
Did you think you could frighten me,
I who many a time challenged death?
Hei, hei! So you sing to my wife
Who once was yours in the days
When kindness you forgot.

Alone she was in those days.
Yet never in combats of song
Did you challenge your foes for her.
Ah, but now she is mine.
Never again shall false lovers like you,
Deceivers, come singing into our tent.
Spewed up from starvation days!
(Qtd. in Radin, "Literature," 625–26)

In Trinidad in the West Indies singing duels of insults are known as *picong* and are part of the famous calypso art displayed most prominently at Carnival in January prior to Ash Wednesday.[3] In the tents where calypso performers gather during Carnival, one performer will "war" on another, challenging, teasing, and taunting. The pleasure of the crowd determines which of the performers is superior in his art, which mixes traditional and improvised material.

At one time such matches may have been used to settle personal disputes, but this is no longer the case. Such songs are thought to have their roots in West Africa, especially in Yoruban forms, and are found also in the Dominican Republic, Surinam, and Venezuela.

Verbal dueling is not confined to preliterate or primitive or adolescent groups. Such duelings have played a role in Western literary satiric tradition. One of the earliest examples of ritual satire in European literature is Fescennine verses, named presumably for the Etruscan town of its origin. Associated originally with weddings, such verses were extemporized exchanges of lampoons that spread to harvest festival times, from rural areas to cities. References to such verses can be found in the writings of Catullus, Seneca, Livy, and others. Ritual satire by dialogue, as Robert Elliott has argued in his *Power of Satire,* may be seen as a domesticated form of the curse, and is the ancestor of invective and other first-person attack satire.[4] The *hija,* extemporized invective verse in pre-Islamic oral literature, was used against enemies prior to battle or as part of duels between poets of opposing tribes. The power of the *hija* ("taunt") came from the ancient belief that satiric words could cause blisters and even death. No *hijas* from pre-Islamic Arabian literature (before A.D. 500) have been preserved, but *hijas* by Jarir in the eighth century and by Abu Tamman, a poet of the early ninth century, helped to establish the fame of each poet. Jarir, one of the most famous of early Arabian satirists, defeated a rival poet with a satire of eighty stanzas, his opponent suffering such ignominy that Jarir made his name a byword for hundreds of years afterward. Abu Tamman, whose fame spread with the defeat of some Egyptian authors in an invective duel, included a chapter of *hijas* in his celebrated anthology of Arabian poetry.

A general word for invective duels, *flyting,* from the Scottish word for scold, has been widely used to describe the duels found in various ancient cultures in the oral tradition as well as expressions occurring mainly in Scottish, Irish, and Italian literatures between the fifteenth and eighteenth centuries. Verbal duels known as *tenzone* were part of the troubadour culture of Provence and Italy in the twelfth century. Called *contrasto* in Italy, among the most famous of such exchanges were those between Luigi Pulci, fifteenth-century Italian poet, and Matteo Franco, chaplain to Lorenze de Medici, for the entertainment of the Medici household.[5]

That *flytings* were entertainment, a kind of acting out of anger, is supported by remarks in the *flyting* between Alexander Montgomerie and Sir Patrick Hume of Polwart, commonly known as "Polwart and Montgomerie Flyting."[6] Montgomerie explicitly denies any personal malice, seeing himself and Polwart as actors who entertain. He says, this "anger to asswage, make melancholy less, / This Flyting first was wrote." An earlier example of *flyting,* this between David Lindsay and James V of Scotland, also illustrates the play acting of anger, although, compared to Polwart and Montgomerie, Lindsay and James are pretty tame. The "Flyting of Dunbar and Kennedie" is the best known example of two accomplished poets haranguing each other. It takes place in two rounds, the first round consisting of three stanzas by each poet, the second round of twenty-five stanzas by Dunbar, thirty-eight by Kennedie. Dunbar brags that the universe will react when it hears what he puts down with pen and ink: the firmament will shake, the air will have a venomous stink, the sea will burn, rocks will rise, "the warld sould hald no grippis." In the exchange the poets denigrate each other's ancestry and life, present a caricature of the other's physical appearance, and mock the other in as many ways as possible, including sexual proclivities, poetic abilities, manner of talking, and political preferences. The last two stanzas of Dunbar's attack contain a string of epithets in a complex mix of internal and external rhyme, assonance, consonance, and alliteration, combined in a climactic shout of defiance and triumph. There is then entertainment in the wordplay and laughter for participants and viewers alike in the acting out of anger.

Verbal dueling is found in many other places and in various forms. Anthropologist Victor Turner uses the word *flyting* to describe the exchanges between men and women of the Ndembu people of northwest Zambia. As part of the *Wubwang'u* ceremony in celebration of marriage, men and women engage in "licensed disrespect" regarding each other's sexual organs and prowess (*Ritual* 78–81). The inhabitants of central Buru in the East Indian archipelago sing songs known as *Inga fuka* that are of a "mocking or teasing nature," as reported by Johan Huizinga. Accompanied on drums, singers of *Inga fuka* take off from a repertoire of traditional poems that are supplemented with improvised verses containing "malicious sallies." Nearby on the island of Wetan mocking songs that are part of the regimen of work may develop into "envenomed singing duels" (Huizinga, *Homo Ludens,* 122–

23). Challenge singing in Fiji Indian communities may arise spontaneously or by arrangement. Small groups of Indians, descendants of those who went to Fiji between 1879 and 1919 to work as indentured laborers in the sugarcane industry, engage in duels using songs that attack the religious beliefs of the other group, often in personal terms (Brenneis and Padarath).

Verbal dueling occurs then in a great variety of cultures and under various circumstances.[7] It can be found among the Mayan descendants in Chamula and Zinacantan in Mexico, among Turkish teenage boys, and among Puerto Rican males. Lina Wertmuller includes a ritual exchange in her film *Swept Away* (1975) between a rich owner of a yacht and her deckhand when he revolts after they are marooned on a desert island. In addition to the sexual insults usually found in such exchanges, Wertmuller enriches the flyting with sociopolitical allusions as well (Wertmuller, *Screenplays,* 214–16).

That anger, outrage, indignation, alone or in some combination, real or simulated, are the emotions behind verbal duels seems to be clear. These emotions also characterize the widely accepted "tradition" of Juvenalian satire. To refer to a piece of satire as Juvenalian may mean one or both of the following: it is a direct and verbally violent attack on something, or it is characterized by a spirit of indignation or outrage. Juvenal wrote formal verse satires, direct poetic outbursts against a person or a group. Formal verse satires are monologues rather than verbal duels, or in effect one side of a duel, a kind of extended piece of invective known formally as a diatribe, a form of direct-attack satire with a long but never wholly respectable ancestry, unlike literary verbal duels which have had a restricted and a largely obscure role in literary history. But the spirit or emotions of dueling and Juvenalian satire share a common emotional source and serve a similar purpose.[8]

Joking Relationships as Satiric Ritual

> In Bali, to be teased is to be accepted.
> Clifford Geertz

If verbal duels are the ritual expression of Juvenalian satire, the joking relationship is the expression of Horatian satire. The joking relationship, the most private and therefore the most ephemeral expression of ritual satire, is a term derived from anthropology.[9] It is a relationship in which a person in one group is permitted by custom to tease or make fun of a person in another group with no offense taken, or at least shown. The relationship may be one-way or reciprocal, it may be based on and defined by kinship or among people who socialize together, or it may occur among persons who work in a factory, office, or store. The joking relationship allows persons who are in sensitive relationships or in situations in which conflict may occur to be friendly *and* unfriendly, to dispel hostility and avoid conflict while getting on with what they have to do.

Joking relationships are found among North American Indian tribes (DeLoria, 147) and among African peoples. Among the clans of the Tonga culture of Africa, "clan-jokers" (Max Gluckman's phrase) perform a moral function by enforcing care for property, by maintaining the rules of marriage and kinship, and by looking after social conduct in general. Clan-jokers may say satirically things forbidden to others because of taboos based on kinship, thereby keeping communication open and helping to maintain morality. The Makah Indians of North America have brought the "art of verbal denigration to a high peak," according to Elizabeth Colson, who studied the tribe in the 1940s. The art is used to enforce values important to the Makah and to maintain social cohesion. On the other hand, the ability to be passive in the face of malice and insult is encouraged and admired.

A. R. Radcliffe-Brown identified the joking relationship primarily with kinship relations, but anthropologists since have found evidence of joking relationships in a variety of groups in which kinship plays no part, as in groups whose only relationship is working together. It is therefore no violation of the concept to extend it to other social groups and periods of time. For example, the Amharic language, a Semitic dialect spoken in Ethiopia, has as a distinct characteristic a figurative ambiguity, *samenna-warq*, which serves as a means of establishing a joking relationship of great subtlety and indirection. It "lends itself readily to puns and hidden meanings, since many verbs can have double and triple interpretations due to the hidden variations in the basic verbal stem and the absence or presence of germination of some consonants. The listener must pay close attention. If he misinterprets the context and fails to discern the pun, he is often the butt of the next tricky joke by those who have heard it before" (Messing, 69; D. Levine, 4–9; Hess, 104–5). Through the use of its techniques insults can be exchanged in a socially approved manner. In a society that strictly controls all expressions of open aggression *samenna-warq* provides a way of criticizing those in authority and serves as a safety valve.

The banter and raillery commonly associated with upper-class English society from the sixteenth to the eighteenth centuries may also be seen as a version of the joking relationship.[10] Shakespeare's plays contain a variety of such relationships, from Beatrice and Benedict to Prince Hal and Falstaff to Hamlet and Osric. Raillery also appears to some extent in verse and prose satires of late Elizabethan writers. To what extent such joking exchanges mirror actual social practice is difficult to determine. But in the late seventeenth and early eighteenth centuries bantering exchanges were a prominent feature of social life in the English court and elsewhere in upper-class life. The "court wits" of the Restoration period were belligerent in deed and word. Their letters show them pointing out each other's failures with taunting references, with the witty rapier-like stroke "that separates the head from the body and leaves it standing in place," to use Dryden's famous phrase.

True raillery was a very subtle process, as references in eighteenth-century conduct books, periodical essays, plays, and novels make clear. Henry Fielding in "An Essay on Conversation" and Charlotte Lennox in her novel *The Female Quixote* agree that raillery should be used sparingly and carefully. Charlotte Lennox claims that it "must be a gift of nature," because "the air, the aspect, the tone of voice, and every part in general" must convey the "full force and meaning" of "many lively and agreeable thoughts." Persons with a "true talent for raillery," she concludes, "are like comets; they are seldom seen, and are at once admir'd and fear'd." Railleurs failed when they lacked humor, when they were motivated by malice, and when they were more interested in showing their wit than in carrying on socially approved conversation. Others lacked the prerequisite of breeding, as Swift makes clear in his poem, "To Betty the Grizette," in which he mocks Betty's attempts at raillery as "scurrilous . . . and rude." In his "Epigram on Scolding," Swift points out,

Great Folks are of a finer Mold:
Lord! how politely they scold;
While a coarse English Tongue will itch,
For Whore and Rogue; Dog and Bitch.

In Swift's hands raillery became so subtle as to become on occasion
a disguised encomium (Peake). But for the elite, raillery was an
antisocial engagement without loss of seemliness. Among equals it
involved some elements of mockery or reproach, allowing one to
comment on another's weaknesses according to accepted social
standards, whether that standard be avoidance of sexual license or
failure to keep up the libertine ideal. Raillery of this sort was not
supposed to give offense, and one was not supposed to take
offense. Or as Richard Steele puts it in his *Spectator* paper number
422 (4 July 1712), "The Satyr is directed against Vice, with an Air
of Contempt of the Fault, but no ill will to the Criminal." In short,
raillery was a social test of ability to adhere to a standard of taste
which bestowed social superiority on those who were successful, a
drawing-room ritual aimed at promoting "delight and pleasure,"
in Fielding's words. Others called it promoting "affability."

   Raillery could, however, be genuinely aggressive if the target
was an affected person. Such a person was of course not playing the
game and could therefore be verbally set upon. John Dryden
discussed "fine raillery" in his *Discourse concerning the Origin and
Progress of Satire* (1693) as including those "nicest and most delicate
touchers of satire." His *Absalom and Achitophel* is a good example of
the spirit of raillery in satire. Raillery itself has been preserved in
passages of plays by Etherege and in plays and poems by
Wycherley and Congreve. But raillery was by no means confined
to the English upper class of the sixteenth, seventeenth, and
eighteenth centuries. Contemporaneously in France there was
Vincent Voiture (1598–1648), whose letters were read by Jonathan
Swift, himself an accomplished railleur in the tradition of Voiture.
Later in France there was Nicholas Boileau (1636–1711), whose
influence on English letters has been well documented. In Italy
Castiglione (1478–1529) in his *The Art of Complaisance* comments
on the need to confine joking to "some little byting" so as not to
offend deeply. That raillery was present in Roman society is
suggested by remarks by Quintilian (first century A.D.) and Horace
(65–8 B.C.), especially in Horace's Satire 1, 9 in which he describes

how wittily he insults a sycophantic admirer. The famous exchanges between Jane Austen's Mr. Darcy and Elizabeth Bennett continue the practice in English literature. And the joking relationship remains alive in twentieth-century British life (Clarke, 203).

In the twentieth century more than one observer of Welsh life has noticed the "finely chiseled malice," as Richard Cobb describes it, of which the neighbors of the English are capable. Such "artistic malice," to use the phrase of the same observer, can be seen as ritual satire virtually imbedded in the language rising to the surface at certain times in certain contexts, becoming a distinguishing feature of the culture or community. Although teasing and kidding in the United States have never attained the social or literary status that some forms of joking relationships have elsewhere, it seems clear that such relationships have been an important form of social expression for a long time. The belief that joking relationships existed primarily in simple, preindustrial societies has slowly given way to the fact that the simplicity or complexity of the society has little to do with whether or not joking relationships exist. Familial, vocational, and professional relationships, equality of status, degrees of intimacy, respect, and formality in those relationships, on the other hand, are a great deal more important than the overall nature of the society itself. In the joking relationship in the United States, as in other societies, "privileged disrespect, mock aggression, and licentious behavior may occur. . . . Everyday rules of behavior are suspended, and otherwise prohibited aggressive and sexual behaviors are commonly the topic of joking" (Alford). Ultimately, "joking relationships, as a form of play, provide tension release, excitement, and opportunities for creativity."

Horace's put-on of the sycophant mentioned earlier is a monologue in which the give-and-take of the joking relationship tends to be one-sided. Yet it serves as one of the best examples of such a relationship. Discussions in manuals and essays on manners and literary criticism from all periods are little help in understanding the relationship itself, and passages of raillery frozen in plays and other pieces of literature tend at best to illustrate the spirit rather than the process. And that spirit, whether it occurs in upper-class English or French society of the seventeenth or eighteenth centuries or in other tribal communities of Africa or North America, is a means of social structuring and control through satire, satire that is itself restrained, even indirect, often witty or clever, generally confined to a social context in which the nuances and overtones in the exchanges are best appreciated by an in-group.

This is in fact the spirit of Horatian satire itself, the other widely acknowledged "tradition" of literary satire, characterized by urbanity, good humor, and avoidance of extremes of tone and subject.[11] Its tone ranges from gentle sarcasm to irony, masking or muting possible threats in the satire. The joking relationship would seem to be a kind of ritual expression of satire and humor in the Horatian mode. Verbal duels, on the other hand, tend to be in the contrasting mode of Juvenalian satire. Simulated anger, outrage, and indignation produce direct and verbally violent attacks, formal verse satires against persons, groups, or institutions. The verse satires of Horace and Juvenal are generally described as monologues, although they could well be described as recessive dialogues since the speakers are addressing and sometimes even reacting to a listener even though that person never speaks. Even more recessive is the dueling element, since the diatribe and the Horatian monologue are in effect the one side of an exchange developed into a form of its own.

Other Duels, Other Jokes

La legge (the law) bears a certain resemblance to verbal duels and for that reason is sometimes coupled with them in discussion of the duel. But if Roger Vailland's description of *la legge* in his novel *The Law* is valid, the Italian ritual is much more elaborate than the usual one-on-one verbal duel. In *la legge* five or more persons may participate, but six is considered a good number, according to Vailland. The game begins with the determining of a "chief" by drawing cards or rolling dice. The chief in turn designates a deputy.

> The winner, the chief, who dictates the law, has the right to speak and not to speak, to interrogate and to reply in place of the interrogated, to praise and to blame, to insult, to insinuate, to revile, to slander, and to cast a slur on people's honor; the losers, who have to bow to the law, are bound to submit without sound or movement. Such is the fundamental rule of the game of The Law. (43)

Part of the ritual of each game involves the dispensing of wine bought for the "chief" by the other persons in the game. He and his deputy may drink the wine themselves or dispense it to others as they wish. How to ask properly for a glass is part of the ritual. A game ends when the wine is gone. The next game begins with the determining of a new chief who chooses a new deputy, dispenses or drinks the wine, and carries on the interrogation. Observers of the game in Vailland's fictional version differed as to whether The Law should direct the attack against one victim or several, whether "wounds should be inflicted as though in sport," or whether the "mortification of the victim should be complete" (51–52). Provided he is lucky enough to win the chief's position, a person whose social or economic position is inferior can use *la legge* to get revenge by commenting unfavorably on another's weaknesses. The reversal of roles of *la legge* is comparable to the same feature in the Roman Saturnalia. *La legge* continues, game after game, until the players have adequately humiliated their victim. "For The Law to be agreeable, there had to be a victim, clearly designated, whom fate and the players could hound until he was exhausted" (60).

Social differences and personal characteristics generally serve as the source of the malice in *la legge*. In the joking imitations of the West Apaches of Arizona and New Mexico described by Keith Basso the source is cultural differences and the "whiteman" is rarely party to the ignominy placed upon him by his attackers. The joking imitations consist of mocking the speech and actions of Anglo-Americans, be they tourists, doctors, VISTA workers, or various kinds of bosses. What is mocked is behavior that implies or states that the West Apaches are stupid, lazy, dirty, irresponsible, and so on. Anglo-Americans also offend the Apaches by behaving socially in ways that to them are gauche and unthinking. Mockery of such behavior through imaginative and creative portrayal is not only a source of humor for the West Apaches but a form of social control in that it can be used to comment on unsocial Apache behavior. The joking imitations are not merely stereotypical but are often tied to particular situations or conditions, such as the intrusion of VISTA workers or an influx of doctors with a specific mission. The imitations always occur in a situation where there is an audience, usually of adult males.

Basso's discovery of the joking imitations of the Apaches was accidental, since ordinarily Apache mockery is not meant to be seen by the "whiteman." Instances of other Indian tribes mocking the white man have been recorded but the instances are not so numerous as with Africans and their relations with whites (Bourke, 4; Bricker, *Ritual Humor,* 189–90; Steward, 196–98). Satirical songs and mimicry occur in many African societies as a mechanism of social control. "Traditional associations, master-singers, work groups, and individual villagers all composed songs satirically alluding to complaints against neighbors and relatives, great men and rulers" (Pierson, 166; Finnegan, 410–11). The Ashanti *apo* has already been mentioned, but reports by Europeans since the eighteenth century have told of satiric songs, sometimes presented in ceremonies, sometimes not, in Sierra Leone, the Gold Coast, and Nigeria. Originally directed at persons in their own societies, satirical songs and other expressions of mockery were directed against the white man as soon as he arrived in Africa. Missionaries and traders were among the first white men to serve as targets. As slaves were transported to the New World the practice of satirical songs went with them. In Brazil, the islands of the Caribbean, and colonies of England, and the states of the United States where slavery persisted, can be found examples of the African tradition in the work and play of the slaves. As William Pierson puts it,

> African satire transferred easily to the New World. Unable to develop formal methods of social regulation under the interdictions of bondage, slaves were quick to adopt the informal controls which accompanied public satire, praise, and ridicule. By cleverly intermixing criticism of their masters with flattery and by combining their praise and criticism with equally ridiculous lampoons of black behavior, Afro-American bondsmen desensitized the seeming impropriety of black slaves satirizing the society of their white owners. (176–77)

This practice is in fact found in Haiti in *combite* songs, improvised work songs in which a leader, the *simidor,* spread gossip and scandal as well as "caustically commenting on the shortcomings of neighbors, or evaluating the hospitality of the owners" for whom they are working. His rhythmic patter is echoed by the workers as they perform their duty. The *simidor,* like all satirists, is feared and respected. According to one native commentator, "The *simidor* is a journalist, and every *simidor* is a Judas!" (qtd. in Herskovits, *Life,* 74).

Satiric songs are in fact a recognized part of the literature of many cultures around the world. Eight of the thirteen cultures included in Mary Finnegan's survey of oral poetry are represented with satiric songs or poems. The eight cultures represent peoples from every continent and include the Maori, Malays, Gonds (from India), Mongols, Somali, Yoruba, Eskimo, and Irish. The satiric songs include Eskimo drum songs already mentioned as well as lampoons against "a conceited man" and "the ever-touring Englishman" (Gond) and "a bully" (Malay). Greed, taxes, injustice, and drunkenness draw satiric comment in forms ranging from quatrains to long narrative poems and songs. The satiric proverb was a specialty of the Ila-speaking people of Northern Rhodesia, according to a study of those people published in 1920 by Edwin Smith and Andrew Dale. Susceptible to ridicule, these people inculcated rules of conduct and an attitude toward life through a large body of maxims and precepts that were felt to embody the wisdom of the people. Disputes, social gaffes, and social misfits were handled by sharply worded put-downs (Smith and Dale, 311–23). Proverbs such as those cultivated by the Ila got their authority from repetition in certain contexts and the willingness and need of people to find a moral structure to their purposes. Similarly, the cultivation of satiric songs circulated orally by those talented in the creation and dissemination of such works in essentially communal contexts places these items in a ritual tradition rather different from a familiar and recognizable literary tradition.

If verbal duels and the joking relationship can be said to embody the Juvenalian and Horatian spirits of satire, it should be noted that "personal" satire also contains the seeds of a variety of literary forms used for satiric purposes. Implicit in the verbal duel and the joking relationship is the dialogue form, one of the oldest and most versatile means for presenting a satiric idea, developed by Lucian and used by Erasmus, Aretino, Swift, and Fontenelle and still a viable form for the likes of Art Buchwald and Jules Feiffer. The satiric songs of Africans and New World slaves have their counterpart in the *sotties* from the medieval Feast of Fools, the *sirventes* of the troubadours, the songs of Gilbert and Sullivan, Tom Lehrer, and Randy Newman.

5

Verbal Aggression and Satire

Verbal Aggression in Ritual and Literature

Verbal aggression is a basic element of ritual satire, whether it be vented face-to-face in a drum match or *flyting* or expressed indirectly in a *sottie* or a Gridiron Club roast. Someone is being criticized, whether violently or more or less gently. The verbal means of such aggression include, among others, invective, abuse, the diatribe, the curse, and the lampoon. Despite their being basic means of communication with traditions that go back to biblical literature with the curse and Greek culture with the diatribe, all have sullied histories. In fact, verbal aggression as an area of study may be said to be largely uncharted territory. Linguists have mostly ignored the topic perhaps because it is too emotion–laden and unquantifiable. Students of aggression itself have had virtually nothing suggestive to say about this most familiar form of communication, even though it might be argued that more violence and aggression are carried out by linguistic than by physical means. Most studies in aggression mention verbal aggression rarely and then in its most obvious forms and only in passing.[1] Literary critics have also tended to ignore verbal aggression. Emanating from what are generally regarded as the less admirable emotions, verbal aggression seems somehow unworthy of serious critical attention. The forms of verbal aggression by their nature fail to show the complexity and subtlety beloved by most literary critics. In effect the forms of verbal aggression exist in a linguistic no man's land between *Terra Crudus* and *Terra Coquus,* between the primitive and sophisticated.

Two studies in an otherwise barren field are Ashley Montagu's *The Anatomy of Swearing* (1967) and Robert M. Adams's *Bad Mouth* (1977), the former a full and entertaining study of one kind of verbal aggression, the other a collection of loosely related papers, the title essay of which has to do with what Adams claims has been the dramatic increase in the use of insult, invective, and other forms of verbal attack in contemporary literature. What Adams sees in literature is paralleled on another level by the increase in the past fifteen years of anthologies of insults and related forms of verbal attack, books aimed at the general public, often in paperback.[2] Such collections supplement the myriad and endless number of jokebooks that collect the put-downs and sarcasms of people in the entertainment world and the mass media and famous squelches by the famous and infamous of history and literature. That there is a market for such material indicates at least a change in standards as to what kinds of utterances should be preserved in book form. Despite the often banal subject matter of much radio and television humor and the circumspect attitude of network officials toward controversial materials, the humor of insult has an established place in popular comedy as was mentioned at the beginning of chapter 4.

In the 1980s insult humor became a virtual flood as cable TV provided more freedom and opportunities to stand-up comics. Radio talk-show performers in some metropolitan areas became widely known for their verbal assaults. On network TV the spirited exchanges of the male and female leads on *Moonlighting* and the put-downs of the waitress Carla on *Cheers,* to name the most obvious, indicate the practice continues there. The *New York Times* recognized the phenomenon in an article by Walter Goodman, "Insult as Entertainment: Cultural Evil or Fad?" (20 May 1984), describing it as a tasteless fad that would run its course. Four years later in the same newspaper Stephen Holden reported that "aggressive, scatological comedians" had reached a "new plateau" (28 February 1988).

Apart from its omnipresence as a linguistic phenomenon, verbal aggression has been a dominant form of expression in much ritual satire. The Bible commends the curse as a weapon of the wronged and oppressed and condemns it for its elemental power to cause harm (Shai). That did not deter the prophets from using invective in their mission. Amos, Hosea, and Jeremiah were masters of name-calling, rhythmic and artful use of language for satiric purposes (Jemiely). Use of the diatribe has earned an unsavory reputation for the Greek Cynics and their twentieth-century counterparts, the Youth International Party (better known as the Yippies), even though both protested against serious social and political shortcomings. Their diatribes offended those who disagreed with them as well as those who did (Windt). Literary satire has persistently used the diatribe, the curse, the lampoon, and other forms of direct attack but mostly as devices rather than as separate forms. The most respectable form of direct-attack satire was the formal verse satire, a staple of Roman literature and imitated in Western literature into the eighteenth century. Whatever the reasons, verbal aggression has been largely ostracized from serious discussion by scholars of satire who have usually admired satire when it was least direct, most successful in the form of fantasy. Since fantasy in some satire has often been dictated by political and social rather than aesthetic considerations, making the satirist's necessity the critic's standard is a questionable procedure. Some critics have denied the status of satire to invective in its various forms. But such satire, whether naked or clothed, is still verbal aggression. Ultimately naked verbal aggression should be asked to face the tests of form and function that all art should face.

Ideally that may be the case, but the conditions already mentioned make it difficult to accomplish. Furthermore the fact that examples from various kinds of ritual satire are nonexistent or fragmentary makes it difficult if not impossible to study verbal aggression in its natural habitat. But examples from Western culture are by no means rare. They suggest that various forms of verbal aggression have long if not particularly honored traditions, that H. L. Mencken may have as much in common with Archilochus as Mencken had with some of his contemporaries. Like his counterpart in ritual satire, the modern practitioner of verbal aggression reacts to personal and social conditions that call for symbolically exorcising the folly and vice that he perceives around him. When the modern satirist is a writer the ritual is attenuated at best, but when the satirist is a performer his separation from ancient or primitive ritual is not that great.

Invective

Invective is a general term indicating direct verbal attack on a person, place or thing through the use of vituperative language or ridicule, often in verse form. Invective in Western culture is coeval with the beginning of the comedy-satire that emerged from the fertility rites of ancient peoples of the Mediterranean basin. Later Archilochus (c. 680–c. 640 B.C.) used the iamb meter to scourge his displeasures, such poetry being, according to Aristotle, one of the lower forms into which poetry divided itself. "Magic, Ritual, Art," the subtitle of Robert C. Elliott's *The Power of Satire,* indicates the early relationship of the power of the word to hurt and destroy and its evolution into the variegated forms of direct-attack satire.

Perhaps because of its spiritual lineage, invective is usually distinguished from verbal abuse as "refined swearing" (Montagu, *Anatomy,* 97) or "inspired vituperation" (Feinberg, *Intro,* 112) and is generally regarded as displaying more originality of expression and greater imagination than abuse. The verbal gyrations and emotional intensity of invective may cause a release of tension that expresses itself in laughter, although that may not be the intention of the creator of invective. Invective removed from its time and place may arouse ironic amusement by the incongruity of spent emotion. But the critical attacks in Nicolas Slonimsky's *Lexicon of Musical Invective* (1953) with its "Invecticon" (Aberration to Zoo) demonstrates that inventive vituperation has a timeless quality.[3]

Invective is usually covered by the umbrella of satire, although Gilbert Highet does not allow invective in his scheme because, he says, the basic emotion behind invective is hatred and the desire to destroy (155). Since purpose and motive are often inferentially arrived at, using them as a basis for distinguishing between kinds of attack raises problems that are difficult to deal with. Hugh Kingsmill in his *Anthology of Invective and Abuse* remarks that irony and satire are separate from invective in that irony demands a detachment that invective clearly lacks. But distinctions based on relative and subjective emotional states are vague at best, oversimplified at worst. The fervent and imaginative attack on a person or group which the attacker reduces to near or actual worthlessness suggests that even invective is not without an ironic touch. In any case, invective is rarely found in a pure state but exists as an element in the work of many satirists from Archilochus to Mencken and after. It appears in such special and ritual forms as *flytings,* pasquins, the Arabic *hija,* the Ashanti *apo,* Eskimo drum matches, and the black American "dozens." The residual "magic" that still lurks in the fear of the curse and the sometime discomfort of some people in the presence of satire are traceable to the element of invective that is never far removed from much satire, as Elliott argues.

An isolated tradition of ritual invective seems to have existed in Roman oratory (Merrill). The tradition supplied orators with a rich vocabulary of terms and themes which could be used in polemical oratory. Handbooks of rhetoric recommended the use of key terms of denigration and charges of disreputable activities. Roman audiences expected to hear exciting accounts of the follies and vices of the orator's opponents. Accusations of sexual misconduct, cruelty, drunkenness, greed, and baseness of birth were typical. Masters of invective include Marcus Porcius Cato (243–146 B.C.), who acquired the name "The Censor"; Scipio Aemilianus (185–129 B.C.), a patron of Lucilius, the earliest Roman practitioner of the formal verse satire; C. Gracchus (153–121 B.C.); and the greatest in the tradition, Cicero (106–43 B.C.) who contributed a handbook of rhetoric *(De Inventione)* in which he recommends the use of the techniques of invective but raised the art to new heights by his powers of invention and imagination.

Outside the Roman oratorical tradition the field is wide open, examples appearing in a great variety of forms from an even greater variety of writers and circumstances. One can choose from Juvenal (60?–140? A.D.) (Satire I among others), the *iambes* of André Chénier (1729–94) and Auguste Barbier (1805–82), or H. L. Mencken (1880–1956), but whichever is chosen, examples tend to be short, since to sustain invective causes it to lose its effectiveness. Mencken's essays on the American scene of the 1920s, "On Being an American" and "The Sahara of the Bozarts," contain several passages of well-sustained invective. The following from "On Being an American" is typical:

> It is, for example, one of my firmest and most sacred beliefs, reached after an inquiry extending over a score of years and supported by incessant prayer and meditation, that the government of the United States, in both its legislative arm and its executive arm, is ignorant, incom-

petent, corrupt, and disgusting—and from this judgment I except no more than twenty living lawmakers and no more than twenty executioners of their laws. It is a belief no less piously cherished that the administration of justice in the Republic is stupid, dishonest, and against all reason and equity—and from this judgment I except no more than thirty judges, including two upon the bench of the Supreme Court of the United States. It is another that the foreign policy of the United States—its habitual manner of dealing with other nations, whether friend or foe—is hypocritical, disingenuous, knavish, and dishonorable— and from this judgment I consent to no exceptions whatever, either recent or long past. And it is my fourth (and, to avoid too depressing a bill, final) conviction that the American people, taking one with another, constitute the most timorous, sniveling, poltroonish, ignominious mob of serfs and goose-steppers ever gathered under one flag in Christendom since the end of the Middle Ages, and that they grow more timorous, more sniveling, more poltroonish, more ignominious every day. (*Prejudices,* 9–10)

This and passages like it caused Mencken to become one of the most attacked writers of his time. Rather than replying in kind he collected the abuse, invective, and name-calling and published it as *Menckeniana: a Schlimpflexicon* (1928), a unique testimony to one man's tolerance for invective. Since most of the contents are rather banal compared to Mencken's own outbursts, the implication was that his critics were of little consequence, a view since corroborated by time.

A British counterpart to Mencken's essay is D. H. Lawrence's poem, "How Beastly the Bourgeois Is," invective being a natural medium for expressing the intense dislike that Lawrence had for early twentieth-century industrial civilization. Lawrence also endowed characters in his novels with the power of invective as can be seen in the exchange between Birkin and Ursula Brangwen in *Women in Love* (1920). Lawrence speaks for himself in his poem:

How beastly the bourgeois is
especially the male of the species—

Presentable eminently presentable—
shall I make you a present of him?

Isn't he handsome? isn't he healthy? Isn't he a fine
    specimen?
Doesn't he look the fresh clean englishman, outside?
Isn't it god's own image? tramping his thirty miles a day
after partridges, or a little rubber ball?
wouldn't you like to be like that, well off, and quite the
    thing?

Oh, but wait!
Let him meet a new emotion, let him be faced with
    another man's need,
let him come home to a bit of moral difficulty, let life face
    him with a new demand on his understanding
and then watch him go soggy, like a wet meringue.

Watch him turn into a mess, either a fool or a bully.
Just watch the display of him, confronted with a new
    demand on his intelligence,
a new life-demand.

How beastly the bourgeois is
especially the male of the species—

Nicely groomed, like a mushroom
standing there so sleek and erect and eyeable—
and like a fungus, living on the remains of bygone life
sucking his life out of the dead leaves of greater life than
    his own.

And even so, he's stale, he's been there too long.
Touch him, and you'll find he's all gone inside
just like an old mushroom, all wormy inside, and hollow
under a smooth skin and an upright appearance.

Full of seething, wormy, hollow feelings
rather nasty—
How beastly the bourgeois is!

Standing in their thousands, these appearances, in
    damp England
what a pity they can't all be kicked over

like sickening toadstools, and left to melt back,
  swiftly
into the soil of England.

Pietro Aretino (1492–1556) engaged in polemics on behalf of
princes and popes, dubbing himself "The Scourge of Princes."
Even an uppity secretary and would-be writer who crossed pens
with him was not immune from his venomous pen as the following
excerpt from a letter shows:

> Then the sodomite, instead of writing my letters, took to
> emulating them and made a book of which not a single
> copy was sold, and which ruined the Frenchman who
> loaned him the money to print it. I do not deny that he
> outdid me in the title, the size, the style, the fine paper,
> the illustrations, and advertising of his book, but not in its
> humanity. *Ecco!* The backbiter turns on me and rips me,
> in return for my defiling my pen by naming the black-
> guard. I thank you for saying that the praise I wasted on
> him redounds to the credit of my goodness and not to the
> defect of my judgment. Certainly, it pleases me to praise
> my acquaintances, even though I rue it as I rue puffing
> this swindler; but compassion is the core of my soul.
> Imagine a desert and you will have the image of my
> long-suffering kindness and the proof of my great
> liberality; but as those who forget offences, which they
> have the power to punish, are magnanimous and strong-
> willed, I shall wait and punish the sot by my courtesy as
> I relieved him by my charity. . . . The stray buffalo ekes
> out his life with two ounces of *pasta* a day; which makes
> Monsignor Lioni say when he gave him a few *lire* for his
> trash, 'I am not paying these notions, I am relieving a
> beggar in need.' And I must tell you what the mistress of
> the ambassador of Mantua said, when she heard the
> scoundrel scolding at me. She caught him by the shirt I
> gave him to hide his nakedness and cried: 'Take it off
> before you abuse the man who gave it to you!' But all this
> is nothing to the boasts with which the ox boosts his
> Dialogues above any that ever were written. 'Here is
> where I pass Lucian,' says the hack. Meanwhile, the stink
> is raging with hunger. Titian says that when the wretch

saw him from afar and had to pass him, he tucked his
bonnet in his shirt so as not to greet him; and yet the
robber would be choking with hunger if the pity of that
most famous man had not found him employment with
the Mantuan ambassador. Let the Jew strut in his rags and
crown himself with chimeras and scrape his brain dry!
The cricket in him made him chirp to Sansovino, the
ornament of our age and the wonder of others: 'What
would you say if, to the shame of your Pietro who draws
200 ducats from the Emperor, I received 400 from the
King?' 'I should be amazed,' Sansovino replied, 'and
meanwhile it makes a good story.' When Serlio, the light
of our architecture, heard that the cur boasted of making
his fame, he said: 'I am happy if he does not rob me of the
little I have.' And Marcolini, the most loyal of friends,
when he learned that the sot was gloating over the
printing of his notions and saying, 'Marcolini has the
profit and Aretino the credit of his *Letters*,' gave him his
answer: 'But for my profit and my friend's credit, Franco
would be a scullion.' But I deserve to have my eyes
plucked out by the pen of Pasquino for wasting good ink
on such scum.

Not surprisingly, invective has often flourished in times of
dramatic ideological differences. Such is the case with *Les Châti-
ments* (1853), a collection of one hundred and one poems by Victor
Hugo against the Second Empire of Louis Napoleon and his
coterie. A complex work that combines epic and visionary qualities, it contains some of the richest invective ever written. Hugo
invokes the Muse of Indignation and is influenced by Juvenal who
is mentioned several times. Hugo himself inspired Vargas Vila
(1860–1933), a prolific but now little-known writer born in
Bogotá, Colombia, whose declamatory and impassioned style in
support of liberalism against the dictators of Latin America made
him one of the most widely read writers in the Spanish-speaking
world in the early twentieth century (Deas). President Theodore
Roosevelt's seizure of Panama led Vila to publish what has been
described as the "archetypal anti-Yankee diatribe," *Ante los
Barbaros*. As a pamphleteer he was unexcelled in his time.
Religious differences have inspired their share of invective, as

witness Martin Luther's *Address to the Christian Nobility* (1520), in which he attacks the pope and the Roman Catholic Church for their corrupt use of power and their perversion of Christianity (Haile, 819–20).

But the minutiae of scholarship have been known to call forth invective also, most notably among the Italian humanists of the fifteenth century (Watt). Bracciolini Poggio (1380–1459), the most bellicose practitioner of *invectivae*, best known for his *Jestbook*, took on Francesco Filelfo (1398–1481) over the reputation of Florence, Guarina de Verona (1370–1460) concerning the comparative merits of Scipio and Julius Caesar, and Lorenzo Valla (1405–57), one of whose students had offended Poggio in a marginal annotation. For Filelfo he piled curse upon epithet, illustrating why his pen was the most feared of its time:

> You stinking billy-goat, you horned monster, you malevolent vituperator, father of lies and author of chaos . . . May Divine vengeance destroy you as an enemy of virtue, a parricide who tries to ruin wives and decency by mendacity, slanders, and most foul, false imputations. If you must be so scornfully arrogant, write your satires against those who debauch your wife. Vomit the putrescence of your stomach.

A century later Julius Caesar Scaliger (1484–1558) responded to Erasmus's criticism of the Cicero-philes of the time with an attack on Erasmus in which he characterized him as an "old buffoon and toothless drybones" (P. Smith, 314). His vituperative orations (1531 and 1536) against Erasmus, coming as they did at the end of Erasmus's life (he died in 1536), failed to gain many supporters for his arguments, even though he demonstrated an ability with invective that puts him in Poggio's class.

The art of invective in politics is a subject all its own, as Leon Harris's *The Fine Art of Political Wit* shows. The American political scene of the nineteenth century from John Quincy Adams to Sam Houston, and including John Calhoun, Henry Clay, Daniel Webster, John Randolph, and Thomas Hart Benton, provides some of the richest examples of invective to be found anywhere. Harris also deals with British political figures from Richard Brinsley Sheridan to Disraeli to Lloyd George and Aneurin Bevan and notes that invective has been a characteristic of political differences in many countries and times.

Because of the fervor expressed in invective and other verbal attacks, it is not uncommon for such aggression to be rejected as the outpourings of a person whose sanity or at least emotional stability is in question. Indeed it is not surprising that some invective does in fact emanate from persons who are near the far edge. Such was the case of Frederick Rolfe (1860–1913), whose bizarre life culminated in exploiting what one writer called a "fabulous talent for invective" (Atlas). Rolfe apparently suffered from a "pathological hostility" toward the world, although this should in no way denigrate the value of his invective, any more than the emotional shortcomings of a Poe or a Dostoevski should detract from the value of their art. But the personal nature of invective tends to eliminate the objectivity afforded other writers when the teller is separated from the tale. Even when invective is evaluated for itself, it is not always easy to separate from abuse, the artless, illegitimate cousin of invective, given the neglect and imprecision from which discussions of verbal aggression suffer. The invectivist has little place in modern society since there is no ritual context for him. But for those who flourish, the passage of time sometimes exonerates their work, taking it out of the partisan and emotion-ridden context so that its verbal felicity can be truly seen. That political differences continue to generate invective is illustrated by the career of Westbrook Pegler (1894–1969), a newspaper columnist whose reason for being sometimes seemed to depend on his disapproval of President Franklin D. Roosevelt and the New Deal.

Carrying on in the spirit of Pegler are contemporary journalists Hunter Thompson, Florence King, and R. Emmett Tyrrell, Jr. Thompson, author of *Fear and Loathing in Las Vegas* (1971) and *The Great Shark Hunt* (1979), arose out of the iconoclastic social furor of the 1960s and 1970s and became known as one of the most virulent of a new breed of invectivists. Thompson's mock-psychotic persona spewed out all the taboo words and inside hipster lingo on a host of popular cultural phenomenon (Hell's Angels, professional football, horse racing) but mainly on politics and politicians. Established figures in the Democratic party he called "a gang of senile leeches" and a "herd of venal pigs" (*Fear and Loathing,* 23). Of Richard Nixon he says:

For years I've regarded his very existence as a monument
to all the rancid genes and broken chromosomes that
corrupt the possibilities of the American Dream; he was
a foul caricature of himself, a man with no soul, no inner
convictions, with the integrity of a hyena and the style of
a poison toad. (*Shark,* 213)

Tyrrell, editor of *American Spectator* magazine and author of
Public Nuisances (1979) and *The Liberal Crack-Up* (1984), invokes
and evokes Mencken (meetings and conventions are *debauches,* the
United States is the *Republic*; slang and multisyllable words are
used studiedly). Tyrrell's description of Jimmy Carter illustrates:

He was a scamp mountebank from jerkwater America
whose knowledge of government and of history was
somewhere between that of a washroom attendant at
"21" and a modestly educated welfare queen. . . . A
peanut farmer from a crossroads village, who had made
his way to the governorship of Georgia playing the
Kluian toot one minute and Negro blues the next, now
had confected a song and dance incorporating Reinhold
Niebuhr, Karl Barth, Bob Dylan, Martin Luther King,
Jr., the Allman Brothers, and a dozen or so Liberal
aphrodisiacs. He wears work dungarees, pole-climbing
boots, and work shirts. (*Crack-Up,* 22–23)

In *He: An Irreverent Look at the American Male* (1978) King says she
is "neither feminist nor Total Woman, just sick of both." But her
gallery of American men is a modern version of Theophrastian
characters—the middle-aged conventioneer, the liberated male, the
misogynist, the confirmed bachelor, among others—feasible as a
result of the feminist ferment of the 1960s and 1970s. Eschewing
the name-calling of her male counterparts, King assesses the
political implications of America's admiration for "regular guys."
A complex, enigmatic, un-regular guy in public office causes, King
says, a "national nervous breakdown." One such was Richard
Nixon who wanted to be considered a regular guy but who
behaved in fact like an "unfathomable Druid." Living through his
administration, King says,

was like going back in time to Celtic Gaul when black-
robed priests practiced government-by-full-moon and

consigned their enemies to the slaughter stone. . . . The High Priest Nixon guarded the secrets of his administration and personality with the same zeal that Druids of old used to guard their Ogam alphabet. The Oval Oak Grove was the scene of time-honored Druidic practices such as weeping, praying, and making human sacrificial offerings. Nixon appeared to be the kind of person who counted time by nights instead of days in the Druid custom: he also played threnodic tunes in the wee hours and prefaced each cryptic Druidic oration with the announcement that soon everything would be perfectly clear. (167–68)

Abuse and Billingsgate

Abuse and billingsgate are direct, usually spontaneous, verbal attacks, usually against a person. In attempting to differentiate between abuse and invective, Kingsmill suggests that abuse most often takes the form of prose, invective the form of poetry. This implies that abuse is pedestrian, colloquial in the main, tending to machine gun-like bursts rather than sustained flights. Abuse is sometimes described as being "heaped" upon its victim, but it does not have the staying power of invective. Although the differences between abuse and invective have not been clearly established either by Kingsmill or Ashley Montagu, there is no question that abuse is looked upon as a kind of linguistic slum, which few respectable critics enter and of which even fewer attempt any clearance projects. Despite its status as a linguistic ghetto, it cannot be ignored. Like the ghetto, abuse does not go away, persisting in a variety of cultures under various guises, even at times occurring in satire itself in the form of caricature, animal imagery, epithets, and obscenity.

Among the Galla, the Tureg, and the Abyssinians, poems of abuse were a special genre in which men and women exchanged impromptu verses ridiculing enemies or unpopular leaders (Shipley). Political figures in England and the United States in the eighteenth and nineteenth centuries used abusive language on their opponents as a normal part of their operations (Harris; Safire). In the twentieth century, however, Parliament and Congress caution their members against the use of abusive language. Informal lists and records of precedents are maintained, and general rules in both institutions warn against overheated language. In 1966 a United States Congressional subcommittee discovered that the telephone had become such a popular medium for abuse that telephone companies, political leaders, and citizens in general were demanding legislation to curb the widespread misuse of Graham Bell's invention. An article in the *Publication of the American Dialect Society* reported that the vocabulary of abusive terms used by certain social groups in Chicago to refer to other religions, races, geographic regions, and ethnic groups ran into the hundreds of words (Pederson). The generous application of abuse to selected groups of young people by the inmates of certain penitentiaries in an effort to deter the young people from lives of crime and reported on public television in a program called "Scared Straight" is an interesting but controversial example of a ritual use of verbal aggression (O'Connor; Kleiman). A similar ritual was carried out against the gangsters of Osaka, Japan, as part of an overall program to shame and ostracize the hundreds of gangs with their thousands of members. Elderly gang leaders were summoned to police stations where they were forced to sit on wooden chairs and listen to verbal attacks denouncing their lives of crime (Haitch).

Abuse may in one sense be looked upon as the clichés of invective. Recourse to the epithets at hand has sometimes been noted as a characteristic of those whose verbal attack fails to indicate either some facility with the language or other redeeming qualities. As Russell Baker of the *New York Times* once noted in a column, Bobby Seale, a leader of the Black Panthers civil rights group during the 1960s in the United States, revealed a minimum of imagination in his attempt to abuse Justice of the Supreme Court Thurgood Marshall by calling him "an Uncle Tom, a bootlicker, a nigger pig, a Tonto and a punk." This primitive name-calling is hardly improved upon by such former members of Congress as Bella Abzug of New York and Ed Foreman of Texas who were rebuked by their colleagues for using the words "racist and demagogic" (Abzug) and "pinko" (Foreman) to describe colleagues (Hunter). Better they should have been rebuked for the banality of their language. Such terms betrayed a minor-league talent for abuse as well as a change in attitude when compared with that of Henri de Rochefort (1830–1913), founder of *La Lanterne,* a

French satiric weekly whose virulence was so great that Rochefort was forced to publish it in exile. Rochefort's verbal violence earned him a prison term in New Caledonia and the titles of "Rochefort the Lurid" and "Rochefort the Vicious." His epithets illustrate a talent for drawing on the resources that satirists have long used. He called M. Jaurès "a decayed turnip"; M. Georges Clemenceau "a loathesome leper"; M. Briand "a moulting vulture"; President Loubet "the foulest of assassins"; and President Fallières "a fat old satyr" (qtd. in McWilliams, 110–11).

The table of contents of Kingsmill's anthology contains the names of the most prominent figures of English and American literature either as abuser or abused. A. C. Swinburne's attack on Emerson is one of the more quotable examples. Having read in a newspaper of some abusive remarks attributed to Emerson, Swinburne wrote to Emerson inviting him to disavow the remarks. Failing to receive any satisfaction, Swinburne wrote again to Emerson attacking him at length but in particular as

> a gap-toothed and hoary-headed ape, carried at first into notice on the shoulder of Carlyle, and who now in his dotage spits and chatters from a dirtier perch of his own finding and fouling: coryphaeus or choragus of his Bulgarian tribe of autocoprophagous baboons, who make the filth they feed on. (Qtd. in Kingsmill, 176)

Abuse has been an element in certain kinds of satire from Archilochus to Lenny Bruce. Some eras, for example, the Elizabethan, have been congenial to abuse as a normal part of satire, whereas the Victorians were offended by personal and aggressive satire, although Kingsmill notes that, after Shakespeare, Dickens was the next greatest practitioner of "everyday abuse" in English literature. When abuse occurs in recognizable or conventional satiric forms or traditions as in Skeltonic verse, pasquinade, lampoon, *flyting*, or the "dozens" in which it functions as a means to an end, it is most likely to be allowed within the pale. When it appears in its purest states, either as *billingsgate* or *diatribe*, or in its more exalted states as *invective* or *raillery*, it is less likely to be welcome. Abuse is a tolerated if not always relished part of satire.

Billingsgate, a synonym for abuse, takes its name from one of the gates of London where the foul language of the denizens of the fishmarket earned them a reputation, especially in the seventeenth century, for scurrilousness above and beyond the call of normal usage. References are sometimes, but not always, to the accomplishments of the fishwomen, as in Marvell's "There is not a scold of Billingsgate but may defend herself" ("The Rehearsal Transprosed," 1. 167 [1672]; Marvell, *Complete Works*, 3:120). But a story involving Boswell and Johnson recounted in Arvine's *Cyclopaedia of Anecdote* (1851) has it otherwise.

> Johnson once made a bet with Boswell that he could go into the fishmarket and put a Billingsgate woman in a passion without saying a word that she could understand. The doctor commenced by silently indicating with his nose that her fish had passed the stage in which a man's olfactories could endure their flavor. The Billingsgate lady made a verbal attack, common enough in vulgar parlance, which impugned the classification in natural history of the doctor's mother. The doctor answered, "You are an article, Ma'am." "No more an article than yourself, thy misbegotten villain." "You are a noun, woman." "You— you—" stammered the woman, choking with rage at a list of titles she would not understand. "You are a pronoun." The beldam shook her fist in speechless rage. "You are a verb—an adverb—an adjective—a conjunction—a preposition—an interjection!" suddenly continued the doctor, applying the harmless epithets at proper intervals. The nine parts of speech completely conquered the old woman, and she dumped herself down in the mud, crying with rage at being thus 'blackguarded' in a set of unknown terms which, not understanding, she could not answer.

Wycherley in *Plain Dealer* (1, 3) equated billingsgate with invective, and Defoe and Thomas Jefferson used it to describe the language of political factions. The *Spectator* (no. 451) denigrated a particular satire by calling it nothing but "ribaldry, and billingsgate." As a synonym for abuse, billingsgate is no longer in common use, although it retains a place in most dictionaries. A little known variation on billingsgate is "water wit," so called from passengers and boatmen on the Thames shouting insults at each other safe in the knowledge that they can get away with impunity. Ned Ward provides examples of billingsgate (chap. 3) and water wit (chap. 7) in his *London Spy: The Vanities and Vices of Town Exposed to View* (1698–1703).

Diatribe

Invective and abuse are general terms used to describe verbal attacks. A diatribe is the term used to describe a particular work of verbal attack, usually against a group, an institution, or kind of behavior. It is often abusive or at least bitter or polemical. Its status, like that of invective, is a bit more respectable than some forms of verbal attacks, say billingsgate, in that its ancestry can be traced to Greek culture. Orginally a discourse or learned speech without critical intent, it was developed into a literary genre by Bion of Borysthenes (c. 325–c. 255 B.C.), a traveling philosopher of cynic persuasion. Bion presented anecdote, animal imagery, parody, character sketch, and a rich wordplay of pun, paradox, and wit in a mixture of tones ranging from the mocking to the serious, a conglomeration of styles from the lofty to the colloquial. He spawned no important followers or imitators, although Lucilius and Horace noted their debt to his spirit and approach. But his use of the diatribe as a medium for direct attack allowed the word to become a term for a lengthy and self-contained direct attack. Gilbert Highet in *Anatomy of Satire* uses diatribe to cover all satire in the first person, including monologues, letters, and formal verse satires in their infinite variety. But to include Bion's diatribes, Horace's *sermones,* Swift's "A Modest Proposal," and Browning's "Soliloquy of the Spanish Cloister" within the same frame blurs some useful distinctions among forms by taking advantage of a loosely used word.

We know of Bion's diatribes today only from fragments of his writings and reports about them. This lacuna may be of little consequence since no diatribes can be found among the immortal pieces of Western literature, nor has any writer made a reputation solely as a diatribist. Chapter 48 in Rabelais's *Tiers Livre* (1548) in which the church is bitterly attacked for its inconsistent practice regarding monks and marriage shows what a master satirist can do with the diatribe. The sermon as diatribe was practiced by Olivier Maillard (1430?–1502) and Michel Menot (1440–1518), widely known in their time for slashing preaching (Disraeli). They attacked the legal practices of the time, the vanities and stupidities of the newly rich and the nobility. Maillard likened evil lawyers to hawks, the terror of the poor. Menot said it was as easy for a lawyer to save his soul as it was for kindling to be in flame and not be burned. Maillard said that if the robes of judges were put under a press, the blood of their victims would flow from them. Maillard even went so far as to attack Louis XI, who then threatened to throw him in the river. Menot was noted especially for a burlesque style and the use of macaronic language. Among the descendants of Bion in the present age, Mencken ranks very high. A vocabulary drawn from languages modern and ancient and an aptitude for catalogues, epithets, invective, and parallel grammatical structures combined with a high sense of the absurdity of American life make him one of the most entertaining of the diatribists of any age. He was most eloquent on the political scene, but he also held forth on journalism, religion, and morality, and what he called the *boobus Americanus* in general. Mencken's best blows were landed in the 1920s and before, and some say that no one can ever take his place. In any case, Philip Wylie's *Generation of Vipers* in 1942 momentarily revived the diatribe but it had been moribund for so long that few recognized it when it reappeared. Wylie's gift for the disabling adjective ("eunuch moms," that is, schoolteachers), satiric imitation ("such stuff as wet dreams are made of"), and imaginative name-calling (Dorothy Thompson as a "she-sachem") impart a verve to his style that has not dated even though his subject matter has.

The tradition continues in G. Legman's *The Fake Revolt* (1967) an attack on the "New Freedom" of the 1960s in the United States, in parts of Eldridge Cleaver's *Soul on Ice* (1968), and in pieces by Thompson, Tyrrell, and King noted earlier.

The Curse

> "I have never made but one prayer to God, a very short one:
> 'O Lord, make my enemies ridiculous.' And God granted it."
> Voltaire to M. Damiliville, letter dated 16 May 1767

Voltaire's curse stands as the wish of all satirists, even though Voltaire is more concerned with making a statement about people than he is about causing harm or injury to the subjects of his curse. As Robert Elliott has shown in his *Power of Satire* the magic of the word—and the curse is one such kind of magic word—was in all likelihood one source of satire in the ancient world and traditional cultures, and its residual force still operates in some kinds of satire. The fear of Archilochus (descended on his father's side from priests of Demeter) and the fear of Hipponax stemmed in part from their use of the curse. The *iambos* meter in which their poetry was cast was sometimes called "cursing verses." A genre of Greek verse known as *arai,* that is, curses, is known to have existed although no examples have survived. A large number of cursing tablets *(tabulae defixionis)* with formulas or words and signs testify to the widespread use of cursing on all levels of Greek society. In Roman culture the *flagitatio* was a specialized curse aimed at regaining property by the use of *maledicta* (curses and abuse) against the offender. The use of the curse for ecclesiastical purposes down through the Middle Ages was known as *anathema.*

Whatever magical powers the curse may have been thought to possess, there is no question that the curse as a social force still exists in some societies. Among the Nuer people of Africa and Kurdish Jews in Israel the curse acts as a form of social control (Evans-Pritchard, *Nuer Religion;* Shai). The Nuer believe that if a person is wronged and curses the wrongdoer, God sees the justness of the curse and allows it to act. Nuer curses tend to run in the family in the sense that kinship obligations and responsibilities are regarded as more important than other social relationships. But curses may also be administered by a man whose wife has been adulterous or by priests and prophets against those who interfere with their functions. Kurdish Jews sanction the curse for use by the weak or by women, even though cursing is traditionally regarded as the province of men. But the public curse involves the community by inviting judgment and reconciliation. Here again the family is central to the functioning of the curse, but it is the status of the family in the eyes of the community that is important to the Kurdish Jews. A curse against a woman who has failed to fulfill an obligation to another family in a society in which "women are deeply involved in one another's domestic lives due to the complicated system of reciprocity in service exchange" (Shai, 45) is a blow against potential social disintegration. Curses against the moral character of members of the family are similarly suggestive of a breakdown in social cohesion. Despite the difference in the concept of what constitutes the community, the Nuer and the

Kurdish Jews use the curse to punish behavior that militates against the normal functioning of the community.

Outside of such special social contexts, and especially in its literary manifestations, it may be difficult to determine whether the curse is functioning as magic, cathartic, contrivance, or some combination. When is a curse a curse, and when is it a parody or mock curse? Two of the best known curses continue to unsettle critics, Horace's 10th Epode, because Horace fails to make clear the reason for the curse, and Ovid's monstrous *Ibis* because the victim of the curse is never named. Horace's poem is concerned with wishing Mevius a terrible ocean trip, with battering winds and final destruction. If this happens, "then a randy goat and lamb shall be offered to the gods who rule the tempest." Horace turns upside down the *propemptikon,* a prayer invoking a safe trip and return. Elsewhere Horace indicates that he knows the *iambics* of Archilochus and Hipponax, but whether the 10th Epode is an exercise in the same kind of *propemptikon* or a genuine curse is impossible to say for sure (Cairns, 55–56).

Equally puzzling is Ovid's *Ibis,* a six-hundred line blast, the *tour de force* of all literary curses, but about whose intention there is no certainty. Based on a missing poem by Callimachus of the same name, Ovid's poem does not mention by name the victim of the curse, but the use of the ibis stigmatizes the victim immediately since the ibis is reputedly a bird of notoriously filthy habits. Ovid's curse is rich in ills and discomforts in life and death for Ibis, noting also the unfavorable signs of his birth. At this point Ovid begins a catalogue of nearly four hundred lines in which he wishes on Ibis the ills and harms and fates of characters and incidents from legend, literature, and history. Written in the elegaic measure, the poem, according to Ovid, is only a preliminary outburst, a warning to Ibis to cease and desist in the behavior that has offended him. If that does not happen, the next curse will be in iambics and the offender will be named. The poem indicates a knowledge of the magical formulas and practices of the curse, but the poem also generates great intensity and shows great skill. Questions about intention and belief cannot be finally answered. As curse or parody, the poem is in a class by itself. Curses or threats of curses also appear in poems by Martial (VIII, lxi) and Catullus (12, 25, 42). These would seem to be literary devices for satiric effect.

Chaucer and Sidney invoke the curse ironically, Chaucer in the

House of Fame (94–108) against any who misjudge his work, and Sidney at the end of *The Defense of Poesy* against those who distrust or disdain poetry. John Donne's use of the curse in "The Curse," "The Bracelet," and "The Expostulation" parodies the ecclesiastical anathema by excommunicating those who threaten his "holy" love affairs (Bryan).

A less witty but also inappropriate curse is Ernulf's curse in *Tristram Shandy*. After Dr. Slop cuts his finger with his knife because his servant has tied his medical bag with tight knots which Dr. Slop could not open with his fingers, Mr. Shandy introduces Dr. Slop to Ernulf's curse, the composition of an English bishop, whose collection of curses was so complete that no one could curse without repeating something from it, a bit of anachronistic antipapal satire.

The use of the formal curse for satire has not been widespread nor has its use aroused enthusiasm. The energy, ingenuity, and imagination expended in Ovid's *Ibis* and Ernulf's curse could be looked upon as almost a perversion of creative effort. The original intention of a curse to do physical, psychic, and spiritual harm to another is an act of aggression that some may find difficult to identify with, even though the use of oaths and swearing which may express what may be called mini-curses is a nearly universal phenomenon. Nevertheless satire and the curse share the characteristic of verbal aggression, differing mainly in the immediacy of the metaphorical attack. Voltaire's curse to make his enemies ridiculous is mild compared to the death and desolation sought by the curses, serious or not, of Ovid, Horace, Chaucer, and Donne. In any case the ridicule comes from the play of language and thus shares the residual magic that Elliott traces in his book. The problematic nature of the curse may be illustrated by this twentieth-century example:

The Curse

To a sister of an enemy of the author's
who disapproved of "The Playboy."

Lord, confound this surly sister,
Blight her brow with blotch and blister,

Cramp her larynx, lung, and liver,
In her guts a galling give her.

Let her live to earn her dinners
In Mountjoy with seedy sinners:
Lord, this judgment quickly bring
And I'm your servant, J. M. Synge._
(299)

The Lampoon

Lampoon may be thought of as a specialized version of invective in that it is a satiric attack on an individual.[4] Many forms of ritual satire may in fact be kinds of lampoons, drum matches, *flyting,* roasts, the Saturnalian freedom described in Horace (*Satires,* 2, 7) when slaves were allowed to lampoon their masters. When a satiric portrait begins to emerge as distinct from a generalized abusive attack, there is the beginning of lampoon, implied, cumulative but secondary perhaps. Personal abuse consisting of remarks made in passing or which are not concerned with portraiture as such and cannot therefore be detached from their context should not properly be called lampoon. When the portraiture becomes a primary means of attack, as it does in some Greek satire, the art of the lampoon has arrived. It may be as terse as an epigram by Martial or Jonson or as elaborate as a scene in a play by Aristophanes or a portrayal in an epistle by Pope.

Archilochus's attack on Lycambes, the man who broke his promise to let Archilochus marry his daughter, is the prototype of all lampoons, here the attack of a disappointed suitor on a man whose word is unreliable. The revenge, both private and public in motive, is personal in tone and vernacular in presentation, using the Greek iambic form suitable to satire. Lampoons with these characteristics appear occasionally in later Greek literature (Hipponax, Simonides, Alcaeus) but rarely in Latin satire. The tradition reappears in England in some poems of John Skelton and Gabriel Harvey, whose lampoons in *Four Letters and Certain Sonnets . . .* (1592) on Robert Greene after Greene's death led to a literary altercation with Thomas Nashe that ended in 1599 with their works among many others being called in by the censor and no works by them ever printed again.

The lampoon received its name and bad reputation in the seventeenth century when poems of personal ridicule were designated *lampoons,* a name derived from the French *lampons,* "drinking song." The social, political and religious factionalism of the last half of the seventeenth century encouraged reckless and violent personal attacks that eventually gave the lampoon a bad name. Thus the seventeenth-century Samuel Butler denigrated the "character of the Lampooner as a Poetaster" whose

> Muse is of the same kind of breed with his that rimes in taverns, but not altogether so fluent, nor by much so generous and authentic as a Balladmakers; for his works will never become so classic as to be receiv'd into a Sive, nor published in the streets to a courtly new tune. He loves his tiny wit much better than his friend or himself; for he will venture a whipping in earnest, rather than spare a man in jest.

In the eighteenth century the lampoon was in such poor repute that critics distinguished between satire and lampoon by characterizing satire as general and reforming, lampoon as personal and malicious. Dr. Johnson includes this distinction in the definition of satire in his *Dictionary.* Thus the virulence of some seventeenth- and early eighteenth-century lampoons invited strenuous reactions. The appearance of the concept of the Amiable Humorist as part of a change in taste and in attitude about human nature made its contribution, as did the growth of libel laws (the word *lampoon* was regularly used as synonymous with *libel* and *slander*). This ostracism of lampoon has continued to the present century when Gilbert Highet in his *Anatomy of Satire* disposes of lampoon as a "parasite which has no life of its own and can exist only through destroying its victim" (152). Since this is true to some degree of much satire, such a statement, rather than disposing of lampoon, emphasizes what lampoon and satire have in common. Both may be unprovoked, personal, and malicious, in which case they are sometimes said to be without socially redeeming qualities. Despite its potential for perversion, the lampoon has had many distinguished practitioners among satirists and writers in general.

Any catalogue of famous lampoons would have to include Aristophanes' lampoon of Socrates in *The Clouds,* Seneca's of Emperor Claudius in *Apocolocyntosis,* Skelton's of Cardinal Wolsey in "Why Come Ye Nat to Courte?", Dryden's of Thomas Shadwell, George Villiers, and others in *Absalom and Achitophel* and *MacFlecknoe,* Rochester's of Charles II in "A Satyr on Charles II," Pope's of Lord Hervey in "An Epistle Dr. Arbuthnot," William Cobbett's (pseud. "Peter Porcupine") of Tom Paine, Byron's of Southey in *A Vision of Judgment,* Shelley's of George IV in *Swellfoot the Tyrant,* Victor Hugo's of Louis Napoleon in *Napoleon le Petit;* George W. Harris's of Abraham Lincoln in three separate Sut Lovingood yarns; Robert Graves's of Robert Bridges in "The Laureate," Ezra Pound's of Arnold Bennett in "Mr. Nixon," Mencken's of William Jennings Bryan in "WJB: In Memoriam," Aldous Huxley's of Middleton Murray in *Point Counter Point,* and Wyndham Lewis's of the Sitwells in *The Apes of God.* Recent examples would include Dylan Thomas's attack on Cyril Connolly in *The Death of the King's Canary,* a novel lost for thirty-five years and published only in 1976; Aleksandr Solzhenitsyn's thoroughly developed portrait of Stalin in *The First Circle;* and Robert Lowell's fourteen-line squib against Irving Howe titled "The New York Intellectual." Hugh Kingsmill's *Anthology of Invective and Abuse* contains (in spite of the title) a sizeable number of lampoons. C. E. Vulliamy's *The Anatomy of Satire* (1950) also contains lampoons sprinkled among the categories assumed by the author.

The examples in the catalogue above suggest two observations. The first is that the lampoon, although somewhat metamorphosed from its Archilochian origins, continues to exist if not to flourish, and second that the novel, especially the roman à clef, has become an important medium for the lampoon. If the lampoon as a satiric form has atrophied, the desire to launch personal attacks has not.

The Fiercest Form

Direct verbal aggression as manifested in lampoon, invective, curse, and so on may be an agreeable literary experience. Such art uses many of the rhetorical devices normally associated with any imaginative presentation of language. It is often humorous, and it certainly may have vitality. Ultimately it serves the same purpose as indirect satire in which the aggression may be managed by irony, metaphor, and allegory, masked with laughter. Why then does direct-attack satire have for the most part a bad name? Is it redeemable, is it worth justifying?

From the writings on toilet walls to the enshrined wit of Alice Roosevelt Longworth or Westbrook Pegler to the art of the Roman verse satirists, direct verbal aggression is a fact of life. From simple name-calling and scatological put-downs to the caustic wit of columnists and iconoclasts, humorous attacks are and have been widely practiced. For verbal attack is one way of expressing anger and indignation, of dealing with frustration, conflict, and other forms of stress, in short, one way of coping. But bare-faced anger and unadorned abuse are rarely worth looking at either in the flesh or on the printed page. Hostile humor in its more malicious and vulgar forms is often embarrassing or unthinking or banal or all of them at once. Hence Samuel Johnson in his *Dictionary* endows satire with some respectability by making it a generalized "reflection" as opposed to the "*lampoon* which is aimed against a particular person." No art has spent more time justifying itself than satire, and in part this is because no matter how hard satirists try they are almost always open to the charge of personal animus or at least general bitchiness. If satire is expressed in strong terms, the sophisticate, the cultivated, the compassionate may be repelled or at best unsympathetic. And yet to close off anger, frustration, indignation, and even hostility as possible motives venting themselves in artistic expression is to narrow the range of art. Ultimately, and this has been the most beneficial thrust of satire criticism of the past quarter century, the value of such expressions should rest on their artistic accomplishment, even, we would urge, those direct expressions of verbal aggression that tend to be relegated to marginal status or wholly ignored.

But critical detachment in the face of strong emotions, especially such threatening emotions as anger and indignation, is not always possible. The victim of direct oral attack tends to react in kind. That such exchanges have been cast into ritual forms by some societies suggests that these societies have a healthy respect for the inherent danger of not letting such emotions be expressed willy-nilly. Such rituals may serve as entertainment even while providing practice in controlling aggression (Triandis and Lambert, 326). Even if the cathartic effect is arguable, a case can be made for ethically justified anger, that is, indignation, according to George Sand, "the fiercest form of love" (70–71). Such indignation may express concern, a desire to lay bare the truth however unpleasant, with the belief that truth is better than lies, better than illusion, better than folly and vice. Whether in fact every satirist's motives are so august is open to question. But the satirist's motives aside, the satire may accomplish the truth-telling function whether or not the satirist has high ideals.[5] Motives are rarely singular or simple, so the satire's the thing, the socially pregnant, linguistically playful artifact that lives or dies according to whether it stirs and strikes its audience, and this no matter whether it be direct or indirect, fable or fiction, simple or complex.

6

Playing the Game of Satire

The Satirist as Playmate

In calling attention to the play element[1] in culture, Johan Huizinga
performed a service whose implications are still being worked out.
One who has done some of the working out is Roger Caillois in his
Man, Play and Games. Rejecting Huizinga's metaphysical interpretation of play, Caillois has elaborated more fully than Huizinga the
play element in games and in the process develops a classification of
games. Caillois's classification in turn can be used to throw light on
the nature of verbal aggression and wordplay that we here call
satire. Play, according to Caillois, is characterized by two "powers," which he calls *paidia* and *ludus*. *Paidia* covers "spontaneous
manifestations of the play instinct" (28). Caillois uses such words
as "impromptu," "unruly," "tumult," "improvisation," to describe *paidia*. It can be destructive, disruptive, and selfish, but
basically it is "the primitive joy in destruction and upset" (28).
Ludus, on the other hand, is "complementary to and a refinement
of *paidia*, which it disciplines and enriches" (29). *Ludus* in turn is
marked by "calculation" and "contrivance." It is an expression of
the "primitive desire to find diversion and amusement in arbitrary,
perpetually recurring obstacles" (33). Caillois's discussion is more
inclusive than this description, since his concern is with characterizing all play, whereas the emphasis here is on those elements
that can be applied to verbal aggression, which, although not
included in Caillois's coverage, can readily be deduced from the
following:

> [Games] can also be placed on a continuum between
> two opposite poles. At one extreme an almost indivisible

principle, common to diversion, turbulence, free improvisation, and carefree gaiety is dominant. It manifests a kind of controlled fantasy that can be designated by the term *paidia*. At the opposite extreme, this frolicsome and impulsive exuberance is almost entirely absorbed or disciplined by a complementary, and in some respects inverse, tendency to its anarchic and capricious nature: there is a growing tendency to bind it with arbitrary, imperative, and purposely tedious conventions, to oppose it still more by ceaselessly practicing the most embarrassing chicanery upon it, in order to make it more uncertain of attaining its desired effect. This latter principle is completely impractical, even though it requires an ever greater amount of effort, patience, skill, or ingenuity. I call this second component *ludus*. (13)

Actual games fall into four categories, *agon* or competition, mimicry or simulation, *ilinx* or vertigo, and *alea* or chance. The latter is obviously an important element in many games but has no application to the discussion here and can therefore be dismissed.

Agon. The contest, on the other hand, is one of the most ancient forms of verbal aggression. Contests in which two participants exchange invective are found in preliterate societies where the exchanges are part of the traditional oral culture. Drum matches, exchanges of *hija,* the *Inga fuka,* and the "dozens" are used to settle disputes and provide a means of catharsis for participants and audience alike. Among Sumerian men of letters a favorite literary composition was the disputation, similar in many ways to what was called elsewhere at a later time *flytings* (Kramer, 217–33; Speiser). Sumerian disputes, however, utilized abstractions as protagonists, summer and winter, cattle and grain, although one involves two school graduates and another two unnamed young ladies. The Old Comedy of Greece incorporated such exchanges into their plays as the dispute in *The Frogs* between "Aeschylus" and "Euripides" about the merits of their poetry and between Just and Unjust Reasoning in *The Clouds*. Aristophanes uses one to denigrate the other, employing everything from abuse to satiric imitation to gain his ends.

The medieval Latin poetic debates cover a great variety of

Table 6.1

	AGON (Competition)	MIMICRY (Simulation)	*ILINX* (Vertigo)
PAIDIA			
"Tumult"*	Drum matches "Dozens"	Ceremonial clowns Saturnalia	Abuse Invective
Improvisation	*Inga Fuka*	Feast of Fools	Billingsgate
"Immoderate Laughter"*	*La Legge* Raillery	Charivari Mumming (New-foundland)	Curse Diatribe
"Agitation"*	Joking relationships *Flyting Hija Contrasto Tenso Picong*	*Holi Fastnacht*	*Apo Terrae Filius* address Lampoon Fescennine Verse *Iamb/Iambs*
Calculation	Debates	*Sottie*	Formal Verse Satire
Contrivance	Contests	The Roast	*Sirventes*
Precepts	Dialogues	Theater Fable/Fiction Burlesque/ Parody/ Imitation	Satiric songs Poetry Essays
LUDUS			

*Caillois's terms (36)

subjects in an allegorical manner, including among others, seasons, flowers, beverages, parts of the body, and kinds of lovers. Rarely are the debates exclusively satiric, but the characters may adopt a mocking attitude toward each other or the form itself which allows for occasional satiric imitation. In *Phyllis and Flora* the young ladies in debating the lovemaking merits of clerks and knights mock each other and their arguments. Another version of the same love debate, *Love-Council of Remirement,* finds the author parodying ecclesiastical style. Versions of the *Debate between Wine and Water* appeared in English, French, Spanish, Italian, German, and Hebrew between the twelfth and sixteenth centuries. Nearly all versions contain humorous elements, but in one, religious satiric imitation is emphasized, while in another the exchange becomes personal and vindictive in the manner of *flyting*.

Such debates were known as *debat* in French (occasionally *estrif*), *Streitgedichte* in German, and *conflictus* in medieval Latin. All may be at times loosely referred to as "dialogues," which differ in being less formal and contentious than debates or contests, although at times the difference between contests and dialogues is unclear.

The debate becomes a rudimentary form of satirical drama in John Heywood's *Witty and Witless* and *The Spider and the Fly*. In the former he attacks his colleague, court fool Will Somers, in the latter he satirizes the Reformation controversy over free will and conscience.

The *tenso* (French, *tençon*, Italian, *tenzone*) was originally a *flyting* contest of the Troubadour culture. Uc de St. Cyr was a notable Troubadour practitioner, and later Dante exchanged sonnets with Forese Donati in an insult combat. In Sicily such insult matches were called *contrasti*, with the sonnet as the weapon, as in those of Giacomo da Lentini and Jacapo Mastacci.

The form that best epitomizes the literary expression of the *agon* is the dialogue, especially as used for satire. Although widely used for presenting philosophical ideas, the dialogue for satire has a rich and varied history. Protean in the extreme, the satiric dialogue may take on the characteristics of the debate, a question-and-answer catechism, a symposium, or become a quasi play or novel, depending on what the writer emphasizes or includes as part of the dialogue. The amorphous nature of the dialogue has probably contributed to its longevity, for the variations that can be worked out in the exchange between two persons seem nearly unlimited. The two speakers may converse as equals or relate as quasi monologist and occasional interlocutor. As equals one may eventually undercut the other, or they may both be condemned by their own words. One may serve as the *eiron* to the other's *alazon*. One may destroy the other by the use of invective and other techniques of verbal aggression. The characters may be as simple as abstractions and caricatures or as complex as characters in some novels and plays. The satirist may speak through either, both, or neither of the characters. The satirist may use real persons, prominent or obscure, alive or dead or in-between, or imaginary persons or animals, all or any of which may enrich the proceedings with ironic or other kinds of overtones. The exchanges may occur any place in this life or the next or no place. The dialogue does not preclude the possibility of a dialogue within the dialogue or of a character's narrating an anecdote or even a picaresque tale in which the satirist may further attack characters, ideas, or behavior.

The dialogue of the dead, developed by Lucian, is the only dialogue form for which there has been what might be called a tradition. This form was picked up in the seventeenth and eighteenth centuries by Boileau, Fontenelle, Fenelon, and dozens of other writers until there was a virtual parade of dialogues of the dead. Erasmus's *Colloquies* represent the dialogue in the service of polemical or ideological dispute, used by him and others in the religious controversy of the time. Voltaire was an able dialogue writer in the Erasmus "tradition." Dialogues by Pietro Aretino, Bernard Mandeville, and Jonathan Swift are used to satirize social mores and practices. Giambattisti Gelli, Denis Diderot, and Walter Savage Landor also created dialogues that were sometimes or in some ways satiric. The satiric dialogue continues as a viable form in the newspaper columns of Art Buchwald, Art Hoppe, and Russell Baker and in the cartoons of Jules Feiffer.

Mimicry.   When the ceremonial clowns of the Dakota people and the Koyemshi of the Zuni become earthling tricksters, they are indulging in one of the most common practices of satire, creating the illusion that they are someone they are not. Whether the illusion is created by disguise, as with the ceremonial clowns or the mummers of Newfoundland, or by temporarily taking on a new personality, as with the Mere Fools or the Lords of Misrule of the Feasts of Fools and *sotties,* or by reversal of roles in the Saturnalia and the *Holi* celebrations, there is the illusion that things and persons are other than they normally appear to be.

Such role playing represents most dramatically the *paidia* element in a ceremonial or ritual context. The clowns and fools are permitted to break the normal rules of society, mocking the gods or the authorities, shouting obscenities at the audience, burning dung in the censers or throwing it at the bystanders from carts. In such festivals as the Roman Saturnalia, the Greek Cronia, and the Babylonian Sacaean the normal relations and hierarchy were turned upside down as slave became master for a day, allowed to mock and affront the real master (as perhaps he might have liked to in real life). That such a reversal carried within it the seeds of anarchy is suggested by the fact that in the most ancient of these festivals the mock king was dispatched in some way so as to imply a return to order. In the medieval celebrations, the victims were those who had transgressed the norms of society, whether an old widow who had married a young man or a prince who had overtaxed the people. The element of *paidia,* "the primitive joy in destruction and upset," potentially present in the assuming of another role or personality is recognized and momentarily cultivated, but only momentarily.[2] It cannot be otherwise.

From the mythical trickster to the most current stand-up comic, mimicry is inherent in the successful functioning of satire. The protean nature of the trickster has been discussed. The trickster's earthly counterparts, ceremonial clowns and other jesters, often appear in masks in order to perform their functions. As representatives of the gods they are a living link with the sacred even as they are laughable and ridiculous. In *Man, Play and Games* Caillois discusses the mimicry of clowns in the festivals held by the Navajos and by the Zunis (138–41). In the Navajo ceremony, masked dancers impersonate the divinities, but one is a clown who dances out of step to confuse the other dancers and acts foolishly. Mostly he mocks the importance of the other dancers, a satiric imitation of a serious ceremony. The Koyemshis of the Zunis portray various characters, each with his own horrible mask, combinations of bumps, horns, various shaped mouths. They too mock the gods as well as rebuke members of the audience for shortcomings, avarice, marital difficulties, living like a white man. In the temple ceremonies of Bali a clown wears a mask that covers the upper part of his face but leaves the mouth free, half masked, half himself. Like the Navajo and Zuni clowns the Bali clown is in touch with the gods as well as serving royalty. But he is free to mock both the gods and royalty, which he does with "earthly humor, obscene jokes and bawdy slapstick . . . [which] are not considered sacrilegious; laughter [being] sacred in Bali" (Jenkins, 20).

Similarly, satirists adopt many guises in the desire to entertain and enlighten. Whether by implied persona or with consciously created characters, satirists have used mimicry as a basic ploy. As persona we have the "little soul" of Thurber and Benchley and Woody Allen, the plain good man of Philip Wylie, the "amiable humorist" of Will Rogers, the sophisticate of H. L. Mencken, the confirmed cynic of Oscar Wilde or Ambrose Bierce, all versions of what Alvin Kernan in *The Cankered Muse* included in the concept of "the satirist" (14–30). From such persona it is a small step to Peter Finley Dunn's Mr. Dooley and Benjamin Franklin, Silence Do-Good and Poor Richard. The final step is into the world of fictional caricatures from Candide and Gulliver to Screwtape and Asmodeus, including Yossarian, Lazarillo, the King of Brobdingnag, Brer Rabbit, Reynard, and others too numerous to mention. (For a fuller discussion of the characters of satire see Chapter 8.) Beyond narrative fiction there is the world of theater where the spirit of *ludus* manifests itself in *sottie,* roast, *fastnachtspiele,* revue, and a variety of dramas, including the mock drama that ridicules the conventions, forms, and tastes in drama itself by means of burlesque, parody, and travesty. For as Caillois says of mimicry in games, "mimicry and travesty are . . . complimentary acts" (21).

This is equally true in literary satire. No literary expression makes such extensive use of other forms as does satire. It can hardly be said to exist apart from the forms that feed it. "Mock" (with its double meaning of imitation and ridicule) is perhaps the single most widely used prefix in satiric nomenclature. There is the mock encomium, the mock pastoral, the mock heroic, the mock Utopia, and so on. Although satire as mimicry may draw upon the genres and modes of literature, it draws equally upon forms from outside literature. Think, for example, of such items used for satire as the dictionary, the obituary, the almanac, the trial, the dinner (*cena*), and the alphabet. There are satiric laws and mock prayers, mock meditations, petitions, sermons, speeches, and testaments. The hoax as satire may be an elaborate piece of theater or an elaborate lie or some improbable combination. Satire is a vast enterprise of mimicry, whether of a form or style (parody, burlesque, or imitations), of a person (lampoon or caricature), or of life and truth itself, the idea that satire merely holds up a mirror to life, an image affirmed by Horace and Juvenal and Swift and made graphic in Holbein's illustrations of Erasmus's *The Praise of Folly.*

From a child mimicking a teacher; a worker, a boss; or David Fry, Richard Nixon to the satirical revue, be it *sottie* or Second City, or *The Beggar's Opera, Dr. Strangelove* or *Saturday Night Live,* through the vast incestuous connection that the satiric impulse maintains with life, the arts, and literature, mimicry is one of the main games played by verbal aggressors, at all stages of life and in many societies.

Ilinx. The kinds of games included by Caillois in this category and emphasized by the English translation, vertigo, are those that involve some physical disorientation as in swinging, spinning, or speeding, whether naturally and individually or in a contrivance of some sort. Ultimately, Caillois says, *ilinx* consists of an "attempt to momentarily destroy the stability of perception . . . (and) reality with sovereign brusqueness" (23). Clearly no linguistic phenomenon can compete with physical activity in inducing this condition, and those that may attempt to do so, chants, for example, take their power more from their similarity to music than from their linguistic properties. But language can shock, inflict pain, induce instability, and otherwise disorient perceptions and feelings in such a way that is as real as dizziness or the feeling of falling. In this category therefore we can place all the expressions of direct verbal attacks, from those in which the element of *paidia* is greatest, abuse, billingsgate, and the invective of the *apo* ceremony, to the diatribe, Fescennine verses, the Greek iambic poems, the formulaic curse, and the lampoon, in which there is some intrusion of the *ludus* spirit. As the *ludus* element increases there is the formal verse satire, *sirventes,* African satiric songs, satiric verse and poetry, the *terrae filius* address, and the satiric essay as practiced by Mencken and Wylie.

Robert Elliott has worked out this "tradition" in his *Power of Satire,* tracing direct-attack from the curse and the primitive belief in the power of the word to kill or at the least raise blisters to twentieth-century manifestations in Wyndham Lewis and Roy Campbell, both of whose works have produced if not vertigo at least strong and unsettled feelings. And this kind of reaction is typical of the way strong and direct attack satire affects its audience. Elliott speaks of Book IV of *Gulliver's Travels* as a "shocking experience," of the "horror of the work." His chapter "The Satirist and Society" is a history of the reactions caused by works of satire, not all of them direct-attack satire, but because such attacks lack the indirections of mimicry and are outside the accepted structure of the contest they seem all the more dangerous and unacceptable. Reactions to the work of Hunter Thompson suggest that invective can unsettle even in an age that seems to subsist on verbal overkill.

But the blast from satire affords only one kind of *ilinx,* even though it is closest perhaps to the organic or physical form; there is, as Caillois points out without actually naming varieties, a "psychological form" (24). This includes the numerous verbal and rhetorical devices and forms appropriated or created by the satirist for his purposes. They vary from most obvious to very subtle, from sarcasm to paradox, from doggerel to zeugma. But all are designed to unsettle, untrack, surprise, or astonish (Nichols, 38–48). One technique is deliberately to dislocate the language or to exploit those dislocations that occur because of carelessness, thoughtlessness, or laziness. Deliberate dislocation of language and reality is nonsense, and "the nonsense poem—if it works— refreshes us by surprise, by invention, or by commenting, in what is said or how it is said, on sense taking itself too seriously or being pompous, or in fashion" (Grigson, 11). Satiric nonsense cannot veer too close to meaninglessness because it must relate to something recognizable, however inverted, surreal, or perverse. Hence satire itself is often taken for nonsense, as when satiric imitation reduces its victim to jibberish, or reality becomes absurd.

But nonsense can be introduced as a kind of *reductio ad absurdum,* as in George Canning's verse in the *Anti-Jacobin Magazine,* or Thomas Love Peacock's "The Wise Men of Gotham," or Ring Lardner's nonsense plays ("The curtain is lowered for seven days to indicate the passing of a week"). M. R. Haight notes that "nonsense literature . . . uses absurdity to amuse. This means that it must either mock (however grimly) or play (with whatever degree of sophistication). Usually it does both. Its characteristic effect is a parody of a play-fantastic kind, carried out at several linguistic levels" (255). A particular form of verbal nonsense is the bull, consisting, as Coleridge pointed out, of a "mental juxtaposition of incongruous ideas, with the sensation, but without the sense, of connection." Such statements as "Abstinence is a good thing but it should be practiced in moderation" and "It is hereditary in some families not to have children" were for a long time ascribed to the Irish, especially by the British, but similar bulls have been attributed to women, the French, Americans, and blacks, depending on who was telling them, so that bulls were once an expression of an ethnic, sexist, or racial slur. Just so in satire the bull is a way to undercut a character, as Swift does in the first Drapier letter, when he has the persona say, "Therefore I do most earnestly exhort you, as men, as Christians, as parents, and as lovers of your country, to read this paper with the utmost attention, or to get it read to you by others."

Various techniques of verse have been used to shock the reader, including the macaronic, the skeltonic, and doggerel. All violate normal expectations for verse either by mixing languages, as in the macaronic, or mixing levels of diction and overusing sound patterns, as in the skeltonic, or by being a kind of aborted poetry, as in doggerel. All of them are in a sense satiric imitations, although their uses have not been confined to that. The macaronic was used by Teofilo Folengo (1491-1544) in the early sixteenth century as an "imitative attack" on the epic and the pastoral traditions and for satirizing miscellaneous local targets (Saintsbury, 65). Macaronics, originally created by mixing Italian with Latin or by making Italian look like Latin, is created by combining two languages. Saintsbury calls Folengo a "satiric realist of remarkable force" (65) and notes that his works were known to Rabelais, who almost certainly borrowed from him.

John Skelton (1464?–1529) is the best known practitioner of the form named for him. But the year before Skelton died, two exiled Franciscan friars, William Roy and Jerome Barlow, used skeltonic verse to attack Cardinal Wolsey, causing Wolsey to order all copies bought up and destroyed. This was the first of many uses of skeltonics in the religious controversy of the second and third quarters of the sixteenth century following Skelton's death. From that time until the present skeltonics has not been much used, satirically or otherwise, although it has evoked the admiration of Coleridge, Auden, Robert Graves, among others.

Macaronic and skeltonic verse must be consciously created. Not so with doggerel. Bad verse may be written by those whose taste or ability or both are not what they might be, but such doggerel would hardly be satire, at least conscious satire, although it might qualify as self-parody. In any case, Chaucer, Samuel Butler, and Swift have used doggerel for satiric purposes, the former in his burlesque *Tale of Sir Thopas,* Butler in *Hudibras,* and Swift passim. Used crudely, like a 2x4 on a donkey, these techniques are so special that they can become a literary Chinese water torture if overly or ineptly used. Their bastard-like status in the poetic hall of techniques can be transferred to those who profess a taste for such satire, which of course affirms the fact that at least they have worked as 2x4s. Doggerel is not confined to poetry in English but exists in German where it is known as *knittelvers*.

These more violent linguistic and logical dislocations can be self-defeating, so that satire has tended to operate somewhere between the unbuttoned level of slang and scatology (although neither is a stranger to satire) and the formal, ceremonial, or learned level of language (also no stranger). Until quite recently the formal level would have included the diction of literature as well. But since Burns and Wordsworth there has been a slow abandonment of the concept of a literary language distinct from the language of general usage. The attempt to maintain a separation of levels of usage in poetry persists, however, as can be seen by consulting the introduction to James Reeves's anthology of satiric verse *A Vein of Mockery,* in which he seriously discusses the question of whether satire can be poetry. His writing off those poets whose "diction is too 'instant' " suggests that even editors of collections of satire may not be among satire's best friends.

Although it is difficult to generalize about the language of satire, Gilbert Highet's statement that "nearly all satiric writing contains colloquial anti-literary words" can be safely defended. On a theoretical level one could maintain that colloquialism is indigenous to the diction of satire. The phallic festivals that were the antecedents of Greek comedy assured that a colloquial diction would be a strong element in Aristophanes and other writers of old Greek comedy. The mixed dish concept of Roman formal verse satire included mixed diction so that from Lucilius to Jerome colloquial idioms were standard equipment for satirists. Horace calls some of his satires *sermones* (that is, conversations) and says in Satire 1, 4 "You can't call a man who writes TALK, / As I like to do, a real poet." Horace started out writing satire under the influence of Bion (c. 325–c. 255 B.C.), whose style is not merely strongly colloquial but slangy, obscene, anecdotal, and parodic as well. The persistence of the colloquial, the inherent necessity of the colloquial in the Goliardic poets, the satire of Aretino and Berni, Byron's *Don Juan,* and Browning's satiric monologues, the mixing of the colloquial and the rhetorical in Gogol, the dominance of the colloquial in Twain and Lardner—all bear out Highet's generalization about the nature of the satiric idiom (Mimker).

The function of such diction has been as a device to shock the reader by its nature and by its ironic contrast with other more widely admired and acceptable styles. It has signaled the fact that satire is in touch with real life as opposed to the diction of the epic, romance, or allegory. To this might be added the highly subjective and politically charged diction of mid-twentieth century poetry, for as Philip Larkin has pointed out, the colloquial nature of John Betjeman's satiric poetry has allowed it to play a subversive role against a literary orthodoxy that did not realize it was being challenged, or, after Betjeman became Britain's poet laureate, that the orthodoxy had been bested.

A special feature of the colloquial is the cliché, and satirists, mostly in the twentieth century, have exploited what can be a kind of linguistic sludge accumulated as a result of the pervasive influence of the technological revolution in the mass media. Used to characterize the ignorant, the unthinking, and the pretentious, Sinclair Lewis, Ring Lardner, S. J. Perelman, James Thurber, and Peter DeVries in fiction and E. E. Cummings, John Betjeman, and Ishmael Reed in poetry have made important use of the cliché. But even before the word itself had come into use, Pope in his *Essay on Criticism* (2, 350–54) satirized eighteenth-century hack poets who relied on clichés to fill out lines and provide easy rhymes:

> Where'ere you find 'the cooling western breezes,'
> In the next line it 'whispers through the trees':
> If crystal streams 'with pleasing murmurs creep,'
> The reader's threatened (not in vain) with 'sleep.'

Frank Sullivan made a career out of attacking the cliché through his character Magnus Arbuthnot, expert on baseball, crime, love, vacations, and war, who invariably responded in clichés. His dialogues, composed by Sullivan from 1930 to his death in 1976, provide a comprehensive catalogue of the clichés that cluttered up the language of banal, unthinking, and uncaring people of the United States in the mid-twentieth century. Newspaper columnists with a satiric bent such as H. L. Mencken, Westbrook Pegler, Art Buchwald, Russell Baker, and William Safire have engaged in intermittent encounters with cliché clutterfication.

Such techniques as doggerel, colloquialisms, nonsense, and skeltonic verse tend to be simple, unambiguous, and direct in their impact, even visual, as in the short lines of skeltonics and the latinate vocabulary of macaronic verse. Complementary to these forms and techniques is the world of what for the lack of a better word can be called wit, the linguistic and sometimes illogical world of paradox, anticlimax, graffiti, aphorisms, compression, and insinuation, the satire of delayed reaction, of little psychological explosions that make wit an exciting area of *ilinx* in every sense of the word.

It is, after all, on the plains of wit that most critics of satire have dallied. Fortified with the handbooks of Cicero and Quintilian and the tradition of rhetoric, critics have argued satire as the art of persuasion (Mack; Rosenheim, 10–34; Paulson, 9–31). Armed with the devices of rhetoric, the satirist goes forth to vanquish the foolish and vice-ridden. But Freud's wit as verbal aggression by indirection helped to bolster the perennial image of the satirist telling the truth to a society that doesn't want to hear it. At different times and places both of these images are and were valid. But it may be that at a deeper level both are encompassed by the concept of wit as wordplay, not the narrow denotation of wordplay of punning that delighted Swift and Sheridan, but wordplay with emphasis on the "play." This goes beyond the "pleasure" derived from speaking the forbidden noted by Freud, expression of those emotions that society seeks to inhibit, hostility and aggression, but which express themselves in some form, directly or indirectly. There is the equally basic expression of delight in language, sound- and meaning-play for themselves and for their social uses (Wolfenstein; Kirshenblatt-Gimblett, 72). Puns, rhymes, stanzaic forms, metaphor, and antithesis are part of childhood language.[3] These and other linguistic patterns fall into the patterns found in the ancient handbooks of rhetoric. In short, the devices of deviousness and indirection are in use long before the satirist is called a satirist. Wit, whether in Cicero's or Freud's sense, is play before it is anything else. Whatever function it may serve in the psychological or social development of the child, it is expressed as play and who is to say that the play function is ever totally lacking when it grows up and becomes satire.

Name-calling and play on people's names is one of the most pervasive forms of wordplay in children (Wolfenstein, 75–77; Opie, 154–73; Jorgensen). In adults they take their place among the devices of abuse and invective. The *ilinx*-y counterpart of word-play on names for the satirist is the charactonym (Malone), an appellation that helps characterize a fictitious person. Exploiting sound and sense (or should it be nonsense?), the satirist creates a device that serves as a kind of instant characterization, a shortcut exposition, immediately establishing a counter or caricature in the satiric sense. Since such charactonyms are humorous, ironic, parodic, dissonant, or some combination thereof, there is playfulness in the sting, a gap between the bite and the pain or pleasure, a tiny *ilinx*.

Perhaps the most widely used kind of charactonym involves personality names. Thus J. J. Morier in *Hajji Baba* gives his characters derogatory names, Mirza Ahmak (Doctor Fool), Namard Khan (Lord Coward), and Mulla Nadan (The Reverend Ignoramus). Gogol coins crippling names for his characters in *The Inspector,* the chief of police, Skvoznik-Dmukhanovsky (Rascal-Puftup) and the judge Lyapkin-Tyapkin (Bungle-Steal). Jonson uses animal names in their Italian form for characters in *Volpone* as well as Italian words with derogatory translations in English, as Castrone (eunuch) and Adorgyno (hermophrodite). John Gay uses seventeenth-century slang and underworld jargon for names in *The Beggar's Opera* that describe not only characters' behavior but their occupations. Filch, Jeremy Twicher, Betty Sly, Nimming Ned, and Ben Budge all bear names that suggest their occupations as thieves. Some of the women carry names suggestive of their occupations as Dolly Troll and Molly Brazen. Thackeray in a different realm came up with "Tiler and Felthan, Hatters and Accoutrement-Makers" and Deuceace, the gambler. The use of charactonym to satirize social status, or, in this case, the lack of same, is Thackeray's Bareacres family which attempts to recoup its status by taking Thistlewood as its family name.

Another important category of charactonyms is the name used ironically. Thus Trimalchio (Semitic, *tri,* trice, play *m-l-kh* meaning king [as in Moloch] yields "mighty monarch") is ironically inappropriate for the tasteless boor of that name. Mayakovsky's Pobedonosiko (Nose for Victory) and Chadakov (Wonder Worker) in *The Bathhouse* are clearly ironic appellations. The use of Loyola Sweeney as a charactonym for T. S. Eliot in "Myra Buttle's" *Sweeniad* makes ironic use of a charactonym employed by Eliot himself for satiric purposes. One of the richest sources of ironic charactonyms are the plays of Friedrich Durrenmatt whose inventions are varied and complex, rich with irony, as with the name of the old woman in *The Visit,* Klara Wascher, whose return to her hometown is designed to cleanse the town of a miscarriage of justice. Durrenmatt crowns a prostitute with the name of Frieda Furst, that is, Peace Prince.

The use of the charactonym as a satiric device is both ancient and widespread. Aristophanes used it for Lysistrata ("Demoboliza") and in *Wasps* for Philocleon and Bdelycleon (lover and hater of Cleon). Renaissance comedy in Italy and Spain in its imitations of Plautus made frequent use of this naming device (Boughner, 53–55, 309). Writers of the eighteenth century in England were especially apt in creating charactonyms, giving us Candide and Gulliver, which stand as classics in the use of the device. In the nineteenth century Dickens's penchant for odd names (Alderman Cutt, Gradgrind, Pecksniff, and numerous others) and Thackeray's facility with foreign names (Jeames de la Pluche for a flunkie, the Count von Springbock-Hohenlaufen, Madame de la Cruchecassee, Mme de Truffigny, and Zeno Poker, the American ambassador) kept the convention flourishing. In the twentieth century the device continues to hold its own, being used in satire in all media. The movie *Dr. Strangelove* (1964) contains General Jack D. Ripper, General Buck Turgidson, Bat Guana, and Strangelove himself. A nightclub routine in the 1950s by Mike Nichols and Elaine May has Nichols interviewing May, who portrays a sex symbol movie star, Barbara Musk. Angela Ravage is Peter DeVries's name for a Hollywood starlet in *Let Me Count the Ways* (1965). The Marx Brothers movies used charactonyms extensively, understandably since S. J. Perelman was one of the writers for some of the early Marx Brothers films. Perelman has a worthy successor in Ishmael Reed, who exploits the charactonym according to his parodic needs (*The Yellow Back Radio Broke-Down, Mumbo Jumbo,* et al.).

Name-calling and wordplay also have their place in graffiti, one of whose many functions is satiric expression. Public and anonymous verbal aggression at its most naked, graffiti also exhibits wit at its most playful. Given its faceless and ephemeral nature, the wittiness of some graffiti is anomalous. Devices of indirection seem redundant in the anonymous world of graffiti. What purpose is served by the use of puns, irony, understatement, and the sound patterns of verse when abuse and billingsgate would do? Why use wit when epithets are so much more direct? The censor and society need not exist for the graffitist. Yet in societies that rely on verbal (as opposed to oral) traditions for communications, graffiti is apparently universal, as ancient as Pompeii, as current as the nearest underpass or public lavatory, illustrating down through the ages in the scratchings and paintings on the wall many of the techniques of verse and rhetoric.

To protest the erecting of so many commemorative arches and vaulted arcades by the emperor Domitian, someone scratched the pun *arkei* ("that's enough") on several of the structures (Kehl, 285-86). Thirteenth-century French students ridiculed Italian students with the symbolism of "illusory courage," the snail, widely used in medieval literature and society (Randall, 362). Antimilitary feelings in the 1960s in the United States used irony in "war is good business—invest your sons." The now largely obsolete privy yielded up an occasional couplet as in the imperious ridicule voiced in an example from Allen Walker Read's collection, "A fitting emblim [*sic*] of his wit / A lofty monument of shit" (75). This reminder of the prominent scatological content of much graffiti should not blind us to the fact that graffiti, like satire, takes unto itself a variety of forms, slogans, proverbs (which are parodied), and, continuing in the tradition of Pasquino and Marforio, the dialogue. Some graffiti and some epigrams seem if not interchangeable in function at least related like kissing cousins. Geoffrey Grigson includes an example of graffiti in *The Faber Book of Epigrams and Epitaphs* and Byron's epitaph on Castlereagh can easily be imagined on a lavatory wall in Ravenna or Genoa:

> Posterity will ne'er survey
>   A nobler grave than this:
> Here lie the bones of Castlereagh:
>   Stop, traveller, and piss.

Satiric graffiti shares a debunking spirit as well as the need to be memorable in expression, causing small explosions by wit and playfulness. In the epigram such devices are obligatory, in graffiti gratuitous, even wanton. Huizinga speaks eloquently of the connections between poetry and play, drawing from folk and literary sources. Graffiti, whether produced by the unlettered, slumming intellectuals, or fast-buck manufacturers of bumper stickers and metal lapel buttons, satisfies a human need for the playfully memorable verbal wit that mocks and ridicules. Despite their transient nature, graffiti have since the 1960s become a ritualized form of communication. On the wooden walls around construction sites, on specially installed blackboards in bathrooms of universities in the United States, and in Stockholm, Sweden, on an official graffiti wall, people are encouraged to express their feelings and ideas. Some bars, restaurants, and coffeehouses have been known to cultivate graffiti in order to attract more customers (Reisner, 10–11). Here ritual becomes commercial. Anthologies and book-length studies of graffiti have appeared over the years, some merely concerned with exploiting the faddishness of wall writing in the 1960s and 1970s. But graffiti will probably survive commercial exploitation as it survived Vesuvius. It is fugitive and universal and can't be all bad—even God wrote graffiti (Daniel 5).

If graffiti is ephemeral, anonymous, and public, the opposite side of the coin is occupied by the aphorism, an individual expression of a general truth. Originally a general expression of a general truth, as in the wisdom literature of Sumeria and Egypt, which flowered in the Old Testament books of Proverbs, Psalms, and Ecclesiastes, all remarkable for their quotable observations on life, the word *aphorism* was first employed by Hippocrates to describe a collection of concise principles, primarily medical, beginning with his famous, "Life is short, art is long, opportunity fleeting, experimentation dangerous, reasoning difficult. . . ." Eventually the term was applied to statements of principles in law and agriculture and extended to other areas, as in James Harrington's *Aphorisms Political* (1659) and Schopenhauer's *Aphorisms on Wisdom* (1850). The aphorism used for satiric comment was coincidental with the origin of the aphorism, as illustrated by the grim humor of Job's "Skin for skin, yea, all that a man hath will be given for his life" and Ecclesiastes' "vanity of vanities." The satiric vein continues through the centuries:

DaVinci: "No member needs so great a number of muscles as the tongue: this exceeds all the rest in the number of its movements."

Montaigne: "Sits he on ever so high a throne, a man still sits on his bottom."

Pascal: "Men never do evil so completely and cheerfully as when they do it for religious convictions."

Twain: "Man is the only animal that blushes. Or needs
                to."

Santayana: "Fanaticism consists in redoubling your effort
                when you have forgotten your aim."

Erasmus was the first writer to grasp fully the satiric potential of
the aphorism, although he did not coin any of his own. In his
Adages, a collection of maxims and tags from classical authors,
which grew from slightly more than eight hundred in 1500 to more
than four thousand by his death in 1536, Erasmus uses the
aphorisms of ancient literature to comment, often satirically, on his
own times. "War is sweetest to those who have not tried it"
(Vegetius, *The Art of War*), for example, draws forth one of the
most eloquent antiwar statements in the history of civilization.

But the satiric aphorism dominates in the aphorisms of La
Rochefoucauld (1613–80) and Georg Lichtenberg (1742–99). Both
writers sting the mind with the sharpness of their skepticism and
their insight, even occasionally seeming to echo each other:

La Rochefoucauld	**Lichtenberg**
However carefully we disguise our passions to look like piety and honor, the mask proves of no avail. Our readiness to think ill of people without sufficiently examining the matter is based on laziness and pride. We want to find people guilty, we don't want the bother of studying their crimes.	Every man has his moral backside which he doesn't expose unnecessarily but keeps covered as long as possible by the trousers of decorum. Condemning people hastily is due mainly to man's instinctive laziness.

La Rochefoucauld's many turns on what he saw as man's
mainspring, self-interest, is paralleled by Lichtenberg's statement
"Actually there were only two persons in the world whom he
loved warmly: one was, at any given moment, his grossest
flatterer, and the other was himself."

La Rochefoucauld's aphorisms are often characterized as cynical.

To establish oneself in the world, one does all one can to
seem established there already.

However well people speak of us, they teach us nothing
new.

> In most men gratitude is only secret longing for greater benefits.

La Rochefoucauld's ability to unearth the worm of self-interest that motivated aristocratic circles of his time outraged the first readers of his aphorisms circulated in manuscript in 1663. Mme de Lafayette said: "Quelle corruption il faut avoir dans l'esprit et dans le coeur pour être capable d'imaginer tout cela [What corruption in the mind and in the heart must one have in order to be capable of imagining all that]," summing up the typical reaction. But like all good satiric aphorists, La Rochefoucauld had merely generated power by concentrating on oversimplification, as any good satirist does (or artist, for that matter). Karl Kraus, twentieth-century Viennese journalist and aphorist, once said that "an aphorism never coincides with the truth: it is either a half-truth or a truth-and-a-half." Either way, as near-hit or as overkill, the aphorism is bound to have an effect. Mme de Lafayette's reaction indicates that.

Lichtenberg's aphorisms are more personal, less abstract than La Rochefoucauld's, being entries in notebooks kept from the time he was a student until his death and discovered only then. Lichtenberg's aphorisms rely more on imagery than the abstractions of La Rochefoucauld:

> There are many people who won't listen until their ears are cut off.

> It's questionable whether, when we break a murderer on the wheel, we aren't lapsing into precisely the mistake of a child who hits the chair he bumps into.

> A book is a mirror: When a monkey looks in, no apostle can look out.

The extreme concentration of the best aphorism is implied in Goethe's remark that behind each of Lichtenberg's jests there was a problem. Karl Kraus emphasizes the same thing in his aphorism: "One cannot dictate an aphorism to a typist. It would take too long." Stanislaus Lec, twentieth-century Polish novelist and aphorist, agreed with Kraus: "Why do I write short aphorisms? Because words fail me."

Part of the power of many aphorisms comes from their definition-like quality, which led Matthew Hodgart to note their often equation-like structure (151). "Health is infectious" (Lichtenberg) shows the equations in its simplest form. In "Medicine: 'Your money and your life' " Kraus omits the copulative word and gives us a definition. But for many aphorisms the two-part structure is more complicated, giving rise to a variety of combinations.

Twain's "Man is the only animal that blushes. Or needs to" uses the second half of the "equation" to undercut the first. Lec's "The weakest link in the chain is also the strongest. It can break the chain" uses the second part to create a paradox. Lec introduces a surrealistic element by elaborating on a cliché piece of advice: "Do not turn your back on anyone. You may be painted on one side only." The unexpected: "When smashing monuments, save the pedestals—they always come in handy." Sometimes the equations become more elaborate, as in Blake's "Prisons are built with the stones of laws, brothels with bricks of Religion" or Shaw's "Democracy substitutes selection by the incompetent many for appointment by the corrupt few." But the well-turned observation in the hand of a master needs no formula: "Some people take more care to hide their wisdom than their folly" (Swift).

It could be argued that the play element—the *agon,* mimicry, and *ilinx*—in a piece of satire determines its ultimate value. After the social, political, historical, and personal disputes and differences, after Aristophanes' disapproval of Socrates, Voltaire's condemnation of Descartes's ideas, Swift's attacks on political and religious vagaries, after the anger, moral outrage, frustration, and indignation of all the satirists, what is left is a work of art. The historical particulars of the time and place, the psychological conditions of the author serve as the pilot fish of satire, like the pilot fish believed by ancient people to guide lost sailors to the shore only to disappear when land was in sight. So history and psychology can help the piece of satire along the way, but satire is finally at home on the mainland of art, the verbal and rhetorical devices, the myriad forms and types, alone or in dazzling combinations playfully entertaining and disturbing.

Evelyn Waugh once said, "I regard writing not as an investigation of character, but as an exercise in the use of language, and with this I am obsessed. I have no technical psychological interest. It is drama, speech and events that interest me" (79). The same kind of obsession can be sensed in Swift's satires and letters on clichés, puns, banter, conversation, and the state of the language. Twain's dicta about the difference between the almost right word and the right word as "a large matter—'tis the difference between the lightning-bug and lightning" (qtd. in Bainton, 87–88) suggests the importance of language to him. The satiric dictionaries of Ambrose Bierce, Gustave Flaubert, Voltaire, Kingsley Amis, and William Safire are further indications that many satirists are extrasensitive to the misuse, corruption, and violations of their languages. Out of the events of their times, out of the satirists' uses of the devices of mimicry, the forms of *agon,* and the turns of *ilinx,* comes the phenomenon known as satire.

Play and Irony

It was a crisp and spicy morning in early October. The lilacs and laburnums, lit with the glory-fires of autumn, hung burning and flashing in the upper air, a fairy bridge provided by kind Nature for the wingless wild things that have their homes in the tree-tops and would visit together; the larch and the pomegranate flung their purple and yellow flames in brilliant broad splashes along the slanting sweep of the woodland; the sensuous fragrance of innumerable deciduous flowers rose upon the swooning atmosphere; far in the empty sky a solitary oesophagus slept upon motionless wings; everywhere brooded stillness, serenity, and the peace of God.

Mark Twain, *A Double-Barreled Detective Story*

But as the animals outside gazed at the scene, it seemed to them that some strange thing was happening. What was it that had altered in the faces of the pigs? Clover's old dim eyes flitted from one face to another. Some of them had five chins, some had four, some had three. But what was it that seemed to be melting and changing? Then, the applause having come to an end, the company took up their cards and continued the game that had been interrupted, and the animals crept silently away.

But they had not gone twenty yards when they stopped short. An uproar of voices was coming from the farmhouse. They rushed back and looked through the window again. Yes, a violent quarrel was in progress. There were shoutings, bangings on the table, sharp suspicious glances, furious denials. The source of the trouble appeared to be that Napoleon and Mr. Pilkington had each played an ace of spades simultaneously.

Twelve voices were shouting in anger, and they were all alike.

No question, now, what had happened to the faces of the pigs. The creatures outside looked from pig to man, and from man to pig, and from pig to man again; but already it was impossible to say which was which.

George Orwell, *Animal Farm*

Satire and irony work together, but discussions about the nature of the irony and of the relationship have produced little agreement. Although the topic of satire and irony will occupy the next two chapters, the playful and gamelike nature of irony should be noted here. Irony, after all, is so basic to satire that its characteristics will color the perception of satire itself. As the passages above suggest, the irony in satire generates a recognizable and significant force of playfulness, despite differences of tone, manner of presentation, and subject matter.

Twain's item is a hodge-podge of botanical and zoological incongruities contained in a swatch of Beautiful Writing, all culminating in the nonsensical image of that "solitary oesophagus" and the "peace of God." Nature has been so violated in this passage that the peace of God should be replaced by the laughter of the gods. Twain was the deadpan comic, telling his story, as he recommends in "How to Tell a Story," "gravely; the teller [doing] his best to conceal the fact that he even dimly suspects that there is anything funny about it." With the straight-faced pose, the biological nonsense, and the sentimental diction and imagery, Twain generates irony by engaging the reader in a series of tiny discoveries or illuminations that tease and amuse in what amounts to a kind of game of hide-and-seek. Twain's target is that special soupy sentimentality of the nineteenth-century middle-class culture that preferred a patina of fantasy to gritty reality, an attitude that Twain battled all of his writing life.

Orwell, on the other hand, presents the reader with an actual game, a crooked card game that reveals its participants for what they are, all animals under the skin and, by means of a now classic image, in appearance as well. And that is often the satirist's game, the game of let's pretend. Let's pretend that animals can talk and walk like people, let's pretend that some people remind us by their looks and behavior of animals. And isn't it funny when we pretend that pigs and humans look alike, behave alike, horribly funny, in fact? But it is only pretend, because however anthropomorphic the imagination, reality will be served, and so pretense and reality cohabit to produce irony. Inside the game of asking the reader to pretend about the nature of the characters, there is the actual card game and the ironies flowing from it, the unwillingness of the players to follow the rules and let chance take its course, the betrayal of trust in the game becoming a metaphor for the betrayal of trust in *Animal Farm* itself, and, ultimately, for Orwell, the betrayal of idealism and hope in all revolution and change, a series, as it were, of concentric ironies resembling a round, flat target similar to those used in various children's and adults' games. (That this image may be fanciful and not at all something that can be attributed to Orwell's artistry suggests the sometimes intractable nature of irony and the riskiness of its use, a characteristic it shares with satire itself.)

These passages by Twain and Orwell, despite essential and profound differences, nevertheless illustrate the pervasive play element not only in satire but in irony as well. A. E. Dyson, in discussing Swift's irony, says that it is "not *only* [sic] a battle, but a game: a civilized game at that, since irony is by its very nature civilized, presupposing both intelligence and at least some type of moral awareness. The 'war' is a battle of wits" (13). The imagery of battle implies an eventual defeat after a period of struggle, a process that seems a bit overwrought if the process of irony is looked at more closely. To be sure, the satirist challenges the reader to discover the irony, but the eventual discovery may unite the satirist and the reader rather than separate them. As Wayne Booth has pointed out, successful closure by the reader of an author's irony produces a unity between them, a "tight bond," in Booth's words, that has important ramifications ("Pleasures," 11). Booth's image for the process of irony is that of the dance, "a fantastically intricate intellectual dance," "an elaborately formal dance" (2, 12; *Rhetoric,* 104). Booth applies the dance image to all irony, although, coincidentally, both he and Dyson are discussing the irony of Swift.

But between the benign dance and the fateful battle there is play, allowing for challenge and competition, for intricate and formal patterns, both a process and a spirit. In it the satirist supplies a series of clues challenging the reader to pick them up and assemble them, not so much in the manner of a jigsaw puzzle, but in the manner of a modern game of charades in which one person acts out a title or idea, word by word, occasionally syllable by syllable, until teammates put them together for a solution. Such a game involves challenge and cooperation, the "solution" coming sometimes after all the clues have been acted out and combined, or sometimes during the process as a particularly imaginative person perceives the drift of the performance or applies special knowledge to the proceedings. Of course the act of equating one thing with another, of attempting to capture the essence and process of irony in a familiar or understandable activity, is a kind of game itself, since readers will immediately examine the appropriateness of the proposed equivalence, challenging, agreeing, modifying. Irony, then, as a process involving wordplay and forms of imaginative literary structures, exhibits the characteristics of Caillois's concept of play, competitiveness, imagination, and revelation, or, in his terms, *agon,* mimicry, and *ilinx.*

7

Critical Irony:
Words and Forms

The Irony of Satire

In short, irony is used in some satire, not in all; some irony is satiric, much is not.

Wayne Booth

The chief distinction between irony and satire is that satire is militant irony. . . . Sheer invective or name-calling ("Flyting") is satire in which there is relatively little irony: on the other hand, whenever a reader is not sure what the author's attitude is or what his own is supposed to be, we have irony with relatively little satire.

Northrop Frye

Perhaps the fundamental distinction between irony and satire, in the largest sense of each, is simply that irony deals with the absurd, whereas satire treats the ridiculous.

Morton Gurewitch

Irony is one of the most powerful devices of indirect satire.

Edgar Johnson

[By the early eighteenth century] the word *irony* had not . . . developed either the philosophic or tragic senses which it carries today. It still referred chiefly to certain devices useful for indirect verbal attack. It was, then, more often, a tool for satire and ridicule.

Norman Knox

Nothing is gained . . . by confusing corrective irony with satire, which need not even employ irony.

D. C. Muecke

Nor would [these poets about to indulge in mockery] care, these creatures, to distinguish satire from irony and sarcasm and cynicism, saying that all these were instruments adapted to the same end.

E. V. Knox

Nearly all satire makes use of irony—ranging from the broadness of sarcasm to the extreme understatement of litotes—to such a degree that it is now very nearly impossible to think of satire without thinking of irony.

Alvin B. Kernan

Unlike play and satire, irony and satire have for a long time been closely associated, although few have been willing to fully sanctify the relationship. Occasionally, as in the eighteenth century, distinctions between the two were not always clearly drawn. If the expansion of the concept of irony since then has successfully eliminated that confusion, it has not helped critics to clarify the nature of the relationship between the two terms. No one disputes the fact that irony is a basic element in satire, but to what extent and what distinguishes irony in satire from irony in other forms and genres are questions that have been scarcely addressed. This is understandable since the works on irony by D. C. Muecke and Wayne Booth have been concerned with rescuing irony from the New Critics, whose usage made it synonymous with art and "truth." Both have helped anatomize the concept into usefulness again, thereby providing a point of departure for future discussions. The concern then is not with the concept of irony but with the irony of satire, how it functions, what its nature is, and to what extent satire and irony are distinguishable.

Satire by its nature and conventions generates irony. Kernan's description of the "satirist" brings together the kind of contradictions that can only be seen as ironic (chap. 2). The "satirist . . . seems to be seeking out and thoroughly enjoying the kind of filth he claims to be attacking" (25). The "satirist's violent denunciations of intemperance and unreasonableness in his victims proclaim his own intemperance and irrationality. Through his sometimes cruel verbal aggression he claims to bring about reform. He displays in himself pride and self-righteousness as he carries out his attacks on vice and folly." The satiric plot which Kernan delineates is another example of irony, displaying constant movement and action but producing no change or resolution. Whatever else satire means to its victims, it "has always conveyed its dubious immortality upon the vermin who are transfixed forever in the amber of its verse" (Elliott, *Power*, 244).

As the plot and conventions produce irony, so does the typical imagery of satire. When humans are pictured as animals or as machine-like, sub- or nonhuman, qualities are played off implicitly or explicitly against what human beings are normally expected to be. If a society is displayed as insane, the contrast is with a society that is reasonable and sane (Pinkus, 37). Whether the satirist attacks from a religious or an ideological position (Partridge; Bloom), the characteristics and behavior of the victim imply a value or set of values, or at the very least assume, in Auden's words, "conscience and reason," which imply a judgment, thereby creating irony by the contrast, contradiction, or incongruity.

This is not to suggest that all works of satire possess clearly distinguishable norms. The word norm implies a standard and regularity that may be neither necessary nor desirable in order to produce irony, depending on the degree to which indirection is involved. Some pieces of satire carry in them explicit norms, others only imply them. But there are some pieces of satire whose norms have never been established or about which there has been no agreement, parts of *Gulliver's Travels* being one example. Some pieces of satire further complicate matters by presenting two mutually unsatisfactory opposites, in which case the reader may become the victim of the satire by making a choice, an interesting irony in itself. What ultimately is necessary is only an opportunity for the reader to perceive a doubleness that is essential to all irony, the two-story opposition that Muecke mentions (19), the "double flow of meaning," as Hodgart refers to it (130). So generally speaking, the imagery, the plot, and the basic contrastive need of satire tend inherently to generate irony.

To be sure, some of this irony may be unconscious and unintended, even undesirable, although the irony of the "satirist" figure seems not to have inhibited writers of satire nor to have alienated audiences. The degree to which the satiric plot is a consciously created irony is difficult to determine. Even the inclusion of fools and knaves as the standard characters of satire may derive as much from a comic intent as from a satiric one. Beyond all this, however, there is an extensive armory of verbal devices, techniques, and forms, all of which the satirist must manipulate in order to be described as a satirist. In his or her hands they generate irony.

Verbal Irony

The nuts and bolts, or better, the ploys and arrows of satiric attack are the various rhetorical devices available to carry on the sportive aggression of satire. Each may be a tiny firecracker of irony, an explosive of *ilinx*. The use of such devices is characteristic of all satire, from the bluntest, most obvious direct attack to the most subtle and invidious fable. What Archilochus, Martial, St. Jerome, Ben Jonson, Jonathan Swift, William Thackeray, and Joseph Heller have in common is their use of the devices of verbal aggression, the linguistic land mines of understatement, oxymoron, anticlimax, and the numerous contrivances that satirists plant along the way of the unwary. All of them are tiny juxtapositions of incongruous details, contradictory ideas, or otherwise incompatible elements that in playing off against each other produce the ironic spark. Some of the best known verbal devices are among the following.[1]

Anticlimax.   The anticlimax produces irony by setting off in one direction and arousing an expectation in the reader that is going to be disappointed. There is a letdown following a buildup, or at least an unfulfilled expectation. Anticlimax may be contained in a single line of poetry, a sentence, or it may be as expansive as the entire action of a plot (Clark):

> Whence flow those tears fast down thy blubbered cheeks,
> Like a swoln gutter, gushing through the streets?
> (King Arthur to Queen Dollalolla in Fielding's
> *The Tragedy of Tragedies* [I, 2, 6–7])

> Well, if that's what we want, walking around half naked
> in some of those midriff dresses I've seen, all right. But
> then we pay the price—rape, whistling, irritability.
> (Peter DeVries, *The Mackerel Plaza* [1958])

An anticlimax that is unintentional and ludicrous produces bathos, the subject of Pope's *Peri Bathous: or, Martin Scriblerus His Treatise on the Art of Sinking in Poetry*.

Catalogue.   Used by the satirist the catalogue, ordinarily made up of objects, persons, or attributes, becomes a way of exemplifying the chaos of reality or at least its incongruity:

> Sweepings from Butchers' Stalls, Dung, Guts, and Blood, Drown'd Puppies, stinking sprats, all drench'd in Mud. Dead Cats and Turnip-Tops come tumbling down the Flood.
>
> (Swift, "Description of a City Shower")

The catalogues in chapter 8 of Evelyn Waugh's *Vile Bodies* intensify the unpleasantness of people and their behavior. The catalogue is readily adapted to comic imitation, as when Chaucer includes seven different catalogues in "The Rime of Sir Thopas," some made up of homely items instead of the conventional heroic ones, others combining incongruous elements. Shakespeare in Sonnet 130 imitates satirically the traditional catalogue devoted to enumerating the physical attributes of the beautiful loved one. Scott Fitzgerald mocks the newspaper gossip column in chapter 4 of *The Great Gatsby* with

> From East Egg, then, came the Chester Beckers and the Leeches, and a man named Bunsen whom I knew at Yale, and Doctor Webster Civet, who was drowned last summer up in Maine. And the Hornbeams and the Willie Voltaires, and the whole clan named Blackbuck, . . .

and so on for another page or two.

The irony of the catalogue device generally comes from the incongruity of the items, as in Swift's series, or in Twain's series from "To the Person Sitting in Darkness":

> Would it not be prudent to get our Civilization tools together, and see how much stock is left on hand in the way of Glass Beads, and Theology, and Maxim Guns and Hymn Books, and Trade Gin and Torches of Progress and Enlightenment . . . ?

Charactonym.   The irony of the charactonym is assured since it may derive from the names being appropriate or inappropriate. That characters may have such appropriately descriptive names as Waugh's Miles Plastic or Vanbrugh's Sir Tunbelly Blumsey of whose meaning the characters are blithefully unaware creates irony. But names that endow their bearers with qualities they do not have (Trimalchio, mighty monarch) or are otherwise inappropriate (Thackeray's Jeames de la Pluche, a flunkie) are overtly ironic.

Imitation.   When Philip Wylie says, "There must be an end to a government of boobs, by boobs, for boobs," he expects the reader to play off Lincoln's statement against the obviously deflated version. Rather than deflating the original as might be the case in some satiric imitations, the original serves as an ironic counterpoint that reinforces the ridiculousness of the new version. Huxley's "In the Year of Our Ford . . . ," and Waugh's "Great State" and "For State's Sake" function in the same way.

Literalization.   This is one of the most widespread but least recognized techniques of the satirist and an effective source of irony. When the pigs in the final scene of *Animal Farm* become like men and men become like pigs, we have literalization rather than metaphor. The same thing happens with newts and men in Karel Capek's *War with the Newts*. The differences among animal imagery, animal metaphor, and literalization are not always as clear-cut as one would wish. Huxley and Waugh each present characters becoming physically ill by their reactions to modern life. John in *Brave New World* vomits during his tour of the Electrical Equipment Corporation with its clonelike laborers. In *Vile Bodies* when Nina sees the chaos and decay of a "straggling red suburb," she too vomits, but not from airsickness (New). Swift was the master of literalization, making more use of it than perhaps any other satiric writer. The cannibalism of "A Modest Proposal" and the floating island of Book III of *Gulliver's Travels* that is used to oppress and suppress are among examples by Swift that come easily to mind (Quinlan). Par Lagerkvist makes the statement "war is childish" literal by turning children into soldiers in his short story "The Children's Campaign." The gross or otherwise unacceptable actions of the literal jar against the preferred, normal, or ideal, the taboo against cannibalism, the "earth of majesty" of Waugh, the "brave new world" of Huxley. The disparity is so great as to be incongruous, hence the irony.

The Pun. In the pun two meanings in a single word play off against each other, one meaning normal, innocent, or even laudable, the other odious or otherwise unpraiseworthy. The Pardoner in the *Canterbury Tales* is described as "in chirche a noble eccelsiaste," but since *noble* means having excellent qualities but is also the name of a gold coin, the pun reinforces the essential greediness of the "ecclesiaste," one meaning undercutting the other. Pope's "Where Bentley late tempestuous wont to sport/ In troubled waters, but now sleeps in Port" puns on the last word, with the image of the blotto Bentley taking precedence over that of a boat tranquilly at dock (Nichols, 107). Mark Twain propagates a double pun in his "To the Person Sitting in Darkness" when he comments on the fact that the Christians in China demanded reprisals for the violence of the Boxer Rebellion in both money and people's lives, payable in Chinese taels and "head for head." Twain says, in mock approval, "Our spirits soar, and we find we can even make jokes: Taels, I win, Heads you lose." The play in a single word makes the pun an unusually concentrated expression of irony, but for a number of reasons one that is not widely used. Capable of debasing conversation and style and seeming to threaten language itself, punning has had a mixed press from writers and critics of the English language. Despite its questionable reputation in English, the pun has flourished elsewhere, two of the greatest satiric punsters being Austrian and Spanish, Karl Kraus and Francisco Quevedo, whose writings rely on the pun to a degree undreamed of in any writer in English.[2]

At this basic verbal level irony is a fundamental tool of the satirist. One could add understatement, overstatement, oxymoron, sarcasm, and paradox as other kinds of verbal play that produce irony. It is the presence of these and other kinds of verbal devices in the works of the first-person, direct-attack satires that makes them eligible for inclusion in the canon. The forms of direct attack—the diatribe, the lampoon, the curse, formal verse satire— do not in themselves usually generate satiric irony, although the fact that the often wild and imaginative wordplay that inheres in much direct-attack satire is expended on targets that are ignominious, degraded, selfish, and irresponsible is not without its irony, however unintended. The difference between the irony of direct-attack satire and the irony of indirect attack is a matter of degree of ironic play and not of kind. Matters of taste aside, the question of what is included under the umbrella of satire can be considerably simplified by recognizing that direct and indirect satire need not be subjected to the same kind of judgment any more than different genres doing the same thing, say a poem and an essay about death and immortality. Both direct and indirect satire use the same verbal devices in the same way with the same results. But indirect satire often uses forms that in and of themselves produce irony, a feature not as readily available to direct attack satirists.

The Irony of Components

The irony of verbal devices comes in many cases from within the device itself. The bipartite elements of the irony are inherent in the statement of the item. The irony of components, on the other hand, requires that this particular kind of satire have a complementary component as a referent which the reader, listener, or viewer must supply from his own knowledge or background. The reader is expected ideally to recognize similarities between the piece of satire and some style, form, concept, or value that is similar to or parallel with the piece of satire itself. Out of special juxtapositioning of the external component and the piece of satire there emerges irony. Such relationships are generally referred to by such terms as parody, burlesque, and travesty and include the mock heroic and other mock forms. For the discussion of irony, however, these terms have limited usefulness.

Parody as a critical term, for example, is in much the same state as irony was after the New Critics got done with it. Parody, in discussions of modern literature and art, carries little if any suggestion of critical mockery of a writer's style or manner. Any use, no matter how idiosyncratic, of another writer's style or of another form may be referred to as parodic in most contemporary critical usage. Uncertain about the nature of reality, dissatisfied with traditions of fiction, and conscious of the need for new modes of fictional communication, some post–World War II writers— Ishmael Reed, Iris Murdoch, Vladimir Nabokov, and John Barth come to mind—have turned to the forms and styles of popular and traditional culture in self-conscious attempts to revitalize their art (Bellamy, 14–15). The word parody comes closest to describing what these writers are doing with the styles and conventions that are part of their art.[3] But it is quite different from what *National Lampoon* and *Mad* in their different ways do to writers, books, other magazines, films, and TV shows, carrying on as has normally been expected of a parodist from Aristophanes on. So parody may operate in at least two different ways, unrelated except for its writers knowingly using another style or form or convention as a basis for a new structure. Dwight MacDonald's parody anthology succeeds because he admitted that "the definition of what exactly IS a parody is subjective" (xv); he goes on from there unencumbered by anything but his own taste and interest. This confusion in the usage of the word is further illustrated by the definition used by John R. Clark and Anna Motto in their anthology of satire, which contains a sizable selection under the heading of satiric parody. They saw that when the caricatures of events "utilize all the mechanisms, legal postures, mathematical certainties, and incongruities but include as well the imitation of style, we encounter what we shall call parody" (Clark and Motto, 27). Their definition suggests that the word parody has so little meaning that it must be defined in context to have any validity.

The term *burlesque* has suffered a fate similar to that of *parody*. *Burlesque* has been most widely used as a way of categorizing a large body of literature of the English Restoration and the eighteenth century in which certain writers mocked other literature. Including such works as *Hudibras, Northanger Abbey,* the plays of Duffett, works by Fielding, and many other effusions, the tendency has been to take this body of literature as a kind of norm for burlesque. Richmond Bond's system of classifying these works has been influential since it virtually eliminated the need for the term *burlesque* by setting up four categories under it: travesty, parody, mock heroic, and Hudibrastic verse. John D. Jump's attempt to refine Bond's scheme by adding "dramatic burlesque" to Bond's categories undercuts both the symmetry and logic of Bond's scheme without adding to the overall concept. Apart from applying the term to literary periods and types of literature, the term has a general meaning synonymous with "mocking," for example, this or that writer *burlesquing* this or that. A cursory survey of handbooks of literary terms and dictionaries reveals that, in addition to the terms already mentioned, *caricature, ballad opera, extravaganza, animal fable, burletta, revue,* and *farce* are used to discuss and define the word. This range of terms suggests a fundamental confusion in usage. Formal attempts to rescue *burlesque* and related words have failed to establish agreed-upon meanings or gain wide acceptance.[4]

Even at that hypothetical moment when there was presumed unanimity about the meaning of these terms, the unanimity was probably an illusion. No terms have ever managed to accommodate the seemingly endless permutations and mixtures that satirists have created out of the conventional, successful, worn-out, indefensible, decadent, overextended (whatever the case happened to be) literature, art, and forms around them. Although parody and burlesque are predominantly literary exercises, they include all other arts as well, as works by John Gay, William Hogarth, Gilbert and Sullivan, and Titian show. Satirists have also taken over nonliterary forms from all areas of culture, such as almanacs, prayers, recipes, memoranda, laws, and reports. Philosophical systems and social conventions that present readily identifiable configurations have also provided useful forms for the satirist to mock or use, as, for example, existentialism, the folklore vogue of Romanticism, or a specific brand of religious fanaticism. The list is nearly endless:

- a particular work of literature, music, or art
- a writer and his or her works
- a literary style, form, or convention
- the ideas, attitudes, or values attached to or exemplified by them
- a great variety of nonliterary or applied art forms
- specific patterns of ideas or conventions of behavior of an era.

These "forms" or patterns are used in two basic ways by satirists. One is to attack a specific form itself, its style, manner, structure, and content and thereby the ideas, attitudes, and values expressed or represented. The other use is as a conveyance for satirizing what satirists usually attack, that is, persons, institutions, behavior, and ideas. In the first instance the satirist is making an aesthetic and usually a moral judgment that involves the technique and form of presentation. In the second case the form or manner becomes a tool for the satirist and not an object of mockery. Both approaches require the reader to know a style, manner, form, set of conventions, a pattern exterior to the satiric work, in order to understand and fully appreciate the satire. The satirist uses the prior knowledge of the audience and the presumed ability of those in the audience to detect the incongruity, contradiction, or incompatibility between what they know of the original style or form and what they perceive before them. Satirists usually present the material deadpan, betraying no indication that what they are presenting is in any way out of order. This feigned innocence is of course a natural element in the creation of irony, as most critics of irony have pointed out. Irony then may be seen as one of the most inclusive expressions of play, involving at once mimicry, *agon,* and *ilinx,* as well as a device for generating laughter by ludicrous or inappropriate juxtaposition.

Unfortunately the two large categories into which this kind of satire falls cannot be described by the standard vocabulary used for such works, nor can the irony generated by the juxtaposing of an exterior "form" with the satiric work be discussed with the conventional vocabulary. Such irony has occasionally been noted, but no systematic or extensive discussion of its nature or its implications for an understanding of satire has ever been attempted.

The discussion that follows assumes that a distinction can be made between style and content, between manner and structure, without losing sight of the intimate and ultimately interdependent nature of the two. The ways in which satirists go about exploiting and attacking the works of other writers suggests that they are not occasionally above making the same distinction.

Irony of Violated Style.   The satiric attack on a style may concentrate on violating the style or on violating its content. Violating the style may be accomplished by exaggerating it, displacing it, or naturalizing it. Exaggeration involves pushing the sentence structure, vocabulary, and other linguistic elements to an extreme. This is the technique used by Wolcott Gibbs in "Shad Ampersand, A Novel of Time and the Writer." In Gibbs's hands Sinclair Lewis's realism becomes statistics; his dialect becomes ultrafolksy; and his charactonyms become ludicrously obvious. Hemingway's *Torrents of Spring* works on Sherwood Anderson's interrogatory monologues and his dreaming characters by expanding the monologues and the stream-of-consciousness passages so that they become noticeable instead of natural, and by including occasional inappropriate details and references. Housman's "Frag-

ments of a Greek Tragedy" multiplies the bookish imagery of
nineteenth-century translations, the plodding renderings down to
the hyphenated adjectives and lumbering antitheses. Such excesses
lead to ridiculousness, inappropriateness, and even sheer nonsense,
as in Swinburne's self-imitation, "Nephelidia," in which the sound
patterns and the rhythm add up to no meaning whatsoever.
Aristophanes in the *Frogs* makes "Aeschylus" and "Euripides"
carefully select tags and lines in order to exaggerate the characteristics of each other's lyrics. Charles C. Calverley in "The Cock and
the Bull" carries Browning's quirky dramatic monologue style
close to incoherence. Henry Reed's "Chard Whitlow: Mr. Eliot's
Sunday Evening Postscript" emphasizes the platitudinous but
pedantic diction of T. S. Eliot, his predilection for foreign phrases
and concern with time, Anglicanism, and Oriental philosophy.

No attack that emphasizes style as these examples do can help
but alter the content as well. But there are some imitations that
deliberately alter the content or the context, thereby undercutting
the original manner and matter, placing it at a disadvantage by
changing the scene of battle or the rules. Such is the case with John
Updike's "On the Sidewalk" in which the souped-up transcenden-
tal prose of Jack Kerouac in *On the Road* is transposed to a children's
world of scooters and skates. Peter DeVries uses the same reductive tactic on William Faulkner in "Requiem for a Noun, or Intrud-
er in the Dusk," which involves a little boy's running away from
home because his father talks like a character out of a Faulkner novel.

Such displacement is the basic technique in Max Beerbohm's
famous collection, *A Christmas Garland* (1912), in which Beerbohm
in the style and manner of a great variety of late nineteenth- and
early twentieth-century writers tells a Christmas story, one of
them the well-known "Mote in the Middle Distance," which
begins in the typically well-qualified Henry Jamesian fashion, "It
was with the sense of a, for him, very memorable something that
he peered now into the immediate future, and tried, not without
compunction, to take that period up where he had, prospectively,
left it." Conrad, Kipling, Wells, Galsworthy, Bennett, Hardy, and
others receive similarly reductive treatment. The collection is the
best sustained and comprehensive set of satiric imitations ever
written.[5] Another version of the displacement technique are those
used by H. L. Mencken and Oliver Jensen. By serving up the
Declaration of Independence in "American" and the Gettysburg

Address in "Eisenhowerese" Mencken and Jensen discredit those peculiar "styles" by means of the grace and clarity of the originals.

Naturalizing a style means squeezing out those elements that make it unacceptable to the satirist, whether it be sentimentality or romanticism. One of the best examples of this approach is Henry Fielding's *An Apology for the Life of Mrs. Shamela Andrews* (1741), in which Fielding boils down Richardson's two-volume set of letters concerning the fate of serving girl Pamela into a hundred pages that mock the original without its sentimentality and unrealistic presentation. Mortimer Collins in "If" applies the same technique to Swinburne's lyric, "The Match," and Anthony Hecht does the same to Matthew Arnold in his "The Dover Bitch, A Criticism of Life." Arthur Guiterman combines the exaggerated style and the realistic outlook in his imitation of John Masefield's "Sea-Fever." With the same anapestic rhythm, alliteration, and feminine endings used by Masefield, Guiterman reduces the wild romance of the sea to a tepid cruise:

Sea-Fever

John Masefield (1878–1967)

I must go down to the seas again, to the lonely sea and
    the sky,
And all I ask is a tall ship and a star to steer her by,
And the wheel's kick and the wind's song and the white
    sail's shaking,
And a grey mist on the sea's face and a grey
    dawn breaking.

I must go down to the seas again, for the call of the
    running tide
Is a wild call and a clear call that may not be denied;
And all I ask is a windy day with the white clouds flying,
And the flung spray and the blown spume, and the
    sea-gulls crying.

I must go down to the seas again to the vagrant gypsy life,
To the gull's way and the whale's way where the wind's
    like a whetted knife;

And all I ask is a merry yarn from a laughing
    fellow-rover,
And quiet sleep and a sweet dream when the long
    trick's over.

Sea-Chill

Arthur Guiterman (1871–1943)

When Mrs. John Masefield and her husband,
    the author of
"I Must Go Down to the Seas Again," arrived here on
    a liner,
she said to a reporter, "It was too uppy-downy,
    and Mr. Masefield was ill." —News item.

I must go down to the seas again, where the billows
    romp and reel,
So all I ask is a large ship that rides on an even keel,
And a mild breeze and a broad deck with a slight list
    to leeward,
And a clean chair in a snug nook and a nice, kind steward.

I must go down to the seas again, the sport of wind
    and tide,
As the gray wave and the green wave play leapfrog over
    the side.
And all I want is a glassy calm with a bone-dry scupper,
A good book and a warm rug and a light, plain supper.

I must go down to the seas again, though there I'm a
    total loss,
And can't say which is worst, the pitch, the plunge, the
    roll, the toss.
But all I ask is a safe retreat in a bar well tended,
And a soft berth and a smooth course till the long
    trip's ended.

Irony of Violated Content. The techniques of exaggeration, displacement, and naturalizing as ways of disparaging style are by no means restricted to specific works or writers. They have been used to violate the form or matter or both of all types of literary and nonliterary prose from popular drama and romance of the seventeenth and eighteenth centuries, and a variety of prose styles from scholarly to journalistic. Various types of music and art have been mocked with the same techniques.

Popular or vogue-ish literature in all ages has regularly come under the gun of satirists who have objected to its unrealism, its clichés and stereotypes, its sensationalism. But as the following list seems to suggest, such attacks have had little influence. Year after year, century after century, satirists have beaten the same horse only to have it revive and flourish.

Charles Sorel in *The Extravagant Shepherd* (1627) mocks the pastoral romance. Henry Fielding in *The Covent-Garden Tragedy* (1732) takes off on neo-classical tragedy.

Charlotte Lennox, *The Female Quixote: or, The Adventures of Arabella* (1752), mocks French heroic romance.

Jane Austen, *Love and Freindship* (c. 1789), mocks the sentimental novel. *Susanne; or, Traits of the Modern Miss* (Anonymous; 1795) mocks circulating library novels.

Edgar Allan Poe, "Metzengerstein" (1831–32), mocks the Gothic tale. William S. Gilbert, *Ruddigore* (1887), mocks the nineteenth-century melodrama.

E. V. Lucas and George Morrow, *What A Life! An Autobiography* (1911), pokes fun at the illustrated shilling book.

Stephen Leacock, "Maddened by Mystery; or, The Defective Detective" (1912), mocks Sherlock Holmes-type detective fiction. Max Beerbohm, *Savanarola Brown* (1919), derides late nineteenth-century imitators of Elizabethan drama.

Stella Gibbons, *Cold Comfort Farm* (1932), mocks novels of primitivism circa World War I and after.

James Thurber, "Bateman Comes Home" (1957), tips its hand with its subtitle, "Written After ReReading Several Recent Novels about the Deep South and Confusing Them a Little—as the Novelists Themselves Do—with *Tobacco Road* and *God's Little Acre.*"

Louis Simpson, "Squeal" (1957), mocks the poetry of the Beat Generation and Allen Ginsberg's *Howl* in particular.

If popularity or vogue-ishness make a style of writing vulnerable, so do its obscurity and uncommon nature. From the mock notes and introduction of Fielding of his play *Tragedy of Tragedies* and the work of the Scriblerus Club down to the present, scholarly writing and its fondness for apparatus have made it a consistently vulnerable target. Thomas De Quincey's "On Murder Considered as One of the Fine Arts" (1827; 1839), Ronald Knox's "The Authorship of 'In Memoriam' " and "The Identity of the Pseudo-Bunyon" (1928), and Frederick C. Crews's *The Pooh Perplex* (1963) may serve as representative examples of the impulse to butcher the products of the scholar. De Quincey gives a scholarly analysis of murder, including its history and philosophy since Cain, and discusses how to choose a victim and the best method for disposing of the remains. Using cryptography, a tool favored by some nineteenth-century Shakespeare scholars, Knox "proves" that "In Memoriam" was written by Queen Victoria and that the second part of *Pilgrim's Progress* was written by a woman. Crews analyzes the Winnie the Pooh stories as Marxist, mythic, Freudian, and several other kinds of critics might, collecting the "essays" in the casebook format, an academic fad in the 1960s. The season for attacks on the scholar is never closed as Herbert Lindenberger's *Saul's Fall* (1979) indicates. The title of the book is taken from the name of a dull historical play that provides a young scholar on the make an opportunity for self-aggrandizement through scholarship, or more accurately, through pedantry replete with notes upon notes, all in a murky academic vocabulary.

Next-door neighbors to the pedant are the denizens of academic journals and little magazines, the special target of many of W. B. Scott's satiric imitations. The peculiarities of some publications are mocked in one of his best-known pieces, "Chicago Letter: Agony, a Sense of Plight" in which "the more precious and insider-oriented snobberies," to use Dwight MacDonald's description (362), are mocked, and "Gaeton Fignole: Pages de Journal," an "article" containing what purports to be the newly published diaries of a recently dead minor French literary figure. Scott's imitation captures the cultlike snobbery and the ultimate trivializing of literature that sometimes seems to characterize the more esoteric little magazines. Such characteristics are not confined to literary criticism or publishing. George Bernard Shaw once discussed Hamlet's "To be or not to be" speech in the style of the academic music score analysis sometimes found in concert programs, beginning,

Shakespeare, dispensing with the customary exor-
dium, announces his subject at once in the infinitive, in
which mood it is presently repeated after a short
connective passage in which, short as it is, we recognize
the alternative and negative forms on which so much of
the significance of repetition depends. Here we reach a
colon; and a pointed pository phrase, in which the accent
falling decisively on the relative pronoun, brings us to the
first full stop. (Qtd. in Henahan)

Other forms of art have also been vulnerable to the technique of
satiric imitation. Alphonse Allais (1854–1905), French humor
writer, and his colleagues at Le Chat Noir cabaret, in protest
against what they thought the lack of technical skill in painters of
the time, held an exhibition for painters who could not draw or
paint. Allais's own contributions included an all-white canvas
called "Anemic Young Girls Going to their First Communion
through a Blizzard." The international Dada movement of the time
of World War I to the early 1920s, in part a protest against Cubism
and Impressionism, also produced its share of works that were
satiric imitations. Dada's anti-art attitude showed up in a "portrait" of Cezanne as a collage-relief of a stuffed monkey, in Marcel
Duchamps's famous reproduction of the Mona Lisa with a beard
and moustache. Sculpture was mocked by mounting "ready-
mades," actual objects, for display. Man Ray's *Gift* was a flatiron
with a row of fourteen tacks fastened to the bottom surface. *In
Advance of a Broken Arm* displayed a snow shovel. Another kind of
art world is shown in Osbert Lancaster's *The Littlehampton Bequest*
(1973), a "catalogue" of the collection of portraits of the Lit-
tlehamptons of Drayneflete, beginning with "portraits" of family
members by Holbein and Cranach the Elder and coming down to
a portrait on an LP record dust jacket. Genealogy, antiquarianism,
art criticism, and the life-styles of numerous generations of the
English upper class are victims of Lancaster's rich mimicry.

Among the satiric imitation of styles and forms, popular
journalism has had its attackers. The early success of the Luce
publishing empire based in part on stylistic idiosyncrasies of *Time*
and *Life* magazines spawned its detractors, especially in the *New
Yorker*. Wolcott Gibbs's history of the Luce publications in
Times-style in the 28 November 1936 issue of the *New Yorker* is

reported to have infuriated founder Henry Luce. Gibbs loaded his account with the exaggerated double-barreled adjectives, inverted speech tags, periodic sentences, sentence fragments, portmanteau words, and multiple parallelism that marked the style of *Time* prior to World War II. "Backward ran the sentences until reeled the mind," Gibbs mocked. The *New Yorker* also published a cartoon version of the "Life Goes to . . ." picture-story series entitled "Life Goes to the Collapse of Western Civilization," in which two pretty young ladies cavort with German and Japanese soldiers as they overrun the United States, thereby mocking *Life* magazine's occasional tendency to trivialize and merchandise the news.

That the vein of mimicry runs deep and wide is illustrated by the following pair of letters, the first received by an applicant from the dean of George Washington University and the second, the applicant's reply:

> The members of the Committee on Admissions have reviewed your application, and I regret to inform you that we are unable to offer you admission to the Graduate School of Arts and Sciences.
>
> The competition for admission for the limited number of spaces has made admissions decisions very difficult. It is unfortunate that this limitation has made it impossible to accept you and other promising applicants.
>
> Thank you for considering The George Washington University and please accept my best wishes for your future studies.

The rejected applicant replied:

> I have reviewed most carefully your recent letter, and sincerely regret to inform you that I am unable to accept your best wishes for the future at this time.
>
> Due to the considerable number of best wishes that I have received for the upcoming year, and the limited number that I can accommodate, competition is understandably quite fierce. As a result, such circumstances have made it impossible for me to accept your best wishes, as well as those from other equally sincere and concerned graduate schools.
>
> I thank you for your genuine interest in wishing me

well, and I would like to take this chance to convey my deepest best wishes for your continued success in future academic endeavors.

The polite and cordial clichés of a rejection letter are exaggerated by the careful addition of several adjectives and the situation altered by the turnabout so that these letters become an excellent example of how satirists use a distorted imitation of style, form, and content to create a two-level structure that generates irony, the counterfeit style or manner running parallel (in the reader's mind) to the original, with a kind of linguistic Gresham's law allowing the bogus style to devaluate the original (Bentley).

Inflicting damage on a style or manner required such close attention to the object that Max Beerbohm's remark that a good parody is an expression of love has been allowed so much credence as to become virtually a critical dictum (878). Whatever the motivation, the successful satirist has a remarkable facility for finding and exploiting the most vulnerable characteristics of a style or form. To be sure some imitations are playful and aim only at humor, but Beerbohm has never been accused of that, thus his remark may be another example of the perennial attempt by satirists to put the best face on their efforts. And imitations that violate the content of a selection or type rather than the style have sometimes seemed to need such apologies. They have often aroused the most vociferous reaction, probably because to violate the material or contents generally means to treat it in a vulgar, commonplace, or disrespectful way. Such is the case with Paul Scarron's *Virgile Travesti* (1648–58), Charles Cotton's *Scarronides: or Virgile Travestie* (an English version of Scarron), and Thomas Duffett's plays, *The Empress of Morocco* (1674), *The Mock-Tempest* (1675) and *Psyche Debauch'd* (1678). Scarron and Cotton take a highly regarded classical work and retell it in earthy and ordinary terms. Duffett takes the tragic highborn personages of opera and heroic dramas and replaces them with lowborn persons pursuing everyday concerns. The same impulse can be seen in Chaucer's "Sir Thopas" in the *Canterbury Tales,* Jacques Offenbach's *Orpheus in the Underworld* (1858), and Mark Twain's "Ode to Stephen Dowling Botts" in *The Adventures of Huckleberry Finn.* A seeming breakdown occurs between major elements of these works when a knight is presented in mundane and unromantic terms, a Greek myth of tragic love is transposed into a modern setting with distinctly French emphasis on sexual hanky-panky, and the death of a young man becomes less than tragic when we learn that he died by falling down a well. Chaucer satirizes the conventions of medieval romance, Offenbach the undue reverence paid to the classics, and Twain the sentimentality of nineteenth-century album verse. Scarron, Cotton, Offenbach, Twain, and others find the original material untrue to their experience and overrated by their audience, in effect, situations crying out for a healthy dose of reality, which the satirist is more than happy to supply.

In doing violence to a style or the content of a selection, writer, type, or form, the satirist is attacking the literary or artistic entity itself. Such attacks rely on the participant's knowledge of the original to help create the irony that undercuts the original by in part creating humor. Popular or pompous, specious or specialized, vogue or vague, literature and art, scholars, critics, writers have always needed the balancing influence of the satirist who carries out the ritual sacrifice of styles, forms, manner, ideas that have been enshrined in usage, acceptance, and value.

Irony of Misused Form.   But true to a tradition that seems to say at times, anything goes, satirists have also turned to literature and art as sources and aids in practicing their subversive wiles. In what can be called the Irony of Misused Form and the Irony of Disparate Elements forms and styles become *not* the targets of the satire but features and forms used mainly as carriers and ploys exploited for generating irony. Here again the reader or viewer is expected to bring to the satire a knowledge of some specific form, style, or subject exterior to but now made inappropriately applicable (or appropriately inapplicable) and therefore incongruous or incompatible. In its original state it tends to provide a norm, a standard, or at least a strong contrast out of which irony can flow. The elements are combined disparately according to their original or conventionally agreed-upon uses. The purpose is not to discredit a style or a form but to use it for the usual purposes of satire, a mocking attack on a person, a group, an institution.

The most widely practiced and least understood type of imitation is the technique in which a form is used in a way not intended, or in other words, intentionally misused. The misuse obviously serves a purpose for the satirist, and although the form may not come away from its use totally unscathed, its demise is generally not the intention of the satirist. The widespread and workaday uses of this technique is demonstrated by the anthology of Alan Dundes and Carl R. Pragter, *Urban Folklore from the Paperwork Empire,* which contains the anonymous work of persons who in no way think of themselves as satirists but who take the materials at hand— conventionalized letters, definitions, typologies, principles, applications for jobs, examinations, bulletin board notes, and office memos—as media for expressing their anger, indignation, frustrations, or just plain discontents. Similarly the anonymous graffitist takes over a nursery rhyme for social comment:

> Ring around a neutron
> A pocket full of protons
> A fission, a fusion
> We all fall down.

Max Beerbohm's use of Walter Savage Landor's epigram works the same way even though the occasion and the subject are different:

On His Seventy-fifth Birthday

> I strove with none, for none was worth my strife
>   Nature I loved, and, next to Nature, Art:
> I warm'd both hands before the fire of Life:
>   It sinks; and I am ready to depart.
>   Walter Savage Landor

Epitaph for G. B. Shaw

> I strove with all, for all were worth my strife.
>   Nature I loathed, and, next to Nature, Art.
> I chilled both feet on the thin ice of Life.
>   It broke, and I emit one final fart.
>   Max Beerbohm

Neither the graffitist nor Beerbohm is interested in mocking the original forms, neither the nursery rhyme nor Landor's "Dying Speech. . . ." But the contrast between the original form and the new content produces irony since the new content is in sharp disparity with the form (and of course the content) of the original (Yunck).

The works and forms that a satirist can appropriate are theoretically endless, but in fact the minds and memories of the audience impose limitations on what the satirist can choose from. Audiences in the last quarter of the twentieth century are less and less familiar with biblical and classical literature and more or better acquainted with the artifacts of commerce, popular culture, and government, the point being that the satirist never lacks for familiar forms to draw on for his faultfinding mission. Until recently, however, forms with religious connections, biblical or ritual, have been among the most persistently used. One of the earliest such uses is the twelfth-century "money gospel," sometimes translated as the "Gospel according to St. Silver Mark." The "Gospel" consists of fragments and echoes of passages from the New Testament used to attack Church officials. The "carmine rebelli" by Gautier de Chatillon (CB, no. 42) from the *Carmina Burana* does much the same thing a century later. The *sirventes* "On the Death of the Duke of Suffolk" puts phrases from the *Requiem Mass* into the mouths of friends of the dead Suffolk which phrases mock rather than celebrate his death. Robert Burns's "Holy Willie's Prayer," Arthur Hugh Clough's "The Latest Decalogue," John Betjeman's "In Westminster Abbey," and Howard Nemerov's "Boom!" are all familiar examples of the same technique, ironic commentary produced by juxtaposing forms carrying religious connotations with disreputable behavior or ideas. The use of biblical phrases for satirical purposes persists to some degree in folk life (Montiero).

The next best thing to a form with moral overtones is a form with built-in respectability, especially if it is a classical form or a well-known work of literature or art. Thus Theocritus could play off his Idyll 15 "Adoniszusae" with its shallow, materialistic city women against the simple country maidens of his other idylls. John Suckling in "A Ballad: Upon a Wedding" presents a mock epithalamium by having a countrified speaker describe a city wedding in a dramatic monologue. Samuel Wesley the Elder's "A Pindarique on the Grunting of a Hog" uses the ode form for an attack on various kinds of music. In each case the form and its conventional content provide a point of comparison with the new content and approach. The same kind of comparison is accomplished by transforming a well-known written work. This is done by Ulrich von Hutten and friends in their *Letters of Obscure Men* (1515, 1517) and by Barbara Garson in *MacBird* (1966). *Letters of Obscure Men* is an upside-down version of *Letters of Illustrious Men,* a series of letters written to support the scholarship of German humanism in its criticism of the Roman church. The 1515 collection of *Letters of Obscure Men* contained forty-one letters, the 1516 edition added six more, and the 1517 edition, contemporaneous with Luther's *Ninety-Five Theses,* added sixty-two more. *Letters of Obscure Men* (the men were in reality ignorant, stupid, and sometimes lascivious) attempted in a satiric way what the *Letters of Illustrious Men* had attempted in a straightforward way. *MacBird* uses the plot of *Macbeth* (and touches of *Hamlet* and *Julius Caesar*) during a time of political disillusionment to satirize Lyndon Johnson, John F. Kennedy, and Robert Kennedy as overly ambitious political figures.

But not all forms in this category are as familiar or obvious in their effect as those cited so far. *La Satire Ménippée* (1594) employs the structure of the "proceedings" of an assembly of religious and political leaders whose connections and sympathies were too closely allied to Italy and Spain, who were, in short, un-French. In a series of descriptions and dramatic monologues the extremists are discredited by their revelations of ambition, hypocrisy, and political intrigue. A more contemporaneous practice is to mock the daily newspaper by turning out look-alike issues, as was done in 1978 and 1979 in New York City and London during prolonged strikes against the *Times* of those cities. *Not the New York Times* and *Not Yet the* (London) *Times* contained satiric imitations of the editorial styles of the respective papers and of their columnists, but the emphasis was on the vagaries of the news.

From the commonplace (letters, newspapers) to the specialized (political proceedings, odes) satirists have been shameless in expropriating other forms. The sampling that follows includes some of the better-known twentieth-century ventures in this manner:

- Transcripts of court proceedings: A. P. Herbert, *Uncommon Law* (1936)
- Dedication of public statue: W. H. Auden, "The Unknown Citizen" (1940)

- Philosophical essay: Paul Jennings, "Resistentialism" (1958)
- Sociological essay: C. Northcote Parkinson, *Parkinson's Law and Other Studies in Administration* (1957); Laurence F. Peter and Raymond Hull, *The Peter Principle* (1969); John Gall, *Systematics: How Systems Work and How They Fail* (1975)
- Report from Special Study Group: Leonard C. Lewin, *Report from Iron Mountain on the Possibility and Desirability of Peace* (1967)
- Corporation Stock: Burton R. Tauber, *Preliminary Prospectus: 225 Million Shares / The War in Vietnam Common Stock* (1970)

Satirists have also used such forms as the almanac, dictionary, recipe, obituary, and how-to-do-it manual in ways that contribute to the creation of irony. Even criminal biographies and eighteenth-century accounts of English low life were turned to good use by Henry Fielding in his ironic *Life of Mr. Jonathan Wild the Great* (1743). Whatever the connotations surrounding the original form, whether they are neutral or charged, the satirist's "perversion" of them forces the original to become if not an ideal norm or standard at least an element whose connotations or emotional value play into his hands.

A special variation on the misused form technique is that employed by George Canning and his colleagues of the *Anti-Jacobin* satiric weekly (1797–98) with poems by Robert Southey providing the medium. The Anti-Jacobites were not interested so much in Southey as a poet as in Southey, spokesman for revolutionary ideas that were anathema to them. Thus Southey's "Inscription for the Apartment in Chepstow Castle, Where Henry Martin the Regicide was Imprisoned Thirty Years," an antimonarchy screed, became in Canning's hands "Inscription for the Door of the Cell in Newgate Where Mrs. Brownrigg, the 'Prentice-Cide, was Confined Previous to her Execution." Southey's sapphics on "The Widow" became "The Friend of Humanity and the Knife-Grinder." Usurping the very forms used by Southey allowed Canning to administer a cold dash of Toryism to what he saw as Southey's sentimental admiration of French Revolutionary ideals.

But the satirist has other elements of literature that can be exploited and perverted. The satirist may manipulate style and content, in addition to form, to create incongruities. A style traditionally used in certain contexts and for certain purposes may be thrust into contexts and used for purposes for which it was not originally designed. Similarly a subject or topic whose value and status is established and well accepted may be treated in a way that violates the reader's expectation. Such a technique is merely a specialized application or expression of a tradition of satire that is found in Aristophanes, Seneca, and Menippean satire in general. Aristophanes in *Clouds, Lysistrata,* and *Peace* inserts tags, words of "high tragic style," into contexts where they are not normally found or expected. In *Lysistrata* he does the opposite, inserting a four-letter word (in the English translation) into a serious discussion of the problem of the women of Athens keeping their oaths to become temporarily celibate (Dover, 72–77). Seneca in his attack on the deification of the Emperor Claudius sprinkles tags from Homer, Horace, and other highly regarded writers; he also uses specialized poetic meters throughout his work but uses them inappropriately (Ball, 62–66), strengthening the case that the *Apocolocynosis* is in the tradition of the Menippean satire, which mixes prose, poetry, levels of diction, and varieties of verse forms and rhythms in a massive attack on its audience's expectation of what is rhetorically appropriate and respectable. Traditionally, Menippean satire has been characterized as a mixture, a potpourri, a *satura,* but its tendency to exploit style and content by placing them in inappropriate contexts or otherwise violating them for ironic and satiric purposes suggests that Menippean satire is another expression of irony by misused forms or disparate elements.

Irony of Disparate Elements.   The main expression of disparate elements is to treat a trivial, mean, or otherwise unredeeming subject as though it were in fact heroic in nature or had epic dimensions. The best examples were produced in an age when knowledge of classical literary models was part of educated persons' intellectual equipment, namely the seventeenth and eighteenth centuries. Thus we find a quarrel between a choir director and a sexton (Boileau's *The Lectern*); any number of second-rate or cut-rate writers (Dryden's *MacFlecknoe* and Pope's *Dunciad*); a wastrel (Guiseppe Parini's *The Day*); and various political hacks (*Criticisms on the Rolliad*). All these figures are treated ironically, endowing them with importance and stature by associating them with heroes and actions of great classical literature, involving mythic gods and goddesses, and using a style generally reserved for presenting such personages. The poems by Boileau, Dryden, and Parini are the "purest" in that the heroic norm is introduced in regular and conventional ways, by no means a discredit to them. Pope, on the other hand, creates a special mythology of his own even while drawing on the epic tradition down to Milton. In *The Rape of the Lock* Pope creates a minimythology that corresponds in size and function to the actions and behavior of his subjects. In the *Dunciad* his pantheon of hack writers behave like stupid, dirty children over which the goddess Dulness exercises authority. Pope's mythic elements are inspired by classical sources, but they emerge in forms created by Pope as more or less conventional parallels to the originals. But whether drawing on traditional sources or creating original parallels, the writer is working against a cultural backdrop that helps to generate irony.

Criticisms on the Rolliad, written by various hands and published in a newspaper, was a device for political satire. Topical in the extreme, concerning party factionalism now forgotten, the *Rolliad* (as it is usually called) is interesting for the elaborateness of its device. The *Rolliad* is in fact a spurious epic poem augmented with a history of the Rollo family and an extract from the dedication to the history. The poem attracts a series of twenty-one articles or commentaries on selected passages from this material which allow their authors to remonstrate on political matters of the time. Since the writers made no attempt to hide their identities or their intentions, the *Rolliad* cannot be classified as a hoax, but the elaborate nature of the scheme has some of the characteristics of the hoax, a device to be discussed later, since it is related to satiric imitation.

Satiric imitations clearly take a variety of forms and allow for many different kinds of attacks. Whether the attacks concentrate on aesthetic or social vagaries, on individuals or groups, is of little consequence. Aesthetic deviations are ultimately expressions of deficiencies of taste or style, aggrandizements of ability or intellect, and as such need to be exposed. Satiric imitation of art and literature is essentially another form of attack on behavior that contributes to a breakdown, a perversion of standards as the satirist sees them.

But no discussion can accommodate the hundreds, perhaps thousands, of examples of the urge to commit satiric imitation.

The examples discussed here have been chosen partly because they are often anthologized or because they best illustrate the ways in which such imitations work. The irony of these examples emerges mainly from the manipulation of components, although such manipulation is by no means the only source of satire in any particular work. (Parini, for example, creates a series of mythic legends to account for several special activities and objects found in *The Day*. The origin and purpose of hairpowder, backgammon, and pleasure are invented increments to the mythic component and as such add an ironic dimension independent of the traditional mythic apparatus.) The overall scheme so far delineated suggests that in general literary selections or their components may be either the targets of attack or the means of attack, in one case (I. and II. below) serving to a greater or lesser extent as literary or social criticism, in the other (III. and IV.) as a servant in straight satire, as follows:

    I. Irony of Violated Style
        A. Style Exaggerated
        B. Style Displaced
        C. Style Naturalized
   II. Irony of Violated Content
  III. Irony of Misused Forms
  IV. Irony of Disparate Elements

Et Alia. No scheme would be complete without a miscellaneous category, especially in a discussion of literary satire, a notoriously recalcitrant subject for neat categorizations. In this category the four techniques listed may be found combined in various ways, sometimes in order to attack a writer or a style as well as nonliterary targets, or sometimes because the writer's "genius" is such that it has produced something that can only be described as unique, or at least more complex than the examples in the four categories above. The techniques of such works and writers do not themselves differ from those of "simpler" examples, but the techniques are yoked together in different ways and combinations, sometimes uniquely so, so that critics run into each other in their confusion in trying to label them with the conventional terminology.

Voltaire's *La Pucelle* (1762), for example, has been described as a "mock-heroic epic" (Besterman, 375), "a burlesque of Joan of Arc" (Meyer, 156), "that gay parody," and a "verse travesty" (Lanson, 52, 80). Voltaire's poem is in fact all of these things, but since no word exists for such a creation, critics are forced to decide which aspect of the poem they wish to emphasize and choose from a, b, c, or d, when in fact the answer is "all and none of the above." Voltaire demythologizes the legend of Joan by mocking the church's concern with Joan's virginity. Yet he tells the story in heroic style. Thus he treats a respected, even revered, subject disrespectfully but in a style and diction that is inappropriate in a story that emphasizes sexual matters in such a way and to such an extent that it has been tagged (wrongly) pornographic. Since Voltaire also includes lines and echoes of lines from an actual poem that idealizes Joan, there is satiric imitation with the "style naturalized," a natural, not to say earthy, presentation of a previously romanticized and idealized subject. But the commendatory poem was by no means Voltaire's primary target. Rather he attacked the veneration paid to (in his eyes) an ordinary albeit somewhat plucky girl (Joan was not elevated to sainthood until 1920). To counteract the mythic venerations he downgrades her by showing her prey to ordinary urges yet overinflates his treatment of her and her era at the same time. Not only has Voltaire's complex ironic handling of Joan's life confused critics of *La Pucelle,* but his approach was seen as so dangerous that it remained unpublished for more than thirty years, parts of the manuscript circulating secretly only among Voltaire's friends. Once published, it was widely attacked, especially by the Catholic Church, and denigrated as irreverent and scatological.

John Gay in *The Beggar's Opera* (1728) combines satiric imitation and Irony of Violated Content to produce his special brand of satire. Swift's suggestion that Gay try his hand at a "Newgate pastoral" provides one entry into the technique of *The Beggar's Opera* in that its plot turns on a satiric imitation of the sentimental novel. More obvious is the satiric imitation of opera itself, especially of those by Handel. In each case, the conventions of the two are put into a new and inappropriate context, low-life characters behaving and performing in ways that were generally reserved for characters of a more heroic cast. Mockery of established and accepted forms was only one of Gay's concerns, however, and the violation of style and context allowed him to satirize the hypocrisy of society and its political leaders.

At first glance Paul Scarron's *Le Typhon* (1644) appears to be a simple case of Disparate Elements, gods behaving in unheroic ways, the technique Scarron was to exploit in *Virgile Travesti* later in the decade. An essential difference between the two is that in *Le Typhon* Scarron is not mocking a specific work but mythology itself. Thus he preserves the heroic tradition in his treatment of the gods even as he makes them behave as French bourgeois of his own time. The Titans, on the other hand, are pictured as children whose carelessness in breaking some drinking glasses provokes a war with the gods. In the obligatory message from Fortune prior to the battle between the giants and the gods, the message arrives in the form of a letter from Tiresias and Nostradamus. Thus are the literary conventions of the fable and epic mocked. But by alluding to contemporary periodicals, putting the battle at the time of the Flanders War, and having Bacchus plug the wines of Burgundy and Orleans, Scarron creates a contemporaneousness that allows him to satirize his own time. Scarron generates irony out of violated content and disparate elements.

By far the most recalcitrant entry in the great scholarly classifying game is Samuel Butler's *Hudibras*. As with Voltaire's *La Pucelle,* critical attempts to categorize *Hudibras* run across a spectrum from "low burlesque" to burlesque to not burlesque with "confusing" and "unique" thrown in as a last resort (Wasserman, 64–65). Butler's basic ploy is similar to the technique of the misuse of a familiar form, namely Cervantes' *Don Quixote,* in which two oddly related characters participate in a series of picaresque episodes. Whereas Cervantes mocks romantic chivalry, Butler satirizes Puritan religion. Quixote and Hudibras are both foolish figures but in quite different ways, the former addled by excessive reading, the latter by trivial piety, both leading to a distorted view of reality. So while Butler uses a familiar form as his point of departure (Cervantes' novel), the play-off between the two is subtly different from the way this technique normally works. The same is true of Butler's use of other techniques. The name Hudibras comes from Spenser's *Faerie Queene,* thereby suggesting a hero with epic qualities. Hudibras's heroic dimensions are insisted upon time and again, but only to be debased by coupling them with the commonplace, as in the following heroic comparison of Hudibras's unsuccessful attack on "fierce Talgol" with his pistol:

> But *Pallas* came in shape of Rust,
> And 'twixt the Spring and Hammer Thrust
> Her Gorgon-shield which made the Cock
> Stand stiff as if 'twere turn'd t'a stock.
>
> (I. ii. 781–84)

Butler also uses the conventions of the heroic in appropriate ways, as when he invokes the muse of Puritan divines Withers and Prynne and creates a catalogue of great bear-baiters. All of this is presented in a doggerel verse that has no redeeming qualities except its humor. Whereas the verses of Voltaire, Pope, and Scarron preserve their essential dignity and value, thereby helping to generate irony out of debased content and subject, Butler's very medium is debased, making it impossible for anything to rise above its linguistic perversions. Since Butler's octosyllabic line is an unnatural medium for presenting even a mock-heroic and antiromantic story, he is able to capitalize on the inherent irony of the contrast between normal expectations and the doggerel and the ability to use it as a debasing agent. It is these quirky uses of standard devices—violated content, misused form, disparate elements, displaced style—that makes *Hudibras* such a bizarre creation and therefore so unaccommodating to the assiduous classifier.

Literary Hoax, Spoof, and Irony

The inevitable coupling of irony and satire is nowhere better illustrated than in spoof and the hoax. In their pure states neither is essentially satiric, combining rather varying degrees of playfulness and deception, the spoof being more playful, the hoax more deceptive. But when a judgmental spirit creeps into either, as it may, then both become expressions of satire as well. The hoax and satire can be found yoked as far back as the trickster figure whose ability to change forms and to assume disguises (as in the Elegba story concerning the inseparable friends) made the trickster perhaps the original hoaxer, even though his intentions were not always satiric. On the other hand, satirists have been drawn to the hoax in a way that suggests that they have seen it as a device that accomplishes what satire in other forms also accomplishes. Swift, Mencken, Bierce, Allais, and Twain are satiric writers who have been attracted to the hoax, and others with satiric inclinations such as Poe, Mérimée, Chatterton, and Ben Franklin have had a go at it. The literary hoax may be both literary criticism and satire, an attempt to debunk a fad or trend, or an exercise in testing the credulity of the public, which almost always fails. Such hoaxing falls under the heading of what Erving Goffman has called "corrective hoaxing" (90–92), hoaxing for fun and morality.

The two most successful literary hoaxes aimed at literary targets have been the *La Guzla* hoax of Prosper Mérimée (1877) and the *Spectra* hoax by Witter Bynner and Arthur Davison Ficke (1916). Both created personas who fronted for the hoaxers, Hyacinthe Maglanovich for Mérimée, Emanual Morgan and Anne Knish for Bynner and Ficke. Maglanovich purported to be an Illyrian bard-outlaw who had collected and translated poems from Dalmatia, Bosnia, Croatia, and Herzegovina. Such was the rage for local color writing that no one recognized that thirty-one of the thirty-two poems were spurious, Mary Shelley praising them and translating three of them into English, Pushkin translating all of them into Russian, Mickiewicz and Chodka into Polish. Only Victor Hugo among the literati of Europe seems to have recognized the hoax, although he may have had inside information (Raitt, 43). Goethe, who had been taken in by a previous hoax by Mérimée and was out of pity tipped off about the second one, ultimately broke the hoax but not before writers and critics had demonstrated that they were no less credulous than other groups against which hoaxes have been aimed.

Equally successful in gulling the literati was the *Spectra* hoax. A book of some sixty-odd pages with a preface announcing its contents as "poetic experiments" by the Spectric group, a new school of poets, *Spectra* was widely reviewed and as widely hailed as exciting new poetry. Where there were reservations, they had to do only with the merits of the verse and the theory behind it. Whatever the evaluation, it was accepted as serious poetry and selections were soon included in anthologies and solicited by the leading literary magazines, including *Poetry* and *Little Review*. Since Morgan and Knish never materialized as persons, the next stage of the hoax involved various poets being accused and accusing each other of having struck off the *Spectra* volume. Nearly two years later Bynner admitted the hoax, having been challenged midway in a lecture in Detroit and unable to deliver a bare-faced lie to a direct question. Bynner and Ficke had succeeded in mocking the literary values and fads of an entire period, the ubiquitous "schools" of poetry that characterized the time, especially the Imagists, most particularly the infatuation with *chinoiserie,* the concept of the "earth woman," the abstract poem, violence, sin, and fast living. Amy Lowell, one of the Imagists most mocked, was accused of having perpetuated the volume of phony poetry while herself accusing others of it and attacking it bitterly. All in all, Bynner and Ficke had made their point (W. Smith).

Literary hoaxes aimed at debunking the sometimes cultlike nature of the literary life operate on the basis of an inversion of the irony of Violated Style. If the hoax is successful, the violation of style is not perceived as such, in which case those who are hoaxed are subject to the irony of not knowing what they are about, a particularly embarrassing irony inasmuch as in the *Guzla* and *Spectra* hoaxes the hoaxed were those who above all others should have recognized the spuriousness of what confronted them. Once the hoax is exposed, the irony doubles by becoming normal Irony of Violated Style as was originally intended.

The insistence by many satirists that in their art they are merely telling some truth, however unpleasant or unwanted, has a natural corollary, the shattering of illusions. A hoax by a satirist may become a testing of a group's ability to penetrate an illusion and grasp the deception. Twain's habitual use of the hoax in his writings involved not only the hoaxing of characters in his fiction but hoaxing of his readers (Ross). The results were never reassuring for Twain who wrote of his *The Petrified Man* that it "was a disheartening failure, for everybody received it in innocent good faith" (qtd. in Weitenkampf, 204). As a hoaxer Ambrose Bierce had mixed success. His passing off a poem as an unpublished original of Poe produced no controversy whatsoever, but his involvement in the publishing of a book called the *Dance of Death,* which attacked the waltz as a seductive influence created a furor on the Pacific Coast. Working with two others in writing and publishing it, Bierce then attacked it in a review that probably helped to boost sales. The book was eventually to be endorsed by a Methodist Church Conference. Jonathan Swift's Bickerstaff hoax of quack astrologer John Partridge and Ben Franklin's variation on it are too well known to retell. Strictly speaking not *literary* hoaxes, they do illustrate the willingness of satirists to turn to the hoax to gain personal ends. Swift's need to publish many of his satires anonymously makes those works a variation of the hoax in that the possibility for deception had to be built into the work and its publication if reaction to it made such deception necessary. These conditions account in part for the numerous personas conceived by Swift (and Franklin). The elements of hoax and satire are inextricably intertwined in the works of these two satirists.

Literary hoaxes that base their satire on violated style run the risk of not being recognized as hoaxes, causing their perpetrators undesirable discomfort. The *Guzla* and the *Spectra* hoaxes were eventually discovered, but such was not always the case, as H. L. Mencken and Herbert R. Mayes learned, Mencken from the so-called Great Bathtub Hoax and Mayes from his mock biography of Horatio Alger. Mencken's article, "A Neglected Anniversary" in the New York *Evening Mail* on 28 December 1927 and Mayes's *Alger: A Biography Without a Hero* published a year later were projected as satiric imitations, one mocking the little-known fact articles once beloved by newspaper editors as fillers on slow news days, the other debunking biography trading on the popularity of such books in the 1920s. Mencken's article called attention to the seventy-fifth anniversary of the introduction of the bathtub into the United States with a brief history of the object. Mayes's book, purported to be the first biography of Horatio Alger, Junior, was based on a minimum of research and emphasized Alger's sexual misadventures, all buttressed with a bibliography containing 135 references, many of them spurious. To the amazement of both Mencken and Mayes no one questioned their research or their veracity (Mayes was the respected editor of *Good Housekeeping* magazine), although both thought they were setting forth japes that would provide only a few laughs. Thereafter both the bathtub history and the biography provided "facts" for serious articles and books, and it was many years later that Mencken and Mayes reluctantly revealed that they were the authors of jokes that failed (Mencken, *Bathtub Hoax;* Bales; Bowerman, 102).

The irony that should have been produced was in fact stillborn since no one recognized the models that were being mocked. The only irony was in the eye of the creator. If there is any irony in such instances, it rebounds against the perpetrators who could be accused of failing in their tasks as satirists. Although one can easily imagine Mencken's delight in having his low regard for the "booboisie" reinforced, deep down there could as easily have been chagrin at not having been a bit less subtle in his satiric imitation. Absent from their intentions, according to both writers, was any desire to deceive so that to call either piece a hoax is incorrect. Deception entered only after each writer realized that what he had intended as satiric had been taken seriously. Allowing the misperception to continue created a hoax after the fact, a natural or unintentional hoax, so to speak, as opposed to a created or artificial hoax. Still, the only irony is that seen by the hoaxer. Even when the deception becomes known, the originally intended irony cannot materialize since the delay has not merely taken the edge off the irony, it has successfully muted it forever. There are other ironies in the situation, but any irony of violated style has become largely irrelevant. The moment of striking determines whether the irony is hot. Unperceived incongruity cannot be ironic.

Similarly, incongruity without an implied judgment cannot be satirically ironic. Such is generally the case with spoof. As a term describing a literary or cultural phenomenon, spoof still leads a marginal existence. The literary dictionaries by Shipley and by Cudden are the only ones to give it space. The entry in Shipley is by Richard Armour, probably the most prolific spoofer in the twentieth century. Articles on the subject attack it as a dishonest and hypocritical expression (Sonstroem; Kael). Like the literary hoax, it may overlap with satire and related forms of humorous critical comment, but only when it includes some tinge of irony, which tends not to be the case. *Spoof,* a British word from the late nineteenth century, originally meant a parlor or card game involving deception, but it has long since left the parlor and become a word of the world referring to certain kinds of books, films, TV programs and skits, magazines, manifestations of the fashion and advertising worlds, and some public events, in all of which playful deception is still an important element. Armour's discussion of the term attempts to establish the roots of spoof in "light" satire, burlesque, and parody of Chaucer, Pope, Byron, and Twain, but his examples from the twentieth century are much more numerous, beginning with Newman Levy's *Opera Guyed* (1923), humorous rewritings of the great and not-so-great operas, coming down to *The Pooh Perplex,* and including Armour's own

"It All Started with . . ." series. He fails to mention the enormous output of humorous imitations of Shakespeare and melodrama in the nineteenth century, although they have all the characteristics of spoof.

But the word has come to describe a wide range of cultural phenomenon that includes the nude Burt Reynolds centerfold in the April 1973 *Cosmopolitan;* the exhibition, "Bicentennial Schlock," which displayed shoddy, cheap, and disposable merchandise with patriotic motifs; TV comedy sketches from the *Carol Burnett Show*; *Belch and Fart* magazine; James Bond movies and others like them; the productions of Charles Ludlum's Ridiculous Theater Company; Woody Allen's early films and most of Mel Brooks's films. As Armour notes, "The spoof makes fun of anything," which may be one of the reasons why so few critics and scholars take it seriously. Shooting ducks in a barrel has never been highly regarded as a sport, and at times spoof is its comic version. Individual movies, movie genres, opera, history, biography, fashions, and fads have all been spoofed, sometimes again and again, from *Cat Ballou* to *Blazing Saddles,* from *Bret Maverick* to *F Troop.* Such spoofs generate little or no irony since the original targets themselves have long since become either clichés or are otherwise of limited consequence. As Richard Eder said of *Stage Blood,* Charles Ludlum's comic imitation of *Hamlet,* "The audience is given no function greater than that of accomplice." And as accomplice the audience's main responsibility is to recognize what in the original is being mocked and to laugh, for that is all that spoof requires. Although the spoof is presented with a straight face, head nodding slightly in the direction of deception, playfulness and getting the laugh are its main goals.

Spoof needed widespread literacy as a seedbed, but it has flowered in a time when the mass media has demanded a constant supply of laugh-getting material that pokes fun without threatening the values of the audience or making undue demands on people's memories and minds. The first outburst of the spoof came in the century with the enormous vogue for "phunny phellows," newspaper column humorists, and vaudeville in the United States and the humorous imitations of Shakespeare and melodrama in England. Much of the spoofery in all of these expressions relied on the ability of the audience to recognize the "schoolmarm literature" that was being mocked. This kind of spoofing is preserved in

Walter Hamilton's six-volume annotated collection of parodies, 1884–99, and Carolyn Wells's collection a generation later (1904), both tributes to the popular taste for spoofing.

But spoof came of age (if that is the appropriate word) with the emergence of the visual mass media and such TV variety shows as *Your Show of Shows* with Sid Caesar and Imogene Coca (in various versions, 1950–58), the *Danny Kaye Show* (1963–67), and the *Carol Burnett Show* (1967–79), TV situation comedies such as *Get Smart* (1965–70) and more recently *Mary Hartman, Mary Hartman* and *SOAP,* the comic mockery of popular songs by Stan Freberg, Woody Allen's films before *Manhattan,* most of Mel Brooks's TV shows and movies, and such movies as *Modesty Blaise* (1966), *Our Man Flint* (1966), *The Russians Are Coming* (1966), *Start the Revolution Without Me* (1970), the Monty Python movies *Holy Grail* (1975) and *Life of Brian* (1979), and *Airplane* (1980). Spoof flourishes in the various versions of *Forbidden Broadway* (1987–current). Renata Adler's description of *Modesty Blaise* as a "kind of all-purpose satire," set out with a "flypaper mood of irony" with the hope that "a lot of funny ideas about things would flutter in from all over and get stuck" can be applied to most films of this kind. She concludes that "all-purpose satire simply doesn't work" (96), and that is because flypaper irony doesn't work either. Its unfocused and fragmented presentation succeeds in arousing a series of laughs, but it works at cross-purposes with any concerted attack on a reasonably identifiable original on which a successful satiric imitation must do a series of turns. Film-length spoofs are often a miscellaneous series of take-offs on the clichés of mass media entertainment and advertising for which the audience becomes a willing accomplice by providing laughter, but out of which no statement of any consequence emerges, lacking, as such bits do, any irony to speak of. Irony in satire cannot be haphazard, fleeting, not even a mere "technical alliance." It is in fact a "necessary structual congruence" (Bogel, 851). Irony springs from two different meanings, different sets of values, contrasting actions, unexpected outcomes, overstatement, understatement, puns, and the other conjunctions that the satirist insists upon. Without irony playful aggression degenerates into spoof, put-on, and take-off, action without meaning, laughter without judgment.

8

Judgment by Irony: Allegory and Caricature

It is ironic in Evelyn Waugh's *Love Among the Ruins* that Miles Plastic, the product of social and educational engineering, is a pyromaniac. It is ironic in Voltaire's *Candide* that after the battle between the king of Bulgaria and the king of Abares each has sung a *Te Deum*. It is ironic in Shirley Jackson's "The Lottery" that a friendly American small town is the scene of a scapegoat stoning ritual. Each of these examples of irony is special to the stories in which they appear, growing out of the circumstances and events of the narrative. Irony as the result of the specific nature of the material itself may be very elaborate as well, as in the minimythology created by Alexander Pope for the *Rape of the Lock,* or the systematic perversion of classical learning attributed to Folly in Erasmus's *The Praise of Folly* (Kay). In all of these cases the satirist has created irony out of the special conditions of the material, be it character, scene or imagery.

But irony is also inherent in the structure of certain kinds of satire and in the use of characters that tend to be typical of, if not unique to, satire. The Irony of Components in which the external style or form is played off against the satiric presentation of that style or form is one kind of irony that inheres in the structure itself (assuming that the audience brings the expected knowledge to the satiric selection). But there are more elaborate structures available to the satirist, an immense collection of characters, situations, ideas, and images that in and of themselves generate irony. This is the area of allegory, a territory so vast that it has led one commentator to say that allegory is "the chief weapon of satire" (Angus Fletcher, 325).

The Irony of Allegorical Worlds

As in the comedy routine in which the impersonator, face-to-face with the impersonated, attempts to convince the latter that he is alone before a mirror by imitating all of his actions, so satire and allegory can be one and the same without losing their individual identities. Together in unison they are an "act," separately they are something quite different, even though at times they may look alike. For satire and allegory are inherently judgmental, and both work (or in the case of satire sometimes works) by indirection. Both set before the audience a work with two levels of meaning, each level representing different realms of experience but which are seen as connected in a unified whole by patterns of details. Allegory is predisposed to control the perceptions of its audience in order to present a particular set of values, be it, for example, Christian morality or Russian Communism. Similarly, the nature of satire does not allow for presenting any side of an argument except that which mocks examples of vice and folly. Allegory presents its messages in terms of something else, a literal set of events, persons, conditions, or images having a corresponding level of existence involving meaning, conceptions, values, or qualities. So in satire there tends to emerge some standard on which the criticism or attack is based, although the degree to which that standard is made explicit varies greatly. Except in most satiric allegories. In many the nature of the allegorical satire causes the norms of the satire to emerge loud and clear, more so than in much nonallegorical satire.

Satiric allegories for which this is most often the case are those in which the satirist creates a fully delineated culture, society, or world that is clearly allegorical. Such a world may include a description of the geography, institutions, customs, and history. Such a culture may be in the present world but only newly discovered, or it may be a society of the future, or it may exist elsewhere in the universe. It may present a near-perfect society, or it may be a society that consists of the worst practices or developments of the present age, or it may present some combination of the ideal and the imperfect. This projected society may be inhabited by human beings, mechanical creatures, animals, or a combination of the three. Whatever the combinations of features, such satire operates allegorically by projecting and playing off against each other two levels of reality: one in which the audience exists, the other the fictive world of satire. Such worlds have been given a variety of names: utopias, dystopias or negative utopias, beast fables, science fiction. They include Thomas More's *Utopia,* George Orwell's *Animal Farm,* Karel Capek's *The War with the Newts* and *R. U. R.,* Zamiatin's *We,* Butler's *Erewhon,* W. Miller's *Canticle for Leibowitz,* Jonathan Swift's *Gulliver's Travels,* and many, many others. Some are "pure" examples, using a single frame for the world, as in *Utopia* and *We.* Others are combinations, as *The War with the Newts* and *Animal Farm,* with animals and humans, *R. U. R.* with humans and robots, and *Gulliver's Travels,* a virtual anthology of different "worlds." Whether pure and simple, mixed or complex, each Janus-like, presents or implies an ideal or norm while projecting a perverted or subverted condition.[1] Unlike conventional allegories in which the levels must be complementary, in satiric allegory the levels are in opposition, thereby generating irony by that very fact.

The allegories of parallel worlds mentioned so far throw into one class satiric works not usually thought of as closely related. Leyburn discusses five different types of satirical allegories, three of which, animal stories, satiric journeys, and future worlds, have been grouped together here under the heading parallel worlds, since the fictional societies in these works are used for contrasting with the actual world. That utopian fiction works in this way is shown by Robert Elliott in his *The Shape of Utopia* when he states that

> The portrayal of an ideal commonwealth has a double function: it establishes a standard, a goal; and by virtue of its existence alone it casts a critical light on society as presently constituted. (22)

Utopia, according to Elliott's theory, is a nonreligious and Westernized expression of the myth of the Golden Age ritualized originally in the festival of Saturnalia. Literary satire is a version of the mockery, ridicule, and invective that were also expressed in the Saturnalia. Satire and utopia are then "not really separable, the one a critique of the real world in the name of something better, the other a hopeful construct of a world that might be" (24). Beast fables, on the other hand, generally do not convey a "hopeful construct" for a better world, although they exhibit the bipartite structure of utopian and similar kinds of fiction. In beast fables one also confronts directly the animal imagery that pervades satire in general. For nowhere does humanity's age-old fascination with animals reveal itself more fully than in satire. From the mythic trickster tales of preliterate peoples and the beast fables in the literature of Mesopotamia through the Aesopian manifestation of Greece, Rome, and the Middle Ages, and *les singeries* of the sixteenth to eighteenth centuries to the fables of La Fontaine, the cartoons of J. J. Grandville, and the tales George Orwell and James Thurber—animals, fowls, insects, and fish have served the satirist as a device for commenting on human behavior. The origin and meaning of this phenomenon has scarcely ever detained either the satirists or their scholarly commentators. Of the latter, those who have touched on the matter of how satirists have used animals, Philip Pinkus (36) is interested in their metaphorical use and Leyburn (chap. 4) in their allegorical dimensions. Neither hints at the complexity or the extent of the satirist's use of animals.

Human identity and relationship with nature are at the roots of human being's attitude toward the animal kingdom. When animals became gods as they did in Egypt, or even earlier when animals were a source of luck and power as in totemism, human beings acted from a mixture of love, fear, and admiration to appease and pacify the forces (gods?) that brought fertility and death. But also present was the assumption that animals were in some ways inferior to humans. Buddha taught that evildoers are nothing but the animals they will become in afterlife, and the ability to domesticate, exterminate, or otherwise control animals seems to confirm man's superiority to the animal kingdom. Although the willingness to endow animals with human characteristics is often thought of as an attribute of primitive peoples, it is by no means confined to them, as animal cemeteries and animals named in people's wills indicate. The controversy over whether animals have souls, feelings, or rights suggests that human attitudes toward animals may be more subtle than they appear on the surface. Even among tribes and cultures in which there seems to be no distinction between human and animal life, there can still exist ironical and mocking relationships alongside fearful and respectful ones, as Edward B. Tylor has told us (317).

Such ambivalence is illustrated in the trickster figure of mythology, which includes more than a dozen and a half different animals among the various forms that the trickster takes, from the spider of the Ashanti, the fox of various South American tribes, the jackal of the Hottentot, the mouse deer of Java, to the rich native American Indian tradition with its raven, rabbit, coyote, wolf, mink, and blue jay. Reynard the Fox of European folklore and literature is a trickster, and Loki of Scandinavian myth, seen mostly in human form, disguised himself as a salmon and bore a wolf child by his second wife. Many of these figures were associated with deeds of bringing benefits to the human race and with helping explain why the things of nature become what they are. They brought fire and water and helped animals and plants take their forms. But many trickster animals are the butt of scatological tales or serve as devices for ridiculing the excesses and weaknesses of humans. The Coyote figures in some creation myths, but he is also the trickster, "the sly, tricky fellow that no one loves or trusts, the 'joker and the butt of jokes' that usually comes out second best, the braggart, the envier, the imitator" (Barclay, 74). As a trickster Coyote was to the Western American Indians what Brer Rabbit was to become to the southern Negro, what Reynard was to become to the European common man. But the literature of the Coyote is much more varied, and according to Lillian Barclay, the animal character portrayed is more vivid (36–37). When tricksters were imitated by tribal clowns, when such tricksters became part of the tribal ceremonies, their freedom to break taboos was a frightening and funny thing, threatening and also liberating (Reichard, 184).

The Greek attitude toward animals expressed in folklore and literature implies a similar ambivalence, although muted and indirect rather than overt as in trickster myths. But the evidence suggests that the Greek concept of animals as expressed in art and customs is not too different from that found later by anthropologists in preliterate tribal cultures. Certainly the spirit of the Dionysia, Aesop's fables, the prehistory of Greek comedy, and the plays of Aristophanes illustrate the pervasiveness of animals in Greek satire and comedy. The Dionysian festival involved the animal-like satyrs and sileni with their world of unbridled celebration. Just as the clown-tricksters of the Dakota and Zuni tribes set aside tribal taboos, so the Dionysia were the occasion for unrestrained verbal aggression and other taboo behavior. Just as there are stories of tricksters with phalluses so long that they had to be wrapped around the bodies of the tricksters in order to be kept out of the way, so the art and drama of Greece show Dionysian figures with abnormally long phalluses. Used for mockery and ridicule, animals and animal-like figures came to represent freedom to the point of chaos.

The dramatic status of the animal chorus in Greek comedy, at least as far as can be deduced from its survival in the plays of Aristophanes, was descended from the Dionysian festival with totemic overtones existing side by side with an autonomy that allowed the chorus to speak and sing in its own right (Dover, 49, 219). Three plays by Aristophanes use animals, *Wasps, Birds,* and *Frogs.* In *Knights* Aristophanes alludes to Magnes of Icarion, a predecessor who "mimicked the music of harp-string, bird-wing, Lydian patois, fig-fly, green-eyed frog." A fragment of a play by Cratinus, also mentioned by Aristophanes, called *Animals* actually exists. Vases antedating Aristophanes by more than fifty years show persons disguised as birds and horses (Kerenyi, 341; Dover, 219). The use of animals for satiric purposes had been going on since the sixth century B.C. when the fables of Aesop began to turn up. Incorporating material from folk tales, including animal tricksters, and domesticating totem myths, the fables allowed the tellers to speak unwelcome truths as well as advocate a practical and skeptical morality. Francis Klingender in his monumental *Animals in Art and Thought to the Middle Ages* traces a change beginning in the sixth century from animals as objects with "magical and mythical associations" to "objects of rational and aesthetic curiosity" (83–86, 91). He sees the fables of Aesop as an expression of and agent in that change, the dissociation being completed by the time of the first collection of the fables around 300 B.C. By the second and third centuries A.D. in Rome, however, there had been a reversion to the pre-Aesopian concept, and humans were once again looking to the "brute beast for guidance." A similar attitude existed in England in 1500, for example, flies illustrating the shortness of life and lobsters providing insights for the invention of military armor. When a speaker in the House of Commons in 1604 was interrupted by a jackdaw flying in an open window, the bill he was advocating was defeated. The omen provided by the bird was too much to overcome. But a century later the clerk of the Royal Society was collecting and studying butterflies and by the mid-nineteenth century some species of birds were on a "protected" list. Although the disappearance of the wilderness came early in England, thereby giving rise to what is now known as the environmental movement, the continuing destruction of wildlife in Brazil, parts of Africa, and elsewhere in the world indicates that the reverence for animal life is not universal. The changes in attitudes toward animals in the Greek and Roman worlds and in England between 1500 and 1900 and the continuing differences in attitudes illustrate the ambivalence toward animals that exists in humans, one attitude dominating at different times, but never overwhelming the other since both have always been present (Keith Thomas).

But no doubt remains as to the liberation of animals from their exclusive role in magic and myth, even though the trickster element and totemic ritual survived in diluted forms. In the late twelfth-century beast epic *Roman de Renart* the trickster figure takes on a literary form that is unmatched elsewhere in the annals of the trickster. In thirty thousand lines of verse consisting of twenty-seven sets of stories animals are used to represent all facets of medieval society, King Noble the lion at the top, his barons, Bruin the bear, Isengrim the wolf, Tybert the cat, and others, including Chanticleer the cock and Tiercelin the rook. Animals represent the rich, the powerful, the orthodox, the polite, the court, and the church of the time. In opposition to these groups representing the establishment stands Reynard the Fox, clever, antisocial, sometimes vicious, a latter-day trickster. He reveals himself in one episode (after twenty glasses of wine) by saying,

> Ever since I was born,
> I've felt bitter scorn
> For worthy respectable people;
> So with merry heart sing
> Here's a fig for the King;
> Nought care I for law, crown, or steeple.
>
> 'Tis my honest belief
> An industrious thief
> Is a blessing to all good society;

> To the humdrumming around,
> Wherein most men are bound,
> He furnishes pleasant variety.

Like the trickster of myth, Reynard is a thief, a murderer, and a rapist who sometimes uses his victims' weaknesses to undo them. He is in short a taboo-breaker. But he is also "an active satirist, exposing [the system] and showing its folly" (Highet, 178; see also Torrance, 83–110).

The *Roman de Renart* is not a single work by a single author but rather an amalgam work-in-process, with numerous contributors, many anonymous, drawing from a variety of sources, folklore, Greek and Roman fables, medieval Latin animal stories, and popular legends. The fable of the sick lion goes back to Aesop. The story of the fox feigning death in order to trap the crows may have come from folk observations and tradition, although the incident appears in a bestiary account. While the fable of the "Jugement de Renart" appeared in early versions such as the *Ysengrimum* (c. 1150) by a Flemish monk, Nivardus of Ghent, and another by Pierre de Saint Cloud (c. 1175). The latter is credited with shifting the emphasis in the tales from Ysengrimus the wolf to Reinardus the fox. The trickster elements can be assumed to have contributed to the popularity of the Reynard stories, which were told, retold, amplified, and modified. In the "Trial of Reynard," one of the best of the stories, Reynard is tried for rape or murder (depending on the version) and is sentenced to be hanged. He will be reprieved if he will take up the cross and journey to the Holy Land as expiation. Once at a safe distance from the court, Reynard throws aside his pilgrim's staff and mocks the court in unmentionable terms. In one version Reynard's victim is venerated into a saint, and miracles are performed at her tomb; in another Reynard escapes to his castle, where besieged, he brings off by a ruse a rape of the Queen, is recaptured, but is freed again when his wife buys his freedom.

Adaptations and translations also attest to the popularity and the usefulness of the Renard cycle. A German translation, *Reinhart Fuchs,* was made as early as c. 1180. A hybrid French-Italian version, *Rainardo e Lesengrino,* appeared in the eighteenth century. Caxton's famous English translation of 1481 was based on a Dutch prose version, although Chaucer's "Nun's Priest's Tale" was an earlier English version of an episode from the *Roman*. Goethe's

Reinecke Fuchs (1794) was a free translation. Although the Caxton and later the Goethe version have tended to fix the cycle for some, it in fact continued to evolve for another century and a half. The last half of the thirteenth century saw three versions, *Couronnement de Renart* (before 1270), *Renart de Novel* by Jacquemart Gielée of Lille (c. 1288), and *Renart le Bestourne* by Rutebeuf (c. 1250–80). The satire of these versions deepens and becomes more direct and bitter. Gielée's poem attacks the Knights Hospitallers and Templars, Rutebeuf's version attacks the king and the religious orders. In the final version, *Renart le Contrefait* (1319–22 and 1327–41), Reynard is an old man who denounces the privileges of the nobles and clergy. In the later version the trickster in Reynard diminishes as the emphasis on ideology increases.

Reynard the Fox was not the only manifestation of animal allegory in medieval life. During the Carnival festivals all over Europe people who were dressed as animals performed allegorical and ritual functions that made various social statements. A manuscript in the Bodleian Museum contains a drawing of five Mummers parading hand-in-hand dressed as an ass, a monkey, a goat, a bull, and an eagle (Rowland, xv). But the symbolism could become socially pregnant, as Ladurie has shown in his *Carnival in Romans*. Not only did actual animals serve as "scapegoats" for collective sins, but men dressed as animals used their costumes to say something about their own status in society, in the case of the *Carnival at Romans,* their discontent with social conditions. "The craftsmen and plowmen took the bear, sheep, hare, capon, donkey (in that order); the patricians, the rooster, eagle, partridge" (214). The patrician birds show positive, aggressive sexual features, while the lower-class animals are castrated (the capon), bad omens (the hare), neutral (the donkey), or weak (the sheep). The bear might suggest aggressiveness, but according to traditional folklore this image was also that of a "weathervane" (compare the groundhog in the United States) and a satyr-like creature. The dual nature of the 1580 Carnival, which eventually led to a massacre, is consistently represented in the costumes and heraldic presentations of the various groups of the city. That this device for symbolizing the social and economic divisions in the city of Romans was, according to Ladurie (318), a congenial form of expression for the people of the times, suggests that so-called primitive attitudes toward animals were not far below the surface of consciousness.

From myth through folklore, from folk culture to popular
literature, conflicting attitudes and concepts of animals persist.
Animals or what they represent may be respected and admired but
also feared and worshipped, or they may represent a lower kind of
existence also feared because by succumbing to bestiality humans
loosen their connection with what is usually assumed to be a higher
reality. This ambivalence was sharpened by the controversy in the
seventeenth and eighteenth centuries by Descartes's claiming as
support for his mechanistic philosophy that animals were machines. As a result La Fontaine and Swift were forced to argue for
the nearness and separateness of animals and humans, adding a
"new dimension to the traditional use of the animal as an image of
man" (Patterson; Renfield; Probyn). Book IV of *Gulliver's Travels*
alone gave us the Yahoos, man-animals, and the Houyhnhnms,
animal-men, adding to the vocabulary of name-calling and insult
and enriching the metaphorical use of animals as well. The humor
aroused by animals incongruously performing acts thought of as
characteristically "human" (as in Houyhnhnm "society") stems in
part from the sense of superiority in humans. Bees, newts, horses,
or spiders carrying on the function of the social order are inherently
funny, if human superiority to animals is assumed. Amy Flint in
John Collier's *His Monkey Wife* laughed, as we do, at the monkey
wife, Emily, "first . . . for being a chimp, and . . . second . . . for
behaving like a human." Yet, as Ellen Douglass Leyburn has
pointed out, successful animal satire is characterized by a nice
simultaneity of human *and* animal traits in animal characters, for at
this point the satirist is exploiting the universal inclination to
project human characteristics into animals. Thus Orwell arouses
pity for the downtrodden of *Animal Farm* and scorn for their
porcine oppressors. We can admire the ingenuity of the newts in
Capek's *War with the Newts,* but we are fearful of their ability to
proliferate, consume, and destroy.

The persistence, popularity, and pervasiveness of animal stories,
satiric or other, rest not merely with the accessibility of animals
into which human traits can be projected and thus dealt with
psychologically. There is the further question of how humans
relate to animals and thus how they define their own humanity.
Writers of animal stories capitalize consciously or unconsciously on
humankind's continuing questions about self-definition. So La
Fontaine in the preface to the first volume of his fables recalled the

legend of Prometheus (a trickster culture hero), noting that when
Prometheus wished to form human beings, "he took the salient
characteristics of all animals; from these so diverse parts he
assembled our kind: he gave form to that work which we call the
microcosm. And so these fables are a painting in which each of us
finds our likenesses."

La Fontaine is at least in part justifying his fables, but only a
century before, Giambattista della Porta (1535–1615), a scientist
and dramatist, and contemporaneously with La Fontaine himself,
Charles Le Brun (1619–1690), an artist, were attempting to
correlate people's characters with their resemblance to animals.
Although such resemblances sometimes exist, probably few people
believe that such similarities are an index to character.[2] Yet the
satirist, but more especially the cartoonist and graphic artist,
exploits just such a connection utilizing a widely accepted and
recognizable visual and physiognomic shorthand. Aesop, La
Fontaine, and other fabulists have helped fix, at least in the Western
"mind," certain animals as exemplifying certain characteristics, the
fox as sly, sheep as mindless, the ass as stubborn or stupid, for
example. The symbolizing of entire nations by animals (the
Russian bear, the English lion, the American eagle) or political
parties (elephant, bull moose, donkey) is a further extension of the
physiognomic relation. Gillray's portrait of Pitt as a fox, Goya's
portrayal of Napoleon as a plucked eagle, and Daumier's of the
wolf in Prussian helmet watching over the sheep (which recalls La
Fontaine's fable of the wolf turned shepherd) all illustrate the
pervasiveness and effectiveness of animals as devices for metaphor
and allegory in both literary and visual satire.

As such, animals have shown themselves to be a rich source of
irony for satirists who have turned them to a great variety of uses.
The simplest use is that in which animal characteristics are applied
to humans. The richest use of animals is that in which animals
stand as full-blown characters in their own world. Between these
poles there are various categories illustrating different ways in
which animals are used, degrees of individuality as animals and
different ways in which human characters figure in the usage (See
Table 8.1). The spectrum covers a range of uses from name-calling
to fully developed dramatic action, the force and degree of the
irony becoming richer as one moves toward and finally into an
autonomous animal world.

Animal characteristics are often attached to humans so as to denigrate them and their activities. When D. H. Lawrence repeats the line, "How beastly the bourgeois is / especially the male of the species," or Philip Wylie calls his book *A Generation of Vipers,* animals provide little more than characteristics for a kind of name-calling one cut above "Off the pigs" and other types of verbal abuse. Working pretty much at the same level are such titles as *The Hairy Ape, Lord of the Flies,* and *This Simian World.* Juvenal in Satire XV uses a similar but a bit more elaborate kind of imagery when he compares the fact that animals do not destroy their own kind to the failure of pity in humans in which the action of the satire leads to cannibalism. But animals may be used as animals without their becoming in any sense characters or individuals. They may serve as symbols, perhaps exemplifying qualities that humans lack, as in D. H. Lawrence's "The Mosquito Knows—":

> The mosquito knows full well, small as he is
> he's a beast of prey.
> But after all
> he only takes a bellyfull
> he doesn't put my blood in the bank.

Other works that operate as Lawrence's epigram include T. S. Eliot's "The Hippopotamus," Robert Frost's "The Bear," Humbert Wolfe's "The Grey Squirrel," Samuel Wesley's "A Pindarique on the Grunting of a Hog," and Belloc's *The Bad Child's Book of Beasts.* In *After Many a Summer Dies the Swan* (1939) Aldous Huxley uses scenes from animal life in much the same way, as, for example, the feeding of the baboons, to which Huxley has one character react, "Aren't they cute! Aren't they *human!*" With this remark Huxley seems intent on establishing the symbolic value of the baboons without being in the least interested in them as fictional characters or even as autonomous creatures. Even though the animals which function in a simple symbolic or allegorical way fail to satisfy the requirement set up by Ellen Douglass Leyburn that calls for animal characters to be simultaneously animals and humans, their use nevertheless generates irony from the explicit contrast between human actions and values and animal characteristics, whether those characteristics be positive or negative. For example, when Robert Graves begins "The Laureate," "Like a lizard in the sun . . ." and extends the simile throughout the poem,

Table 8.1

1. ANIMAL CHARACTERISTICS:		3. ANIMAL SYMBOLS:
Metaphorical Reinforcement	2. Symbolic Function	Dramatic context with humans
Lawrence, ". . . beastly bourgeois . . ."	Lawrence, "The Mosquito Knows"	Aristophanes, *Frogs; Birds; Wasps*
Wylie, *A Generation of Vipers*	Eliot, "The Hippopotamus"	Brer Rabbit stories
O'Neill, *The Hairy Ape*	Frost, "The Bear"	Capek, *The War with the Newts*
Golding, *Lord of the Flies*	H. Wolfe, "The Grey Squirrel"	Twain, "Jim Baker's Blue Jay Yarn"
C. Day, *This Simian World*	Belloc, *The Bad Child's Book of Beasts*	de Assis, "The Most Serene Republic"
Graves, "The Laureate"	S. Wesley, "A Pindarique on the Grunting of a Hog"	Spenser, *Mother Hubbard's Tale*
Pope, passim		Heywood, *The Spider and the Fly*
Berman, *The Politician Primeval*	Lydgate, "Debate of the Horse, Goose, & Sheep"	France, *Penguin Island*
Archilochus, passim	Southey, "Ode to a Pig while his Nose is being Bored"	Mandeville, *Fable of the Bees*
Animal names: Volpone, et al.	Bestiaries; Aviaries	James Gillray
		Thomas Nast
		Edward Sorel
		Singeries

he is not being complimentary. Henry Reed's use of peaceful nature imagery, including references to bees and sheep, in "Lessons of the War" denigrates the violence and brutality, the unnaturalness, of military life. The animals do not have to exist in their own right but must merely stand for some quality or characteristic that helps to create irony.

But animals as characters seem to have had the greatest attractiveness for satirists, if number of works in which they appear is any criterion. As characters they may be little more than allegorical figures or they may exist independently in their own world in which their allegorical value is muted and covert. They may coexist with humans, be subservient to or independent of them. For example, in several plays by Aristophanes animal life emerges as independent of human life, but animals also exist as

Table 8.1 (Continued)

4. ANIMAL/ HUMAN CHARACTERS: Dramatic context	5. METAMOR-PHOSES: Human to/from animal	6. ANIMAL CHARACTERS: Humans minor or implied	7. EXCLUSIVE ANIMAL WORLD: No humans
Peacock, *Melincourt*	Kafka, "A Report to an Academy"	Chaucer, "Nun's Priest's Tale"	*Roman de Renart*
Collier, *His Monkey Wife*	Ionesco, *Rhinoceros*	Orwell, *Animal Farm*	*Batrachomyomachia*
Maloney, "Inflexible Logic"	Lucian, *The Ass*	Marquis, *Archy & Mehitabel* poems	Rostand, *Chantecleer*
Munro, "Tobermory"	Apuleius, *The Golden Ass*	Burman, Catfish Bend stories	de Vega, *Gatomaquia*
Heine, *Atta Troll*	Swift, . . . *Travels,* IV	Soseki, *I am a Cat*	Casti, *Gli Animali Parlanti*
Swift, *Gulliver's Travels,* IV		Cervantes, *Dialogue of the Dogs*	Anon, *Ecbasis Captivi*
Wireker, *The Book of Daun Burnel the Ass*		Bergerac, "Story of the Birds" in *Voyage to the Sun*	Updike, "Under the Microscope"
Gelli, *Circe*		Lao She, *Cat Country*	Twain, "Three Thousand Years among the Microbes"
J. F. Cooper, *The Monikins*			Neidle, *Fables for the Nuclear Age*
Some trickster tales			Most beast fables

members of the Chorus complementary to it. In *Birds,* Aristophanes introduces a variety of winged creatures using them not only for comic purposes, as when they explain the advantages of having wings, but also for serious comment in which the harmony of bird life puts them in a realm superior to human life. In *Wasps,* the Chorus represents the old and vulnerable jurymen who sting the rich with fines but who are themselves capable of being victimized by demagoguery. Despite their ambivalent role, they are probably more effective than the animals in Spenser's *Mother Hubbard's Tale,* Heywood's "The Spider and the Fly," Anatole France's *Penguin Island,* and Mandeville's *Fable of the Bees*—in all of which the allegorical value of the animals tends to dominate the action and precludes any sense of animal life.

But in animal satires in which the narrator is the only human, animals may begin to take on a life of their own, emerging as fully delineated characters. Not only do they carry normal allegorical value, but they may be used as "satirists," characters who mock, ridicule, and criticize. In the Brer Rabbit stories, the Panchatantra series, Capek's *The War with the Newts* and *The Insect Comedy,* and Machado de Assis's "The Most Serene Republic," animals assume a new and separate importance but are still tied directly in one way or another to the human world. The line between such usage and those stories in which animals and humans mix more or less equally is not a distinct one.

But the latter category (see column 4 of chart) contains the highest percentage of animals that are members of the ape family, used apparently because of their primateness, as in Peacock's *Melincourt, or Sir Oran Haut-ton* (1817), John Collier's *His Monkey Wife, or: Married to a Chimp* (1930), and Russell Maloney's "Inflexible Logic." Included here also are the *babouineries* in which monkeys are pictured aping human activities, a tradition in French art that goes back to medieval manuscript decorations and lasted into the nineteenth century. Peacock's *Melincourt* is one of his less successful fictions, using Sir Oran to mock the upgrading of apes and others on the animal scale (as argued in Lord Monboddo in *Origins and Progress of Language,* 1773–92) but also to attack the politics of rotten boroughs, Parliament, and mobocracy, and the boorish and crass behavior of British lords. Although a useful device, Sir Oran does not emerge as a wholly successful character in the way that Emily does in Collier's *His Monkey Wife.* In this very clever and funny novel, much of the story is told from Emily's point of view. Long-suffering, patient, all in enforced silence, Emily is on one level a satiric imitation of countless Jane Eyre–types, seemingly unworthy women who fall deeply but silently in love with an unnoticing and unsuspecting male. Emily is also a contrast to the feminist but unfeeling and selfish Amy Flint (note the name) who wants to reverse the double standard so that her fiancé cannot show passion but she can (but not to him). The final paragraph of the novel (too good to be spoiled by quoting out of context) is a brilliant example of Leyburn's dictum of the necessity of maintaining a balance between animal and human characteristics in successful beast stories. H. H. Munro ("Saki") in "Tobermory" and Maloney in "Inflexible Logic" conduct less ambitious exercises in combining human beings and animals as full-fledged characters.

A different kind of equality operates in stories in which men are metamorphosed into animals and vice versa. In Kafka's "A Report to an Academy" an ape reports on his transformation to a man while Ionesco's *Rhinoceros* shows men succumbing to mass suggestion and rule and becoming lumbering, destructive animals. In Lucian's *The Ass* and its later version, Apuleius's *The Golden Ass,* a young man is accidently turned into a jackass. Lucius, the young man, remains a human being in thought although he is tempted to accommodate his form at times. As he seeks seriously to regain his human shape and his humanity, the society around him becomes increasingly beastly. Without the metamorphosis and much less accomplished than Apuleius is Nigellus Wireker's *Speculum Stultorum* (c. 1180), known widely later as *The Book of Daun Burnel the Ass,* in which the worldliness and hypocrisy of the clergy are attacked through the device of a peripatetic donkey.

The most famous attempt at a human-to-animal metamorphosis is Gulliver's unsuccessful try to become a Houyhnhnm in Book IV of his *Travels.* If the attempt fails, it is not because he doesn't have a well-developed model and society to follow. In this way Book IV is typical of a whole category (column 6 of table 8.1) in which human life begins to recede and autonomous animal life with well-developed characters emerges. Chaucer's "Nun's Priest's Tale," Orwell's *Animal Farm,* Ben Lucien Burman's Catfish Bend stories, Don Marquis's *Archy and Mehitabel* poems, and Natsume Soseki's *I am a Cat* are examples of animal worlds in which humans no longer play a dominant role, being subordinate to Napoleon, the tyrannical pig, Chanticleer, the boisterous cock, and Archy, the poetic cockroach. In such works the allegory becomes nearly absolute, nearly so, because while humans are still present, they are on the periphery or in the distance, physically as in *Animal Farm* and the Catfish Bend stories, or psychologically as in Soseki or Marquis, in which the world of the author is seen through the eyes of a cat and of a cockroach.

But in the final groups of animal satires allegory becomes absolute. Animals and humans merge, humans disappear completely, and a new world is created in which humans and their world exist only in an allegorical sense. The dominant mode is narrative or dramatic fantasy. In this category are the *Roman de Renart* cycle, most beast fables, the *Batrachomyomachia*, Rostand's *Chantecleer*, Lope de Vega's *Gatomaquia*, Casti's *Gli Animali Parlanti*, and the *Ecbasis Captivi*.

Satiric use of animals by graphic artists has not been as extensive as that by literary satirists, but such uses have been by no means negligible. Graphic artists have used animals as writers have, as symbols, as full-fledged characters, with humans and without them. They too have observed the characteristic noted by Leyburn of combining the animal and the human world simultaneously. In some cases, the artist places animals in human contexts performing human acts, as in Heinrich Kley's "Politicians" in which two unsavory lizards put their heads together across a restaurant table, or in the drawings for the fables in Fritz Eichenberg's *Endangered Species*. In such cases the animals tend to become symbols, as in Eichenberg's "Total Disarmament" or "Endangered Species," in which the predatory nature of beasts is emphasized. Thomas Nast made obvious political use of animal symbolism with his Tammany tiger, the British lion, and the elephant and the donkey, a practice that is by no means extinct. By far the most extensive use of animals for satire is that by J. J. Grandville in *Metamorphoses of the Day* (1829) and *Scenes of the Private and Public Life of the Animals* (1840). (Grandville also illustrated an 1840 edition of *Gulliver's Travels*.) Grandville tends to place animals in human contexts and activities, clothing the animals in the fashion of the time. They are animals in form but humans in dress and action. But Grandville also includes a variation in which human figures appear with animal heads. Ultimately Grandville's practice was to put human and animal forms together in any manner that would be effective, even in one instance combining a human hand and an animal paw on a female spaniel singing while accompanying herself on a piano. The human face on an animal form, used by Grandville, is the technique most widely practiced in political cartooning. This is also the device favored by James Gillray and Thomas Nast. The face of Charles Fox affixed to the body of a rattlesnake, the face of William Pitt atop the body of an octopus, the head of Boss Tweed on a vulture's body are among the most striking creations of these political cartoonists.

Although animal allegory or symbolism is only one among several techniques used by these artists, such techniques help to produce some of the most memorable of their works. Nast's cartoon of Tweed and his cohorts as vultures sitting on cliffs as lightning strikes around them with the caption "A Group of Vultures Waiting for the Storm to 'Blow Over'—'Let us Prey' " is one of his best-known works. In "The Crowning Insult to Him Who Occupies the Presidential Chair" Nast expresses his sympathy for President Grant but in an allegorical fashion with the presidential lion being "crowned" with a goat's head labeled "scapegoat" by a fox standing on the back of a donkey. In the distance are the barking dogs of the "Press," including a giraffe symbolizing the New York *Tribune,* an ass representing the New York *Herald,* and a unicorn wearing a monocle, the *New York Times.* Although the politics of Gillray's time is at greater remove, some of his drawings have a universal quality, such as "More Pigs than Teats, or, the New Litter of Hungry Grunters, sucking John-Bulls-Old-Sow to death" (1806), the sow being of course the national treasury. "Market-Day" shows steers with men's faces being herded into stalls. Next to the title are the quotations, "Every Man has his Price, Sir Rt Walpole" and "*Sic uter ad astra*" (Thus do we reach the stars). Purchasing the favors of members of a legislative body was not confined to Gillray's times.

Francisco Goya's use of animal allegory is all his own and seems to follow no recognizable pattern. "No more, no less" shows a monkey painting the portrait of a donkey as a judge. The only human artifacts in the picture are the pallet, paintbrush, and canvas on its tripod. Monkey and donkey are portrayed more or less realistically. "Look, are we not wonderful!" contains four figures in which animal forms and human forms are united with no discernible logic, except that of grotesqueness. One figure with the lower body and paws of a bear has an ass's head. On his back is a figure with the body of a human, the head, hands, and feet of a vulture. A third figure is similar to the first, but he is carrying what appears to be a human being with the ears of a donkey. Both of these are part of the *Cappricios* series. "The charlatan's swindle" in *The Disasters of War* shows a birdlike figure with a parrot's head addressing an audience of humans and animals. "The Carnivorous Vulture" shows a huge Cock of France being routed by a horde of Spanish people led by a man with a pitchfork. Goya's work is not always so topical as this one or as those of Gillray and Nast, but tends to create a nightmare-like symbolism that combines realism and fantasy. This is shown in one of his best-known animal drawings, "The Dream of Reason Produces Monsters," in which owls, bats, and cats hover around the head of a man sleeping with his head on a table.

The place and fate of *homo sapiens* (that is, wise primates) in the universe has played into the hands of satirists. Whatever attitude human beings have taken toward themselves, that attitude has been portrayed in animal form. Whether animals provide descriptive details, as in "ratface" or "stubborn as a mule," or whether they serve as actors in elaborate animated cartoons such as Ralph Bakshi's modern rendition of the Brer Rabbit stories in the controversial *Coonskin,* or his satire on sex and violence in the X-rated film *Fritz the Cat,* animal characteristics and behavior provide a parallel world that produces the irony so indispensable for successful satire. To imagine satiric art without animal imagery and animal life is to realize that such satire would be an art whose very existence would be in jeopardy.

The Irony of Character

All humankind is capable of the stupidity and folly presented in satiric works, and so there would seem to be no bottom to the well from which to draw material. This richness of resources turns out to be illusory. The satirist is compelled by his or her vision to deal generally in caricature, to present characters in simple rather than complex terms. Subtle, complicated characters tend to impede action, to blur moral distinctions and contrasts, to center on the subjective, the psychological, the introverted as opposed to the secular, the social, the worldly. Raskolnikovs and Hamlets are out of place in satire. The reliance on caricature is a major source of humor in satire, but critics, unable to accept satire on its own terms, that is, that caricature is inherent in satire, find caricature a baneful rather than a charming feature of the mode, a minus quality that helps to keep satire among the lesser art forms. Despite what some see as a limitation, the gallery of characters in satire is rich with types and stereotypes, the sycophants of Horace and Juvenal, the social climbers of Jonson and Thackeray, the various misfits of *Catch-22,* the originals of Wilde, to mention a few. Out of this richness satirists have tended to rely on three types, which appear in various guises as major characters or personas. These are the ingenu, the *eiron,* and the iconoclast. Each of these types is a source of irony, in some cases directly so, in others indirectly. Such irony is inherent, inevitable with the concept and appearance of the characters. All of these characters are out of place in the scenes in which the satirist casts him, unable or unwilling to function in or accept a world of selfishness, ignorance, intolerance, or injustice. Each becomes a foil to the unsocial activities around him. What the ingenus, the *eirons,* the iconoclasts are, do, and say is played off against the world into which they can never fit comfortably, alienated by their innocence, honesty, or skepticism. Directly or indirectly their person, their behavior, their words are an ironic judgment on the malice and vice of the world.

The Ingenu. Voltaire's *Ingénu* (1767) is the story of a handsome young man, born of European parents in North America, reared by Huron Indians, then transported to Europe. Speaking Huron, English, and French, he is a deistical noble savage, at once wise and innocent, and while in trouble with French society for speaking as he thinks, acting as he wishes, all out of natural goodness. But as a person who cannot proceed by the pointless conventions of society, the prejudices and power of sects and classes, he is bound to come to no good end. Such naïveté makes an unfavorable comment on the guile and artificiality of society. And so Voltaire's Ingénu gives his name to one important and widely used satiric character type.[3] The innocent childlike nature of the Ingenu is perhaps his most obvious and charming characteristic and has been much noted. But in fact the Ingenu is not a simple, monolithic type but one that offers, prismlike, a variety of slightly different faces, all looking out on a fallen world that in turn looks upon the Ingenu, sometimes as a threat, sometimes as a dupe. That both reactions comment on the values of the world is part of the satirist's strategy to get the audience to condemn those values. Either way the Ingenu is a victim, often violently so, always unjustly so. Always there is something childlike in the Ingenu, even when he is driven sexually as Voltaire's Ingénu or Candide occasionally are. But actual children are rare among the Ingenus, being perhaps too vulnerable to take the thwacking that is often the lot of the adult Ingenu. But Lewis Carroll's Alice and Raymond Queneau's Zazie do to some extent serve as Ingenues. In one sense the most primitive Ingenu is Grimmelshausen's Simplicissimus, who "knew neither God nor man, heaven or hell, angel or devil; nor yet the difference between good and evil." He is a true blank slate, but he remains so for only a short time. But while he is totally innocent, he is unable to see the rapine and pillaging, greed and dishonor that go on around him for what they are. He joins in the agonized laughter of his tortured father and is amazed by the wealth of his father that the torturers uncover. But Simplicissimus the Ingenu gradually becomes Simplicissimus the opportunistic survivor, in short a picaresque rogue, although in his original state he is the best example of a true Ingenu.

In some ways similar to the German original is Seba Smith's Jack Downing more than two centuries later. Downing, like Simplicissimus a rustic, is described by Smith as a "green unsophisticated lad from the country." His untutored and witless commentary on local and national politics of the United States in the 1830s laid bare the hypocrisy and other idiocies of legislations and political figures from Portland, Maine, to Washington, D.C. But Downing was also a Yankee and in keeping with the mythology of the day was not above an occasional piece of trickery. The uses of Simplicissimus and Downing imply that the Ingenu is a rare and delicate character, difficult to sustain, especially in a mode as motley as satire. Thus one finds an occasionally fugitive example, as in Addison's American Indian king in No. 50 of the *Spectator* papers (27 April 1721), used to make miscellaneous comments on English society of the time.

More usual is the Ingenu produced by a background that fails to prepare him for the world in which he finds himself, or one so gripped by a set of values that he cannot synchronize with the values of the world. Such Ingenus are childlike and innocent in that they generally trust those about them, often to their own discommodity. They are naive in that they are unable to fathom the reason for their troubles. But these characteristics are symptoms really, however valid as descriptive terms. The real source of their problem is that they are possessed by values and beliefs that cause them to behave in ways that are self-defeating. Unlike the biblical prophecy, they do not inherit the earth, but given the choice between the typical Ingenu and the society mistreating him, the audience tends to wish him better treated than is usually his fate.

Such are the characters of Candide, Lemuel Pitkin, Chauncey

Gardiner, and Paul Pennyfeather. All but Chauncey are young men, but all share backgrounds that can only be described as sheltered. Candide is ejected from the baronial "estate" of Baron Thunder-ten-tronck in Westphalia, hardly a center of learning and sophistication by Voltaire's description; Pitkin sets out from Ottsville, Vermont, hard by the Rat River; Paul Pennyfeather is expelled from Scone College where he had been reading for the ministry; and Chauncey Gardiner is thrust out of a big-city mansion where he had been a gardener and handyman all his life when not being entranced by the television set. Candide, of course, is inconvenienced by the teachings of Pangloss that everything is for the best, this being the best of all possible worlds, and that all events have a cause. These teachings fail to prepare Candide for the physical and emotional buffetings that he encounters trying to live by them. Lemuel Pitkin in Nathanael West's *A Cool Million* sets out to make his fortune, burdened with the Horatio Alger myth of honesty, hard work, patriotism, and a never-say-die optimism not unlike Candide's. Neither Candide nor Pitkin realizes his dream, the latter destroyed by being slowly dismantled physically, the former finding not a beautiful romantic lover but an excellent pastry cook. Paul Pennyfeather in Evelyn Waugh's *Decline and Fall* and Chauncey Gardiner in Jerzy Kosinski's *Being There,* on the other hand, do not leave their nests voluntarily. Pennyfeather leaves because he is the victim of a prank that caused him to appear in public without his trousers, Gardiner because his employer died and left him homeless. Both are decidedly passive characters, victims of those who are forceful, stupid, or dishonest. Pennyfeather is unable to cope because of his simple English gentleman morality, and Gardiner because of a very literal simplicity.

On the other hand, the satirist himself is not above victimizing his Ingenu. Even as the audience sympathizes with the unjust treatment that the Ingenu receives at the hands of society, it sees that the Ingenu has to some extent brought it on himself. But the audience's willingness to forgive the Ingenu his simplicities is what distinguishes him from those characters whose excesses are without redeeming value or are otherwise unalloyed. Candide and Pangloss share the same limited view of reality and are mocked for it, but only Pangloss receives the audience's total condemnation. Lemuel Pitkin and Shagpoke Whipple share the same American myths, but it is clear that Whipple is a hypocrite of the worst kind.

Neither Pennyfeather nor Chauncey Gardiner are heroic in any sense of the word, and the audience cannot help see the limitations of their positions, but those limitations do not justify the treatment they receive at the hands of society. So the satirist is able to have it both ways, mocking the Ingenu even as he uses him as a foil for exposing the weaknesses of the society in which he attempts to operate.

Through the actions and the reactions of others to the Ingenus, Voltaire, West, Waugh, and Kosinski make the audience see the inadequacy of certain social values, attitudes, and behavior. The Ingenu's needs and wishes—romantic love, fortune, a vocation, to be let alone—are simple and harmless and not without a charming reasonableness. But discommoded by values or backgrounds or both that unfit them for existence in societies dominated by vice and folly, they are doomed. Blessed by their simplicity, they are at the same time cursed by it. They accept and trust what they see, are undone by what they cannot see or understand. They mean well, but they participate in or are agents of violence, exploitation, and death. As characters they are simple in the extreme, but they produce an inescapable irony, however unsubtle and uncomplex it may be at times. The use of the Ingenu character does not guarantee a satirist success, but the type has appeared to good advantage in a variety of successful satires and so clearly has its uses. Do not naive, innocent people in the throes of unrealistic ideas exist? Do not such events as happen to the Ingenus of satire—earthquakes, dismemberments, seductions—occur? Is the artist not allowed to unite the Ingenu and such events in order to express his or her view of reality?

The Eiron.   True to his Greek origins, the Eiron is a two-faced type. The face seen by the world may appear innocent, ignorant, foolish, bumbling, stupid, although the world can never be sure whether the appearance is real or feigned. The truth is of no consequence, because the mask allows the Eiron to act and speak from behind it in ways that would otherwise be forbidden. This forbidden behavior is the main reason for the Eiron's existence, for the audience eventually becomes aware that of such is the kingdom of the satirist. Out of this discrepancy between appearance and some more important reality behind it, emerges another expression of the irony of character. The relationship between what is shown and said and what is really meant is generally more complex than the simple reversal or opposite here described, but this is one expression, and all others, however complex, start from this point. The Eiron-like pose is the pose of the mock encomiast, smilingly praising what in fact is trivial or evil.

The Eiron is the role of Horace as he allows the sycophant in Satire 1.9 to dominate the conversation while managing by sarcasm and understatement to cut him to ribbons. It is the mark of the bore's obtuseness that he is unaware of what Horace is doing. The Eiron is the pose taken by Socrates the teacher. Unprepossessing, even homely, dressed in the same coat no matter the season, wearing no hose or shirt, Socrates represented himself as dull, a slave to his passions, and a person who hears "voices" which occasionally advise against certain actions. Such behavior disarmed some, attracted some, irritated others, left scarcely anyone indifferent. His role allowed him to attack moral and intellectual pretentiousness so that wisdom and truth might emerge. Chaucer assumes the role of Eiron when he seems not to recognize some of the other pilgrims for what they are, worldly, materialistic, and impious in the cases of the prioress and the monk. Chaucer presents them nevertheless as charming and dynamic persons, playing, in the words of Talbot Donaldson, "the latent moralist and the naive reporter" (13).

Blaise Pascal used the traditional Eiron when he created Louis de Montalte, the persona writer of the *Provincial Letters* (a series of fifteen pamphlets issued between January 1656 and April 1657) in which Pascal attacks the Jesuits as a way of defending his friend Antoine Arnauld, a Jansenist. In Letters 4 to 10 Pascal has Montalte engage in a dialogue with a Jesuit father whose benign arrogance and "scholastic formality" (Topliss, 60) make him a ready target for an ironist like Montalte. Pretending to seek information and clarification on Jesuit views, Montalte traps the priest into contradictions and monstrous statements, into defending bribe-taking, usury, and murder. Seemingly naive and curious, argumentative only in search of truth, Montalte's occasional open sarcasm and irony never penetrate the convictions of the blissful Father who becomes his own worst enemy and that of the Jesuits. And finally some manifestations of the Eiron can be seen as a literary projection of the mythical trickster. Protean, clownish, anti-authority, combining contradictory kinds of behavior, existing on the edge of respectable society, and representing the potential for—sometimes the fact of—chaos, the list of characters who have been dubbed tricksters is a virtual who's who of comic and satiric characters: Tom Jones, Sebastian Dangerfield, Lazaro, Huck Finn, Falstaff, Sut Lovingood, and Holden Caulfield from literature, Brer Rabbit and Till Eulenspiegel from folklore, the Marx Brothers in the movies, and Dennis the Menace and the Katzenjammer Kids in the comic strips. Many of these are to some degree also the agents of satire, exhibiting the doubleness that is the essence of the Eiron and his irony.

The above list implies an infinite variety of Eirons, but a closer look suggests that in addition to the pure or traditional Eiron already mentioned, Eirons of the type in this category tend to center around either the wise fool or the picaresque rogue. To be sure these types are not invariably nor inevitably satiric, but they lend themselves readily to satiric purposes and have therefore been widely appropriated by satiric artists.

The wise fool is the most readily identifiable of Eirons. Acknowledged to be or pretending to be a fool in some manner, his actions or statements express some truth or wisdom that satirically reveals the moral weakness of society. The freedom to speak forbidden, unwanted, or unrecognized truths is a widely acknowledged freedom bestowed upon the fool, although some fools, say, in the form of clowns, do not always avail themselves of the privilege. The richest manifestation of the fool in the service of satire occurred in the late Middle Ages, a period in which the idea of folly permeated society. One particular expression of this fascination was the *sottie,* or fools' play (Arden). Because the *sotties* are an important source of information about the phenomenon, they illustrate in concentrated form the nature of the fool. In the *sottie* all the characters are fools whether they represent some abstract quality (*Ordre, Sancte,* Malice) or some particular social group or institution (*Sergents* [churchmen]), various *gens nouveaux* (new middle-class groups). Sometimes the fools of a particular *sottie* are presented as opposing groups, that is, foolish fools and wise fools, so to speak; sometimes characters change from one kind of fool to another; and occasionally a character is both at the same time. Those who were truly evil are "destructive to themselves and to society" (164). The fool then could serve in the roles of "evil-doer, accuser and victim" (163), "truth-speaker, wrongheaded, and lowly" (164), all at the same time or in one capacity or another, as an individual or as a member of a group.

The *sotties* were at once an expression of allegory and of satire, a form of ritual, and finally, "profoundly ironic," a unique combination in one sense but not unusual in another since the wise fool existed as a character before the *sottie* and would continue after the *sottie,* for the fool is a serviceable type. Bringing together the opposing traits that the *sottie* often presented separately, satirists have created a great variety of characters in the guise of the wise fool. They have exploited the freedom that has always gone with the role of combining some form of foolishness with satiric revelation, a source of unavoidable irony. For example, the Madwoman of Chaillot, in Giraudoux's play of that name, unwilling to cooperate with a society that devalues beauty, romance, and innocence, becomes in the eyes of that society an eccentric of immense presence, a virtual madwoman. But when confronted with a situation that threatens to result in another case of alienation and disappointment such as hers as well as the destruction of her milieu, she functions effectively to destroy the enemy, the speculators, the engineers, and their toadies, momentarily saving and serving those values that have been the cause of her eccentricities.

But not all wise fools are so self-conscious as the Madwoman of Chaillot. Some are simple in the extreme, therefore foolish, but still capable of seeing through or otherwise revealing the stupidity and injustice around them. Such is the case Jaroslav Hašek's Josef Svejk in the *Good Soldier Svejk.* A Czechoslovakian and "certified cretin" in the crumbling Hapsburg Empire on the eve of World War I, he is charged with treason for pointing out fly dirt on the picture of the Emperor. Apart from that, he is victimized by doctors, military officers, and others in positions of power. If he is a victim, he is also a survivor with a genius for landing on his feet after adversity. In trying to satisfy those in power, he reveals their stupidity; in explaining his bungling and ineptness (he's a cretin after all), he comments obliquely on the irrational nature of the society around him; in gulling the vain (as he does in his dog business), he reveals further follies of the rich and powerful. In short, the mask of simpleness, ineptitude, and victim is the public side of the Eiron who is thus able to reveal by situations and statements the failings and immorality of those in power. Even though the doctors in the army certify Svejk as a cretin and send him to an insane asylum, the doctors there classify him as a "malingerer of weak intellect" and send him back to the army. Thus the nature and extent of his foolishness remain open.

Such is also the case in Brocca and Boulanger's film *The King of Hearts* (1966), set in a small town in France just prior to the end of World War I. When the Germans retreat and leave the town unoccupied, the occupants of an asylum are accidentally set free. Indulging their suppressed playfulness and desire for beauty and illusion, they conduct a mock coronation of an Allied soldier sent to the town to scout for explosives left by the retreating Germans. Despite the threat of destruction, the inmates refuse to leave the town and eventually return to the asylum when the explosives are defused and the town is occupied by the Allies. They and their values have no place in a brutal and stupid world, a realization finally shared by their adopted "king" who deserts his job as the keeper of carrier pigeons (to whom he reads Shakespeare) and joins the inmates in the "insane asylum."

By far the richest and most concentrated use of the wise fool figure is that in Erasmus's *Praise of Folly* (1511). In a lengthy monologue Folly claims all life as her province. "The whole of life," she asserts, "is nothing but the sport of folly"; she is the "source and seed of existence." Despite her "divine" status, she admits that no temples have been raised to her, nor is there any formal worship of her. But she crows that she has no need of these things since "the entire world is my temple," and "I'm worshipped with truest devotion when all men everywhere take me to their hearts, express me in their habits, and reflect me in their way of life—as in fact they do." In a satiric imitation of the classical encomium, she establishes her birth, upbringing, and early companions, all of which are either disreputable, undesirable, or at least suspect. She is the daughter of Plutus, the blind god of wealth; she was suckled by Drunkenness, daughter of Bacchus, and Ignorance, daughter of Pan; and her boon companions are Philautia, or self-love, and Kolokia, or flattery, among others. She praises those who are dominated by instinct, committed to ignorance, and stoned on illusions. For these she is the "true bestower of 'good things,' called STULTITIA in Latin, MORIA in Greek" (sec. 4).

But Folly's praise is not only for the seven deadly sins and other traditional pleasures of the flesh and society. She praises men and women from all walks of life, hunters and their rituals, gamblers and their superstitions, hack writers and their vanities, lawyers, statesmen, scholars, and merchants. Folly's comments on the theologians are closer to sarcastic attack than to mock praise, and the last part of her monologue fluctuates among passages of direct praise, direct attack, and exhortation. The last part especially becomes a plea for the folly that comes from the Pauline commandment that Christians be fools for Christ. This is not the kind of conduct that Folly had praised earlier, but for Erasmus it is the true folly, so that the irony becomes not the irony of mock praise, but the irony of discrepancy between the ideal and the real. Men everywhere have not taken Paul's plea into their hearts, expressed it in their habits, or reflected it in their way of life, as earlier Folly had claimed men do for the false folly. In the conclusion of her speech, Folly recognizes that she has veered sharply away, has even done a complete turnabout from her original approach, for she says, "I've long been forgetting who I am," and concludes with the command to her "distinguished initiates of FOLLY" to "clap [their] hands, live and drink," thereby putting on again the mask of the fool.

If there has been any question about the character of Folly (and apparently there was in Erasmus's time, as indicated by his famous letter to Martin Dorp, rector of the University of Louvain, who wished Erasmus to answer his *Praise of Folly* with a Praise of Wisdom), the conclusion should remove any doubt that she is a wise fool.

Folly had noted at one point in her speech the practice of kings keeping fools who are encouraged to speak the truth. She praised Democritus, the laughing philosopher, and quoted Horace concerning the fact that truth and laughter are not mutually exclusive. Horace, Erasmus, and others who have believed that humor and truth may be yoked have run the risk, as does the wise fool, of being misunderstood, since truth and humor are generally seen as separate from, even antagonistic to each other. There remains for the puzzled the question, where does one leave off and the other begin? Unfortunately, the English language can offer only the oxymoronic "wise fool" as a way of capturing the unitary power of truth and laughter, of foolishness and wisdom.

Numerous characters and personas of the wise fool as Eiron have flourished among the satirists and humorists of the United States. The widespread presence of such types from Ben Franklin to Art Buchwald suggests that it may be one of the distinguishing features of the humor of the Republic. A somewhat pale and toothless version of the wise fool can be seen in Will Rogers, although there is no doubt that Rogers's typical pose produces an Eiron character. Physically his role was that of a Western cowboy with a wide-brimmed, well-worn slouch hat, bandanna neckerchief, and worn, relaxed trousers. As he confided to his audience, he chewed gum and occasionally did tricks with a lasso. His pose was that of a common man, or, as he styled himself, "an old country boy." Grammar and he got along as well as a "Russian and a bathtub." His acquaintance with fiction consisted of reading the newspaper, which, he claimed in one of his most famous statements, was the source of all he knew. In fact, he said, "I don't make jokes, I just watch the Government and report the facts and I have never found it necessary to exaggerate."

His disclaimers, his aw-shucks modesty, his slouch, all worked to disarm his audience and make them receptive to his jokes at the expense of the persons and issues of the 1920s and 1930s— Coolidge, Lindbergh, Prohibition, the Depression, and both houses of Congress. Few were fooled by the pose, which was probably not too distant from the real Will Rogers in any case. But the ruse allowed him to catch the contradictions, hypocrisies, and other absurdities of political and social life of the time and hold them up to the light of common sense and the traditional values and prejudices of persons like himself. His message was rarely revolutionary or even very disturbing, although he spoke out for the victims of the Depression, a safe subject since so many were affected by that spectacular economic dislocation. He shared and voiced the skepticisms and sentimentalities of his audience, which believed him when he encapsulated this contradiction in "I joked about every prominent man of my time, but I never met a man I didn't like" (qtd. in Brown). Rogers exemplified a type that is as old as humor and satire on the shores of North America, the effaced or unpretentious or ordinary person whose straight-faced or deadpan delivery takes the edge off comments that under other circumstances might wound or unsettle an audience. Such a pose served well on occasion the satiric purposes of Franklin and Twain, and more recently Harry Golden and Art Buchwald.

If there is an element of mock innocence in the Eiron of Will Rogers, a single turn of the screw produces another indigenous type, the Eiron as victim. Variously described as "the little man" or "the little soul," the victim is unable to cope successfully with life, whether it comes in the form of the Post Office in the case of Robert Benchley, a to-be-assembled toy in the case of S. J. Perelman, sex in the case of Woody Allen, or a Tupperware party in the case of Erma Bombeck. Bombeck is closest to the "average" person in her pose as suburban housewife harried by crabgrass, real estate salespeople, stray dogs, and station wagons. Like Rogers she denies any special talent: "I live my books 90% of the time, and write the other 10%. But I don't make them up—I'm always observing" (qtd. in John Baker, 9). But anyone who turns out a successful syndicated newspaper column and more than half a dozen equally successful books is no victim; nor was Robert Benchley, whose career included editing, writing, speaking, and acting, among other related activities. Woody Allen's career began as a comic writer for TV shows, moved into performing as a stand-up comic, turned to acting, writing, and directing for films, all the while turning out comic sketches and books, all activities that hardly suggest the biography of a victim.

Perelman's career is no less varied than that of Benchley and Allen, and it is equally as successful. Beginning as a mediocre cartoonist, he moved into a full-blown career with several early Marx Brothers movies and nearly two dozen books beginning with *Dawn Ginsberg's Revenge* in 1929 and ending with *Eastward Ha!* in 1978. Yet the role each adopted in his or her writings and other productions was that of a victim, inept physically, poorly adjusted psychologically, put upon by nearly everything and everyone they are forced to deal with, thwarted in their desires and aspirations, figures whose plight mirrors an aspect of the lives of millions of inhabitants of the United States in the twentieth century. The image of self-deprecation is ideal for producing laughter at the expense of the victim, and so these four who play the role of victim are primarily humorists rather than satirists. Openly fighting back is not one choice available to them by virtue of their roles, but reducing their problems and tormentors to absurdity or escaping into fantasy can be forms of fending off problems, and so these are the reverse side of the role of victim that they tend to adopt. They retreat only as far as their common sense and basic integrity allow them. Against the advances and blandishments of advertising, cultural snobbery, suburbia, intellectual faddism, and other excesses of the last half century of life in the United States, they offer a zany interpretation of reality that ultimately makes more sense (or is it less sense?) than the original. In "My Speech to the Graduates," Allen addresses the "predicament of modern man . . .: How is it possible to find meaning in a finite world given my waist and shirt size?" Like Benchley in "How to Understand International Finance" who approaches high finance in terms of a family budget, Allen sees cosmic questions in terms of his personal problems. Perelman has the same kind of sanity and integrity, opposing "bombast, conceit, pedantry, and strutting pomposity," as he backhandedly describes his own books in the introduction to *The Best of Perelman.*

In *Aunt Erma's Cope Book, or How to Get from Monday to Friday . . . in 12 Days,* overexposure to self-help books produces no improvement in biorhythms and a large dose of boredom—with herself. "If I never hear another word about me it will be too soon. . . . If I ever say the words, 'share with you,' or 'at this point of time in my life,' I hope my saliva runs dry." She discovers that she is not permitted to get depressed nor to age. Each of these writers presents a persona that is attempting to protect and maintain an individuality against an encroaching world. The most effective way to do so is to pretend to be its victim but at the same time to fight back through language, absurdity, and common sense, thereby keeping that individuality inviolable. This role is by no means the only strategy for humor and satire which these writers adopt, but it is the main technique by which they are readily identified, a version of the Eiron.

Eiron characters in the literature of the United States often tend to be marginals, socially and mentally. Polly Baker and Edith Bunker seem to share very little in the way of values and behavior, although both are to different degrees and in different ways sexually exploited. But Polly Baker in Franklin's famous hoax is able to turn that exploitation against the exploiters, her speech being a classic statement against the sexual double standard. Although she appears naive, she seems slowly to have learned the truth of her helplessness and the ability to use it and other arguments against the conventions and her exploiters. Similarly, Edith Bunker is able to use her status as "dingbat" in the eyes of her husband, Archie, to undercut him and his usually troglodytic ideas. The extent to which Polly and Edith are conscious of their innocent deviousness is difficult to say, but the discrepancy between the face they present and the results they achieve is a strategy for satirizing ideas used by Franklin and the writers of the *All in the Family* series alike.

Other American marginals may be on the edges of mainstream society socially, racially, or physically. Mark Twain's Jim Baker has spent so much time alone, alone, that is, as regards other humans, that he has departed slightly from his normal faculties. He believes that birds and other animals talk to each other and that he can distinguish them by their facility with language. Their behavior is suspiciously like that of human beings as well. He enjoys total identification with his nonhuman neighbors, further evidence that his mental equilibrium is not all it should be. But in fact his blue jay yarn reveals such "chuckleheaded" behavior that the animal-human identification becomes totally acceptable and what on one hand appears to be sheer idiocy becomes on the other satiric insight into human stubbornness and stupidity.

Similarly, Langston Hughes's Jesse B. Semple (generally referred to as plain Simple) lives a marginal existence in New York City's Harlem, troubled by lack of money, too many women, omnipresent landlords, and assorted do-gooders, politicians, and bureaucrats. Hughes endows Simple with some of the characteristics and behavior bestowed on all blacks by bigots, such as womanizing, rioting, and lack of education. For Hughes the last two are part of the proletariat heritage of many urban blacks, the first a convention that is more cliché than a mark of racial distinctiveness. But out of his racial heritage Simple has learned skepticism, clarity of vision, and what may be called defensive fantasy, an ability to conceive of a black "nude-out" designed to force Americans "to scrutinize our cause" ("Pose-Outs" in *Simple's Uncle Sam* [1965]), or to picture a segregated planet Moon unless there are black astronauts ("The Moon" in *Simple's Uncle Sam*). But above all Simple is a survivor, having been, as he describes it, "laid off, fired, and not rehired, Jim Crowed, segregated, insulted, eliminated, locked in, locked out, locked up, left holding the bag, and denied relief." But through it all he maintains an optimism or at least a hopeful simplicity, not a simple-minded simplicity but a simplicity that cuts through hypocrisy, stupidity, and all expressions of racism. "Me, I speaks simpler myself," he once says to his friend Boyd, his interlocutor, who is college educated and speaks without a street dialect. When Boyd points out that sometimes simplicity may be more devious than learning, Simple anwers, "Of course" ("Concernments" in *Simple's Uncle Sam*). His simple rejoinder implies that his simplicity is an acquired characteristic. Simple can be seen then as a wise fool in the true sense of the word.

Another socially marginal character who would never have shown much sympathy for Simple's predicaments but who shares with Simple a discerning dislike for hypocrisy and vanity is Sut Lovingood, the central character of mid-nineteenth century stories by George Washington Harris. Lovingood revels in being a "nat'ral born durn'd fool" with a talent for coarse and cruel practical jokes. Some of his humor is directed at people he doesn't like, and it is calculated to get even. But some is directed at figures of authority, sheriffs, lawyers, preachers, and parsons, people who not only bedevil him but also exhibit more than their fair share of hypocrisy and vanity, making them vulnerable to this latter-day trickster. Although his jokes seem at times like a combination of the fantasy-like violence of modern animated cartoons and the irrelevant ingenuity of Rube Goldberg creations, his redneck view of society is not without some validity (the satirist's view of society is after all only one possible view). No one, least of all Lovingood, would deny that he is a fool. But if it is possible to imagine a perverse kind of wisdom born of deprivation and alienation, then Sut also qualifies as a wise fool.

All of these made-in-America Eirons play a role, consciously or otherwise. Some play the fool, others play the victim. Whatever their public role, it allows them to point out the lapses, quirks, and faults of society, generating along the way humor and irony. In any case, they illustrate a variety of wise fool, whether they are labeled full, semi-, demi-, hemi-, or quasi.

Another kind of Eiron is the picaro or rogue, an ideal although by no means inevitable strategy for satire. He is in the first place mobile, unable or unwilling to stay in one place very long. He exists, moreover, on the underside of society, usually as a servant, involved in crime to a greater or lesser degree, or otherwise making his way in a catch-as-catch-can manner. Living by his wits and wiles means developing a detachment so that he can evaluate his master and his circumstances and act to his best advantage. This detachment may lead to satiric observations, "a stance," according to Robert Alter, "easy to adopt in the picaresque situation," but "not an absolutely necessary characteristic of the picaresque hero" (15). The rogue becomes, whether by force of circumstances or force of character, an Eiron, his destiny to manipulate his often *alazon* masters in order to survive or, if lucky, to flourish. Lesage's Gil Blas and Thomas Mann's Felix Krull are such Eirons, although neither comes from the severely deprived background and circumstance that produce such picaresque characters as Lazaro in *Lazarillo de Tormes,* Pablos in Quevedo's *La Vida de Buscon,* or Simplicissimus in Grimmelshausen's novel of the same name.

Gil Blas's parents are respectable, and an uncle provides him with an opportunity for a limited education. Felix's father is a champagne manufacturer who lived the good life which Felix partakes of until his father commits suicide following the collapse of his wine business. Both Felix and Gil are clever, intelligent, ambitious, yet in a very special sense innocent, or at least simple. Except for his service as secretary for the Duke of Lerma, Gil Blas remains an essentially decent and honorable person even though he pretends to be otherwise with the band of robbers who capture him, with Doctor Sangrado, and with the fop Don Matthias. Which is not to say that he is unsullied. He robs, his patients die, and he imitates his foppish employer, but he never sees his masters for anything other than they are. This doubleness of vision allows Lesage to satirize through irony various elements in the social structure (Carson). Like other Eirons Gil Blas becomes a satiric butt when he panders and plunders in the service of the Duke of Lerma, becoming as greedy and corrupt as those he once served. But generally Gil Blas keeps his distance from those around him so that at times he is an ironist himself (Alter, 18; Bjornson, 217), as when he describes how he attempts to maintain his dignity as a "doctor" despite his wearing a cloak that is too long and a doublet and hose that are too big.

While Gil Blas dissembles in order to survive and prosper, Felix Krull performs his roles because illusion is for him a superior reality. Felix was rarely what he appeared to be, not unlike his father's wine. Called Loreley Extra Cuvee, it was dispensed in bottles sealed with silver wire, gold cords, and purple wax and bore a label full of coats of arms, gilt lettering, and a monogram. But it was in fact such bad wine that the champagne company reeled into bankruptcy. So Felix was rarely what he appeared to be, feigning epilepsy in order to avoid military service, working as an elevator boy while living the life of a man about town, or passing himself off as the Marquis de Venosta on a world tour. Felix's single-minded dedication to, at times obsession with, the truth of illusion keeps him detached from the sordidness and decadence around him even when he is part of it, detached as an artist who incorporates or rationalizes everything for his own purposes. An "infinitely plastic creature" (the phrase is Alter's), Felix literally becomes anything he wishes to become, thereby serving as a foil against which Mann plays off a variety of characters who reveal themselves in all their vanity and pride: Diane Philibert, wealthy and famous writer whose joy is to be sexually humiliated by athletic young men; Professor Kuckuck, paleontologist and director of a museum who is completely taken in by the image of nobility projected by Felix and spends the evening telling his eager listener his nihilistic theory of existence.[4] Mann's portraits are very Horatian, allowing his characters to reveal themselves to a credulous, cooperative, and eager-to-please Felix, producing thereby "polished, whimsical satire" (Apter, 122). Despite his service as confidence man as foil for satire, Felix reveals directly in his narrative that above all he is his own best (or worst) victim. When he indulges in petty thievery from a candy store, he does not deny that he is a thief but says only that "I will simply retreat and not confront anyone who chooses to take the paltry word into his mouth," implying that somehow his doing it endows the act with a fine significance that separates it from similar acts. Sexual desire he labels "the great joy," finding desire preferable to its enervating satisfaction. Later, when presented with Professor Kuckuck's philosophy of cosmic meaninglessness, he experiences again "The Great Joy, a secret formula of my innocence used at first to denote something special, not otherwise nameable, but soon endowed with an intoxicating breadth of significance," the longing for which kept him in his own words, "my whole life long a child and a dreamer." And an excellent Eiron for Mann's satire. His role as an eager military recruit with a supposed history of epilepsy allows Mann to satirize doctors and the military. Felix's description of how he and the audience are transported by an actor, Müller-Rosé, incredibly impeccable and handsome on the stage but sweaty and pimple-covered backstage, satirizes the gullibility and vacuity of an image-worshipping public. But Felix is so caught up in his own perception and understanding of these things that his mind is incapable of being violated by satiric irony. Diane Philibert likens Felix to Hermes, the patron of thieves, although she is not aware at the moment how fitting the name is. She is thinking rather of Felix's shapely legs which remind her of Praxiteles' famous statue of Hermes. Felix has never heard of Hermes, and he later introduces the name gratuitously into his conversation with Professor Kuckuck, who, taken aback by the reference, tries, without much success, to make some sense of the matter. Although it is appropriate that Felix, the master impersonator-thief, be associated with his Greek patron god, it is ironic that he be associated with a god whose identifying symbol is the phallus. Although Felix idealized the desire for sex, he was always the sought-after, the instructed, the seduced rather than the aggressor. Sexual activity for Felix was to be husbanded even though he was never a husband, or a father. In short, Felix is a somewhat tame version of his patron god, although in other respects he is a fitting protégé of the ancient trickster.

Mann's identification of Felix with the mythic trickster can be extended to many Eirons already discussed, although it would be inappropriate to identify the trickster solely with the Eiron. But certainly the trickster was a master at dissembling as is the Eiron, and both occupy the same territory on the fringes of society and view it with a similarly disrespectful and cavalier attitude. Since there is danger in the territory and risk in the attitude, the Eiron prefers to dissemble regarding his true attitude, and out of this discrepancy comes the irony that is typical of the true Eiron.

The Iconoclast. Ambrose Bierce, Lord Byron, Charles Churchill, Karl Kraus, Duc de La Rochefoucauld, Mary Mc-Carthy, H. L. Mencken, and Oscar Wilde. In background, talent, and literary reputation a varied group, but sharing the use of the persona of the Iconoclast to express irony in their satires. Unlike the Eiron and the Ingenu in whom and through whom irony is created indirectly, the Iconoclast is the ironist directly and designedly so. Irony is a basic weapon in the armory of the

Iconoclast, a weapon that he or she cannot dispense with and perform the duties of the Iconoclast. Iconoclasts come in various forms, literary characters, and public figures, but more usually and importantly as personae, personae that range from those that are fully conceived and acknowledged to others that are barely, poorly, or often not recognized.

For the Iconoclast as persona immediately raises again the question of the validity of the concept of the persona itself.[5] With some of the writers mentioned above, Bierce, La Rochefoucauld, Mencken, for example, little attention has been paid to the possibility that each may have been writing through a persona. With others there is uneasiness about the nature of the persona or a lack of understanding of the role and kind of persona involved. Admittedly, the line between the writer and his or her persona is not always easy to set down. In fact, to assume that writer and persona are totally different would hardly be valid. They may be separate, but they will overlap and have characteristics in common. On the other hand, what may be part of the actual personality of a writer may have little or no place in a persona created for a special purpose. The persona will likely be as much a caricature as most other characters in satire. Thus Mencken has puzzled and disappointed those admirers who have attempted to find coherence and consistency in his persona and his writings. His unsavory ideas regarding Jews, Germans, and the United States government expressed during World War II strained his relationship with the upper echelons of his employers at the Baltimore *Sunpapers* and are difficult to reconcile with James Farrell's report of him during the same period as "courteous, friendly, genial," carrying no grudges, and frequently helping writers with whom he disagreed (55).

Karl Kraus presents an equally dramatic case. The lyrical and idealistic Kraus revealed in his love letters to Didonie Borutin is very much at odds with the satirist-editor of *The Torch*. For the thirty-seven years between the decline of the Hapsburgs at the end of the nineteenth century and the rise of National Socialism in the 1930s Kraus savagely attacked the follies and crimes of Austria and his countrymen. Or as Harry Zohn (19) notes, "In his private life, Kraus was, by most accounts, kindly, uncomplicated, natural, and charming rather than egocentric, petty, or irascible."

The question of the connection between the persona-satirist and the writer is not a new one, as Maynard Mack, Alvin Kernan, and

others discussed it some years ago. Even longer ago, La Rochefoucauld noted in his *Maximes* that

> On all occasions we assume the look and appearance we
> want to be known for, so that the world in general is a
> congregation of masks. (256)

Byron in *Don Juan,* or at least his persona, proclaims the very idea
in

> 'Life's a poor player,' —then 'play out the play,
> Ye villains!' and above all keep a sharp eye
>   Much less on what you do than what you say:
> Be hypocritical, be cautious, be
> Not what you *seem,* but always what you *see.*
>
> (11, 86)

Delacroix, the Romantic painter and admirer of Byron, says in his
diary, "I have two or three, perhaps four friends, but I am forced
to be a different man with each of them, or rather, to show each the
side of my nature which he understands. It is one of the saddest
things in life that we can never be completely known and
understood by any one man."

Role playing and the concept of the "real self" have been raised
to serious psychological and philosophical concerns since the times
of La Rochefoucauld, Byron, and Delacroix. But despite that and
the fact that La Rochefoucauld shows awareness of the phenomenon in other maxims (81, 233, 289), he himself is not the least of
those who continue to suffer from commentators' failing to suspect
that the voice of the speaker of the *Maximes* may not be exactly the
man La Rochefoucauld. One commentator notes the differences
between La Rochefoucauld's *Réflexions Diverses* and his *Maximes,*
the former "relaxed, not at all cynical, and much more positive
than the *Maximes. . . ,* written with a studied moderation . . . and
understatement" (Moore, 107–8), a difference that hints at, if it
does not prove, the possibility of a persona lurking somewhere in
La Rochefoucauld's sophisticated and justly admired artistry.

Nor does the case of Oscar Wilde contribute to the unsnarling of
the author-persona problem. A famous mocker of social mores and
behavior in his own person, Wilde also created in his four comedies
a series of characters who share his unconventional and iconoclastic
conversational profligacy. Whether this is an example of life

imitating art or vice versa is something commentators of Wilde
have yet to agree upon. There is less uncertainty about Wilde's ca-
pacities as a poseur, although its relationship to some "real self" is
less settled, and probably never will be to everybody's satisfaction.

The critic's task would be less irksome if writers were conscious
and clear in their use of a persona, but that is asking of writers what
critics probably do not ask of themselves and their writing.
Humphry Osmond, clinical professor of psychiatry, has said that
"the normal person can, at very high speed, adopt the role that
others expect. Much of one's social assessment entails perceiving
and judging the role and allowing other people to assume their role
with you" (qtd. in Collins). With the Iconoclast (and with much
satire in general) the failure of the audience to perceive the role and
react appropriately is at the root of much misunderstanding and ill
feeling directed at the Iconoclast. For the closer a piece of writing
is to the direct conveyance of facts, opinions, and ideas, which is to
say reporting, reviewing, criticism, and other nonfictive writing,
the less apparent is the presence of a persona. Bierce's dictionary
entries, La Rochefoucauld's and Kraus's epigrams, Mary Mc-
Carthy's criticism would seem to be the direct expression of their
authors, hot from the "real self," no fiction involved. Yet if it is
valid for B. F. Skinner, the behaviorist psychologist, to speak of
"two or more selves, in the sense of congeries of responses," from
which a "real you" is built up in a particular environment
("Notebooks"), how much more valid is it to speak of a persona
for a writer, a satirist, who is attempting to entertain or to persuade
or both, working within the boundaries and means of that
particular art.

The tendency to confuse the art of the satirist with the writer's
life and times is seemingly inherent in satire itself, especially in the
symbiotic relationship between the works and times of a Mencken,
a Kraus or a McCarthy, for it is with such writers as these that
failing to recognize or consider the possible presence of a persona
causes reviewers and other commentators to react, often overreact,
to the wrong elements in the works. Biographers of both Mencken
and Kraus have fallen into the trap and have reacted in the same
way. Douglas Stenerson attempts to reconcile Mencken's persona
with some "real" Mencken by calling part of chapter 1 of his study
"Loving and Loathing American Life." Harry Zohn actually calls
chapter 1 in his study of Kraus "A Life Between Love and Hate."

More recently, however, Edward Timms has traced in detail the development of Kraus's concept of a persona, revealing the decisive influence of Oscar Wilde in that development (part 3). But for the most part, when commentators should be considering a satirist's art, they are instead uncovering contradictions and attacking or apologizing for what they perceive as the "real" person, someone in fact as fictional as the persona that they failed to perceive in the first place. When the writer fails to project a clear sense of a persona, as seems to be the case with Mencken and Kraus, and when the writer is so deeply involved in the controversies of his time as to arouse strong reactions, as again with Mencken and Kraus, the more difficult it is for commentators to see or at least acknowledge that the writer is or might be playing a role. When, as with Iconoclasts, the art is redolent of irony, skepticism, or cynicism, it is difficult indeed not to focus on opinions and ideas and easy to ignore the art of the satire.

The aggressive spirit of the Iconoclast tends also to evoke a pugnacious reaction. Such a spirit is basic to much satire, perhaps all, but for the Iconoclast it is a mark of distinction. Satirists may attack their targets from bases of varying presuppositions, but the Iconoclast, as distinguished here, is not any ordinary satirist. Some satirists, for example, may attack those who degrade and misuse what in society is good and venerable, as Juvenal does in his Third Satire when he sees Rome becoming Hellenized, or as Erasmus does in *The Praise of Folly,* or as Waugh does to what he sees as barbaric forces at work in modern England. Neoclassical satire, on the other hand, as W. H. Auden reminds us, "owes allegiance to certain eternal laws that are known to human reason and conscience; its purpose is to demonstrate that the individual violates these laws out of presumption, malice, or stupidity" ("Life," 135). For still other satirists their own times may represent a falling off from some former golden age. But over and against such satirists are those for whom the traditional, the conventional, the venerated, the eternal, restrict, entrap, entomb and so represent a threat to freedom and a richer reality. Or to quote Auden again, such satire, and he calls it "Byronic" satire, is the "weapon of the rebel who refuses to accept conventional laws and pieties as binding or worthy of respect. . . . It speaks in the name of the individual whose innocence of vision has not been corrupted by education and social convention."

In short, the Iconoclast contradicts the bromide that all satirists are conservatives. Hence he is neither the *vir bonum* described by Maynard Mack nor the "satirist" of Alvin Kernan. The former, "stable, independent, urbane, wise," is guided by "personal moral insight" (Mack, 200). The "satirist," in all ways as moral as the *vir bonum,* tends on the other hand to be more homely, less urbane, and burdened by a private personality that could undercut his public figure if revealed (Kernan, 258–59). Needless to say, the Iconoclast is at the opposite end of the spectrum from the Ingenu, one simple, the other complicated, one innocent or unknowing, the other sophisticated, witty, and skeptical (Feinberg, *Introduction,* 239–40). Neither does he dissemble as the Eiron, nor does he have a hidden side to his character as the "satirist." Despite differences in degree of forcefulness and uses of irony, audiences seldom have trouble recognizing what the Iconoclast stands for, what judgments are being made. To hide anything or equivocate would be contrary to the spirit that makes the Iconoclast what he is.

Despite the cognomen Iconoclast, this character is no simple-minded mauler, laying about indiscriminately. Icons may be destroyed on the altar with bludgeons or from a distance quietly with a sharpshooting rifle. Either method works. So unanimity in method of attack does not distinguish the Iconoclast. What Iconoclasts share is the status of being outsiders in their societies, of being suspected, rejected, reviled even, for seeing and saying things about their societies that are unwelcome. Iconoclasts share a special facility with their language and compound this with a special interest in the use of the language that is unique among virtually any literary characters, let alone satiric types. And finally they display an attitude that is marked by irony, skepticism, and cynicism about the values of their society and the behavior that such values give rise to. All Iconoclasts may not display each of these characteristics to the same degree, but the traits are present in all Iconoclasts. Such characteristics may be present in other satiric or literary types, but the Iconoclast is unique in the traits he or she combines and in his or her stance and preoccupations. The persona of *Don Juan* and the pose of Oscar Wilde portray to some degree the figure of the dandy, although the dandy is not necessarily an Iconoclast. Flashes of the railer, the misanthrope, the rogue, the man of the world, and the honest man *(honnête homme)* may also appear in the Iconoclast from time to time (Kronenberger, *Polished;*

Stanton; Godfrey). Again none of these is synonymous with the Iconoclast who is above all else his or her own person.

For the Iconoclast is first of all an outsider, although this is not to imply that the Iconoclast is an outcast or pariah; he or she is just never completely at home in society. The Iconoclast obviously has reservations about his or her society and is not shy about voicing them often and forcefully. Bierce, Churchill, Byron, Kraus, La Rochefoucauld, McCarthy, Mencken, and Wilde: all of them for their personae have suffered the slings and arrows of outraged society. Mencken's *Schlimpflexikon,* a collection of verbal blasts directed at the "Baltimore Bad Boy," memorializes reactions to his differences with the verities of society at large. La Rochefoucauld's epigrams stirred strong reactions, causing him to cancel some of them for the second edition. Mme de Sevigne referred to him, perhaps in jest, perhaps not, as "ce chien de Barbin" (Barbin was the publisher of the *Maximes*), but there was no ambiguity in the *Maximes* themselves being called "galimatias," that is, balderdash, a word that dismayed La Rochefoucauld (17).

Quite apart from stating unwanted and unwelcomed truths about society, the Iconoclast tends to hand them down, adopting an attitude of superiority that clearly does not endear him or her to an audience. La Rochefoucauld was by birth the "grand seigneur," but his piercing insight into the coils of human motivation make him appear haughty, not to say cynical, in his view of his society. Less exalted but nevertheless a position endowed with authority and remove is Bierce's role as lexicographer. Invested with the authority given by society to the dictionary, Bierce pronounced a series of demonic definitions that cut through the hypocrisy and stupidity of many widely accepted truths. Doris Grumbach speaks of Mary McCarthy as a "displaced person, the 'stranger to this ground,' orphaned, excluded, the Westerner come East, the Catholic among Protestants, the end girl of the rooming group, the American abroad. Despite this, she makes very little effort to gain acceptance except on her own strict terms" (215; Trouard). Charles Churchill "presents himself as a solitary figure of righteous opposition," according to Thomas Lockwood in his *Post-Augustan Satire* (45).

The Iconoclast also sets himself or herself apart by being an individualist. The ultimate good for the Iconoclast is the individual inviolate. Any group or institution that attempts to thwart the individual makes an enemy of the Iconoclast. For Karl Kraus it was the military and the established church; for Mary McCarthy, it is intellectuals (as in *The Oasis*), the "sensibility school" of women writers, and the literary establishment; for Mencken it was the "booboisie," "school marms," and fundamentalist religion, all variations of "mobocracy." The persona of the "satirist" seeks the public, the social good, according to Kernan, despite the possible threat that he poses. As a magician without portfolio, the "satirist" serves society by exposing and scourging those who would dissolve social ties and undercut social efficiency.

For the Iconoclast the emphasis is reversed, the individual good taking precedence over the immediate social good. This attitude was expressed perhaps most dramatically in Oscar Wilde's concept of art and society embodied in himself and some of his characters as dandies. For them art is the supreme value since it gives form to the crass and chaotic society around them. The public figure that Wilde presented was perhaps his greatest creation, the dandy, the cynic, the wit, the sinner, a kind of monster that finally destroyed itself. What else Wilde was beyond this pose and how any other self or selves related to the public role have always troubled Wilde's biographers and critics. There must be something else, they say, but the nagging question has been what and how that else is. In Wilde the persona dominates, and because it is a role it is rejected or at least questioned as the "real" Wilde. At the heart of the trouble is the unwillingness of the commentators to accept Wilde's disenchantment with the world, his belief that life is merely the stuff of art. Where and how such an idea fits into some overall pattern of Wilde's thought is open to endless discussion, but that it is to some degree part of the public pose is not. Wilde's paradoxical attitude toward the frauds and follies of Victorian society, his witty inversions of the accepted values of his times, and his glorification of art without conventional morals indicate that individual form was more important than social mores and conventions, the pose more important than the audience, the playing more important than the message. Aesthetic judgments replace moral judgments, individual expression overrides social coherence (Ganz; McCormack).

Equally as dramatic as Wilde's espousal of individualism is that of the persona of *Don Juan,* although the word persona hardly does justice to Byron's creation. At the least there is, according to Leslie

Marchand, the "author, embodying whatever fictional character or persona we may wish to ascribe to him, certainly . . . the dominant character in the poem [who] endows it with its chief interest and value" (42). Beyond that there is virtual chaos because *Don Juan* is one of those poems so rich in content and imagery that readers seem sometimes to discover and reveal as much about themselves as they do about the poem, thereby reducing the chances for a reasonable consensus. The narrator, of course, keeps the reader off balance in such statements as

> Few men dare show their thought of worst or best;
> Dissimulation always sets apart
> A corner for herself; and, therefore, Fiction
> Is that which passes with least contradiction.
>
> (15, 3)

and

> Of all the Muses that I recollect,
>   Whate'er may be her follies or her flaws
> In some things, mine's beyond all contradiction
> The most sincere that ever dealt in fiction.
>
> (16, 2)

But of his individualism there is no doubt. He says,

> And I will war, at least in words (and—should
>   My chance so happen—deeds), with all who war
> With Thought;—and of Thought's foes by far most rude,
>   Tyrants and sycophants have been and are.
> I know not who may conquer: if I could
>   Have such a prescience, it should be no bar
> To this my plain, sworn, downright detestation
> Of every despotism in every nation.
>   . . . —I wish men to be free
> As much from mobs as kings—from you as me.
>
> The consequence is, being of no party,
>   I shall offend all parties:
>
> (9, 24–26)

He even provides an excellent image of the individualist as outsider:

Thrice happy he who, after a survey
  Of the good company, can win a corner,
A door that's *in* or boudoir out of the way,
  Where he may fix himself like small 'Jack Horner,'
And let the Babel round run as it may,
  And look on as a mourner, or a scorner,
Or an approver, or a mere spectator,
Yawning a little as the night grows later.

                              (11, 69)

A century later, far removed from the aristocratic world of Byron, Mencken in the *American Mercury* expressed his own brand of individualism by identifying with a "maverick and outlaw strain" in American life which caused "certain men [to] find the restraints of what is called Christian civilization unbearable, and break into insurrection against it" (Mencken and Nathan, "Hero," 126; the sentiments are Mencken's, despite the dual byline.) In the first number of the magazine Mencken pictures himself as an iconoclast who "by his blasphemy that this or that idol is defectively convincing—[will cause] . . . at least *one* visitor to the shrine [to be] left full of doubts" (Mencken's emphasis) (Mencken and Nathan, "Clinical," 75). Thus the readers of the *Mercury* were encouraged to think of themselves as an elite who shared the editors' skepticism about American institutions and practices. Mencken's persona was a minority of one tuned to the phoniness of a stodgy plutocracy and the inanities of a herdlike "booboisie" (Yates, chap. 9).

The Iconoclast's role of outsider is strikingly reinforced by an attention-getting style and a special interest in the state of the language. The satirist's art is often marked by vividness in the devices and strategies of rhetoric, from the magical curse and *flyting* to the subtlest epigram or novel. But the pose of some "satirists," as Kernan notes, is that of a simple, plain, truthful, outspoken person without guile or art. Not so the Iconoclast. The Iconoclast is a conscious, assertive stylist, often reveling in his or her facility with the language. But more than being aggressive stylists, Iconoclasts may conceive of themselves as guardians of the language, a proprietary attitude based on the recognition that perversion of the language is the first resort of the knave.

It is no coincidence that the Iconoclasts are famous for their wit,

for being among the most quotable of writers. Kraus, La
Rochefoucauld, and Wilde are noted for their epigrams, and Bierce
in his *Devil's Dictionary* operates in adjacent territory. Byron and
McCarthy tend toward the epigrammatic in their styles, and
Mencken combines hyperbole, neologisms, figurative and allusive
language for a unique blend of invective. Charles Churchill
roughed up the polished heroic couplet perfected by Pope and
made it a device for his special brand of invective. Churchill and
Mencken are latter-day practitioners of the ancient art of *flyting,*
while other Iconoclasts polish and compress their words into
special combinations that have a magic about them that is part of
their memorableness.

The Iconoclast's idiosyncratic style asserts at its most basic level
his or her claim to individuality and status as an outsider. The
distinctiveness in choice of words, levels of diction, and imagery
are essential to the expression of the sometimes eccentric ideas and
opinions of the Iconoclast, reinforcing his or her individuality.
Their epigrams and their epigrammatic styles are designed to shock
audiences and to differentiate their creators from society and its
commonplaces. La Rochefoucauld understood the objections to his
startling and outrageous ideas when he said,

> What provokes so much objection to aphorisms that
> expose the human heart is our fear of being ourselves
> exposed in turn. (no. 524)

But the fears and objections of the audience rarely if ever inhibit
the Iconoclast. He unleashes the unwanted truth with wit and flair.
Thus La Rochefoucauld could write, "The subtlest folly is
fabricated of the subtlest wisdom" (no. 592). Kraus could
challenge political complacency with: "Democracy means the
permission to be everyone's slave." Wilde's stylistic trademark is
the outrageous epigram, such as, "The only thing that ever
consoles man for the stupid things he does is the praise he always
gives himself for doing them" *(In Conversations)*. Bierce's definitions are occasionally as compressed as any epigram: "Impunity, *n.*
Wealth," "White, *adj.* and *n.* Black." The style of Mencken, on the
other hand, while endlessly quotable, is built on a rich and allusive
vocabulary, a variety of verbal devices and the unique ability to
exaggerate and render absurd, as illustrated in the passage from the
blast at William Jennings Bryan in "WJB: In Memoriam":

Wherever the flambeau of chautauqua smoked and guttered, and the bilge of idealism ran in the veins, and Baptist pastors dammed the brooks with the sanctified, and men gathered who were weary and heavy laden, and their wives were full of Peruna and as fecund as shad (*Alosa sapidmissima*), there the indefatigable Jennings set up his traps and spread his bait.

Memories of a Catholic Girlhood, Mary McCarthy's look back in anger at her family and education, contains a number of descriptions of teachers and relatives, but none more pointed than that of one of her grandmothers:

An ugly, severe old woman with a monstrous balcony of a bosom, she officiated over certain set topics in a colorless singsong, like a priest intoning a Mass, topics to which repetition had lent a senseless solemnity: her audience with the Holy Father; how my own father had broken with family tradition and voted the Democratic ticket; a visit to Lourdes; the Sacred Stairs in Rome, bloodstained since the first Good Friday, which she had climbed on her knees; my crooked little finger and how that meant I was a liar; a miracle-working bone; the importance of regular bowel movements; the wickedness of Protestants; the conversion of my mother to Catholicism; and the assertion that my other grandmother must certainly dye her hair.

McCarthy's fondness for the ironic catalog and her cold eye for the reductive detail demonstrate why one commentator could call her a "conscious stylist of the first rank" (Grumbach, 215).

But the Iconoclast's style is not merely a way to show off, to get attention, or to keep an audience in its place. Iconoclasts often show an interest in and concern for the language that goes beyond the sensitivity that is generally assumed to be part of the make-up of most writers. Mencken's study of the American language is the best example of the Iconoclast's care for his medium. *The American Language,* first published in 1919, occupied Mencken for the rest of his life. His study reflected his delight in the American idiom used so cogently by Twain, Lardner, and humorists of the early twentieth century. Behind that idiom Mencken detected an

irreverence similar to his own. The term "rubber-neck" he said
was "almost a complete treatise on American psychology."

> It has in it precisely the boldness and disdain of ordered
> forms that are so characteristically American, and it has
> too the grotesque humor of the country, and the delight
> in devastating opprobriums, and the acute feeling for the
> succinct and the savory. (*American Language,* 19, 23)

Espousing the concept of an American language as opposed to *the*
English language was another way for Mencken to unsettle the
school marms of the Genteel Tradition, those of the literary and
academic establishments whose habitual tilt toward the language
and literature of the British Isles Mencken found untoward. But all
this was merely another way to right the imbalance in the
perception of reality dominated by an American Victorianism that
failed to acknowledge or even recognize a part of its own literary
and linguistic heritage. Mencken's linguistic nationalism was one
expression of his need to uncover what he saw as a diverted and
polluted branch of the American mainstream. Despite his mockery
of the mob, Mencken was a journalist who wrote to be understood, whatever the idiosyncrasies of his style might suggest. His
attacks on "Gamalielese" and other perversions of the tongue
indicate his concern with language that obscures and misleads. As
an Iconoclast then, he sought not only to capture the richness and
variety of his medium but also to avoid those disorders that inhibit
communications of ideas and opinions needed in what he saw as a
traditionally repressive culture.

What Mencken was attempting to do in the United States for its
language, Kraus was trying to do in Austria for the German
language. But Kraus's concern with his language sprang from a
mystical belief that trapped in the German language was a clarity
and rightness that could be discovered by dedicated writers who
would be unable therefore to utter the clichés and jargon that
burdened the conversation and writing of the time. Such linguistic
perversions were not merely inefficient, they were, for Kraus,
immoral. "My language is a common prostitute," he says in one of
his many aphorisms on language, "that I turn into a virgin." "The
German language is the deepest," he notes, "German speech the
shallowest." Unlike Mencken who found originality and vigor in
ordinary speech, Kraus saw only violations of some mythical

purity. "Heinrich Heine so loosened the corsets of the German language that today every little clerk can fondle her breasts," he claimed. In Kraus's epic, *The Last Days of Mankind,* a play of nearly two hundred scenes in almost eight hundred pages of printed text, he created numerous monologues to allow characters to reveal the amorality, the lack of feeling, the vulgarity, the banality that he saw all around him. The violence done to the German language was for Kraus at the heart of the breakdown of his times, a view similar to that argued by George Orwell regarding English during the period prior to World War II.

Also on the linguistic firing line of journalism among the Iconoclasts was Ambrose Bierce. Bierce, a columnist for various California newspapers, never suffered bad writing gladly. Bierce's "blacklist" of imprecise and improper usage in *Write It Right* (1909) aims at the "narrow etymons of the mere scholar and loose locutions of the ignorant . . . alike." In such essays as "Word Changes and Slang," "Writers of Dialect," and "For Brevity and Clarity," Bierce attacked sloppiness and imitativeness in literary writing. The use of artificial and phony dialects and the kind of pronunciation that Frank Sullivan was later to dub "Slurvian" found a harsh critic in Bierce. His strictures sound so dogmatic that Mencken attacked *Write It Right* as being "full of puerilities" for its advocacy of a "mere set of rules" that failed to recognize that "language is a living thing" (422). But Bierce in the *Devil's Dictionary* had also attacked the linguistically stultifying effect of the "Dictionary" by defining it as "a malevolent literary device for cramping the growth of a language and making it hard and inelastic."

As newspaper writers and magazine editors, Mencken, Kraus, and Bierce were sometimes close to but certainly always aware of the sources and forces that tended to corrupt their languages. But La Rochefoucauld, member of a closed and elite society, was equally as aware of the need for linguistic health. In "a society in which compliments were conjoined rapiers, in which men bowed suavely to one another at two o'clock and ruthlessly betrayed one another at four; and having participated in so dishonest a spectacle no less than observed it" (Kronenberger, *Polished,* 26), it is not surprising that the art of conversation be of great concern. "There are," he points out, "various airs, tones, and manners which often determine what is pleasing or displeasing, delicate or shocking in

conversation; few people possess the secret of using them."
Conversely, he says, "There are some people who, by a kind of
instinct of unexplained origin, . . . always make the right choice.
. . . In such people everything acts in concert. This harmony allows
them to make sound judgments and gives them a true idea of things"
(qtd. in Stanton, 140, 203). In his *Maximes* he puts it, "True
eloquence means saying all that is necessary and only what is
necessary" (250). Although expressed in the vocabulary of another
era, such sentiments suggest that La Rochefoucauld shared the
Iconoclastic concern for the state of the language and the way it
was managed.

But however varied their verbal mannerism or different their
attitudes toward their language, Iconoclasts share a regard for,
sensitivity to, and creative capacity for style in their use of language
that sets them apart from most other personae, satiric or other.
Their special styles are of course inseparable from their essential
and in some cases most characteristic attitude and satiric technique,
namely, irony and wit.

Satiric irony is a dangerous technique in any circumstance but
for the Iconoclast it is extra hazardous. As an outsider whose
standards and behavior put him or her at odds with society, the
Iconoclast is likely to be seen as a threat in any case. But wielding
a style that mocks and cuts is inviting the most violent kind of
reaction, total rejection. And for the most part this is what the
Iconoclast gets. At best he or she is accused of skepticism, of being
a doubter, a questioner, one who is unwilling to fall in line with
convention and tradition. That is the generous reaction to the
Iconoclast. At worst and most commonly he or she is accused of
cynicism. All Iconoclasts have had this label plastered on them.

One of the most famous attacks on an Iconoclast, although the
word cynic is only implicit throughout, is the *Blackwood's*
reviewer's reaction to *Don Juan*. Byron is described as a "cool,
unconcerned fiend, laughing with a detestable glee over the whole
of the better and worst elements of which human life is composed—treating well nigh with equal derision the most pure of
virtues, and the most odious of vices—dead alike to the beauty of
the one, and the deformity of the other—a mere heartless despiser
of that frail but noble humanity." Even though such a reaction may
seem beside the point, it is typical of what Iconoclasts are exposed
to. Mencken's *Schlimpflexikon* preserves the colorful and vitupera-

tive reaction to his equally colorful and vituperative ideas and opinions. Ambrose Bierce's name has become inseparable from the epithet "bitter" which all of his commentators dutifully report. La Rochefoucauld's insistence on the essential selfishness of much social behavior has similarly laid him open to the treatment commonly received by other Iconoclasts.

For most Iconoclasts the main technique for irony has been the shocking statement, the attention-getting device of pulling the rug out from under the audience, sometimes slowly, sometimes not, but in any case leaving the audience disoriented and threatened. The paradox, one such technique, turns up in a variety of forms. Some of Bierce's definitions in his *Devil's Dictionary* fall into that category. For example, "MARRIAGE, *n.* The state or condition of a community consisting of a master, a mistress and two slaves, making in all, two." Mary McCarthy in *Memories of a Catholic Girlhood* disingenuously (presumably) says, "I am driven to the conclusion that religion is only good for good people, and I do not mean this as a paradox, but simply as an observable fact. Only good people can afford to be religious. For the others, it is too great a temptation—a temptation to the deadly sins of pride and anger, chiefly, but one might also add sloth" (23). The very essence of the epigram as practiced by La Rochefoucauld is paradox, and his art is rich in antithesis and wordplay: "Our evildoing arouses less hate and persecution than our good qualities" (29). "To establish oneself in the world, one does all one can to seem established there already" (56). One of Wilde's techniques for shocking was the reworking of a cliché, turning it upside down or inside out: "If one tells the truth, one is sure, sooner or later, to be found out." "Work is the curse of the drinking class." "I live in terror of not being misunderstood." Kraus's paradoxes sometimes offend doubly, turning biblical quotations bottom side up: "Lord, forgive them, for they know what they do." "They judge lest they be judged." Like all good satirists, Iconoclasts insist on rubbing the audience's noses in the discrepancy between appearance and reality, in the fact that the king is unclothed. Since such discrepancies are presumably endless, the Iconoclast can agree with Mary McCarthy when she says that a paradox is eternal (B. McKenzie, 99).

Such verbal irony is typical of the Iconoclast, although it may not always take the precise form of the epigram or aphorism. Bierce's *Dictionary* is an anthology of satiric imitations with violated styles and content, misused forms, and disparate elements. He uses heroic diction and imagery to define "Abdomen," biblical style to define "Abnormal," a trivialized imitation of "Locksley Hall" to define "Weather" (Highsmith). Mencken and Churchill, unlike most Iconoclasts, favor invective more than irony, but both can deal in irony as a variation on their otherwise direct-attack technique. Mencken's favorite devices for irony are animal imagery and inappropriate diction. In "The Husbandman," his attack on the quasi-mythological status accorded the farmer in American life, Mencken concludes,

> What I sing, I suppose, is a sort of Utopia. But it is not the Utopia of bawdy poets and metaphysicians; it is not the familiar Utopia of the books. It is a Utopia dreamed by simpler and more virtuous men—by seven millions of Christian bumpkins, far-flung in forty-eight sovereign states. They dream it on their long journeys down the twelve billion furrows of their seven million farms, up hill and down dale in the heat of the day. They dream it behind the egg-stove on winter evenings, their boots off and their socks scorching, Holy Writ in their hands. They dream it as they commune with *Bos taurus, Sus scorfa, Mephitis mephisti,* the Methodist pastor, the Ford agent. It floats before their eyes as they scan the Sears-Roebuck catalogue for horse liniment, porous plaster and Bordeaux mixture; it rises before them when they assemble in their Little Bethels to be instructed in the word of God, the plots of the Pope, the crimes of the atheists and Jews; it transfigures the chautauquan who looms before them with his Great Message. This Utopia haunts and tortures them; they long to make it real. They have tried prayer, and it has failed; now they turn to the secular arm. The dung-fork glitters in the sun as the host prepares to march. . . .
>
> (*Chrestomathy,* 364)

Despite the surging parallelisms and the pretense of praising a Utopia of husbandmen, Mencken manages to undercut them with a felicitous choice of details, juxtaposing biblical and animal imagery, creating a rich verbal irony.

Churchill's irony comes from shifting from one role to another, varying his usual pose of oratorical outsider armed with bruising invective with that of one who praises and admires. But the praise is never unalloyed and the reader soon sees that it is all ironic. In his *Prophecy of Famine* (1763), an attack on the Scots who Churchill thought threatened England, the speaker of the poem pretends to admire the Scots and enumerates England's "indebtedness" to its northern neighbor:

> To that rare soil, where virtues clust'ring grow,
> What mighty blessing doth not ENGLAND owe,
> What *waggon-loads* of courage, wealth and sense,
> Doth each revolving day import from thence?
> To us she gives, disinterested friend,
> Faith without fraud, and STUARTS without end.
> When we prosperity's rich trappings wear,
> Come not her gen'rous sons, and take their share,
> And, if, by some disastrous turn of fate,
> Change should ensue, and ruin seize our state,
> Shall we not find, safe in that hallow'd ground,
> Such refuge, as the HOLY MARTYR found? (111–22)

Churchill attacked Bishop Warburton of Gloucester several times in retaliation for the Bishop's attack on Churchill's friend John Wilkes. Attacking Warburton directly in *The Duellist* early in 1764, Churchill tried the ironic approach in his "Dedication to Warburton," published posthumously early in 1765, although earlier publication had been scheduled. Churchill used the pose of the "ironic eulogist" (Lockwood, 126–42) in a section (lines 547–58) of his *Epistle to William Hogarth* (1763) as well as in lines 148–55 of *The Apology*. But irony can be a much more pervasive technique for Churchill than these examples suggest (R. J. Smith, 57–62, 127, 147). In *Night* (1761) he displays a variety of techniques for creating irony. The poem is usually seen as a defense of loose living, a charge to which Churchill was vulnerable despite his being a curate. But the poem becomes a bold and unorthodox defense of individualism supported by a variety of ironic sallies. Night, for example, is preferable to day, loose living to prudence, disengagement to political activity. In short, the poem turns conventional values and behavior upside down. A nocturnal perspective puts the affairs of life in their true light, allowing the poet to see that prudence is hypocrisy (307–24), that kings contending for territo-

ries are no different from squirrels fighting over nuts (195–206).
Thus only individualism is worthwhile:

> Stedfast and true to virtue's sacred laws,
> Unmov'd by vulgar censure or applause,
> Let the WORLD talk, my Friend; that WORLD, we know,
> Which calls us guilty, cannot make us so.
> Unaw'd by numbers, follow Nature's plan,
> Assert the rights, or quit the name of man.
> Consider well, weigh strictly right and wrong;
> Resolve not quick, but once resolv'd be strong.
> In spite of Dullness, and in spite of Wit,
> If to thyself thou canst thyself acquit,
> Rather stand up assur'd with conscious pride
> Alone, than err with millions on thy side.
>
> (371–82)

One of the richest sources of irony perpetrated by an Iconoclast
is *Don Juan,* the illustration par excellence of all that the Iconoclast
stands for, shot through with irony from its ottava rima stanzaic
form to its epic-like but unfinished state. Like the epigram or
aphorism that frequently uses balance and antithesis for irony, the
ottava rima allows Byron to build an idea or a picture in order to
undercut it in the closing couplet, a technique that is repeated in
various ways throughout the poem (see 1, 42, 43, 44, in which
romantic love is set up in each stanza only to be undercut by
biological or digestive considerations; or 1, 218, 219, 220 with the
meditation of fame reduced to the mundane; or description plus
offhand editorial comment):

> To Norman Abbey whirl'd the noble pair,—
>   An old, old monastery once, and now
> Still older mansion,—of a rich and rare
>   Mix'd Gothic, such as artists all allow
> Few specimens yet left us can compare
>   Withal: it lies perhaps a little low,
> Because the monks preferr'd a hill behind,
> To shelter their devotions from the wind.
>
> (12, 55)

A description of Catherine of Russia's figure can be turned awry by
inappropriate imagery:

Though somewhat large, exuberant, and truculent,
   When *wroth*—while pleased, she was as fine a figure
As those who like things rosy, ripe, and succulent,
   Would wish to look on, while they are in vigour.
She could repay each amatory look you lent
   With interest, and, in turn, was wont with rigour
To exact of Cupid's bills the full amount
At sight, nor would permit you to discount.

                                     (9, 62)

But as D. C. Muecke has shown (41), Byron's irony can be very complex, as in stanza XI, 6, in which a series of attacks of illness bring a temporary surge of piety:

The first attack at once proved the Divinity
   (But *that* I never doubted, nor the Devil);
The next, the Virgin's mystical virginity;
   The third, the usual Origin of Evil;
The fourth at once established the whole Trinity
   On so uncontrovertible a level,
That I devoutly wished the three were four—
On purpose to believe so much the more.

Although the narrator makes himself the object of mockery, the irony is also directed at the mechanical accumulation of dogma. Ultimately even these fail to satisfy, since the speaker wants more ideas to believe in, presumably to prevent or allay future illness. Ordinarily the "uncontrovertible" establishment of the Trinity shouldn't lead to a "devoutly wish'd" for additional element to accommodate "belief." But irony is also used to attack "a whole complex of English evasions and hypocrisies" (Ruddick, 129) as well as a way of playing fast and loose with the poem itself. Nothing, in short, is exempted from the revealing light of irony. For example, Byron's hero Don Juan is not the person of legend, not the rake and libertine, but an energetic, somewhat idealistic victim, overshadowed by the narrator whose brilliantly witty and pervasive commentary become a main, if not the main, source of interest in the narrative. In stanza 187 of Canto 1 he says, "Here ends this canto,—" and then continues for thirty-five stanzas more. He had already promised that his "epic" would be in twelve cantos, but the poem remained unfinished—at the sixteenth. The poem includes numerous references to Byron's family, his friends, public figures, and real events, including his swimming the Hellespont (6, 105). But the narrator is at once Byron and notByron, or perhaps more than Byron. "Again and again, he invents attitudes, fanciful responses for the benefit of the reader. He poses, and then parodies, his own assumed role, creates as well as records a complex personality" (Barton, 20).

> Few men [he says] dare show their thoughts or worst
> > or best;
> Dissimulation always sets apart
> A corner for herself;
>
> > > > (15, 3)

But that is too simple. Later in the same canto (stanza 87) he says,

> Whene'er I have expressed
> Opinions two, which at first sight may look
> > Twin opposites, the second is the best.
> Perhaps I have a third too, in a nook,
> > Or none at all—which seems a sorry jest:
> But if a writer should be quite consistent,
> How could he possibly show things existent.

He argues further,

> If people contradict themselves, can I
> > Help contradicting them, and everybody,
> Even my veracious self?—But that's a lie:
> > I never did so, never will—how should I?
> He who doubts all things nothing can deny:
> > Truth's fountain may be clear—her streams are
> > muddy,
> And cut through such canals of contradiction,
> That she must often navigate o'er fiction.
>
> > > > (15, 88)

By this time in the poem, such sentiments are in the way of justifying what has already been occurring. In Canto 9, 21, he had posed,

> But I, the mildest, meekest of mankind,
> > Like Moses, or Melancthon, who have ne'er

Done anything exceedingly unkind,—
   and (though I could not now and then forbear
Following the bent of body or of mind)
   Having always had a tendency to spare,—
Why do they call me Misanthrope? Because
They hate me, not I them:—

From time to time, irony is laid aside and direct attack becomes the manner, as in 13, 94, and 95, or 11, 87, the following:

But how shall I relate in other cantos
   Of what befell our hero in the land
Which 't is the common cry and lie to vaunt as
   A moral country? But I hold my hand—
For I disdain to write as Atalantis;
   But 't is as well at once to understand,
You are *not* a moral people, and you know it,
Without the aid of too sincere a poet.

From the sarcasm of "too sincere" to the ironic juxtaposing of love and infidelity, idealism and cannibalism, cosmogony and lycanthrophy, romanticism and materialism, *Don Juan* serves as an anthology of the range and depth of irony, from techniques to attitude, all of it couched in the witty epigrammatic style of the skeptical outsider that is the persona of the Iconoclast.

But the Iconoclast as persona, while most exemplary and best known, is not the only form the Iconoclast takes. A small and exclusive group of literary characters can also be called Iconoclasts. On the whole they tend to be less auspicious than the Iconoclasts discussed so far, but they exhibit most of the same characteristics and present some of the same problems. If the differentiation between the author and his or her Iconoclastic persona is sometimes vague and uncertain, Iconoclastic characters also struggle to be their own persons. They also invariably suffer from being seen as mere mouthpieces for their writers, even though they are always recognized as distinctly individual characters. Since their stock-in-trade is ideas and opinions rather than actions and deeds, and since they appear in works in which there is little or no opportunity for actions, the overlap between the author and character is understandable. M. Bergeret in Anatole France's tetralogy, *Histoire Contemporaine* (1896–1901), the Man in Black in Oliver Goldsmith's *The Citizen of the World* (1760–61), Rica in Montesquieu's *Persian Letters* (1721), and certain characters in the comedies of Wilde are usually seen as to some extent the alter egos of their creators. Only Mirabell in Congreve's *The Way of the World* (1700) succeeds in being his own man, although he clearly represents a concept that Congreve is attempting to establish in the play. The close relationship between the character of the Iconoclast and the author is reinforced by the fact that the character is often immersed in the events of the author's own time. Goldsmith's *The Citizen of the World* contains references to the death of George II, the coronation of his successor, and the publishing of such sensational pieces of literature as *Tristram Shandy* and the *Rosciad*.

France's novels refer to the notorious Dreyfus Affair and the various factions pitted against each other. The death of Louis XIV, the regency of Phillipe d'Orleans and other political and social events of the early decades of the eighteenth century are referred to and serve as a background for the *Persian Letters*. The close tie to actual events of France's and Goldsmith's times results in part from their works having been published serially in newspapers. The *Persian Letters* were published anonymously as a collection, but their controversial nature made it necessary to publish in Holland in order to protect the author and the publisher from prosecution. The letter form of Goldsmith's and Montesquieu's works and the ideological and philosophical monologues of France's works give them a digressive quality similar to some of the works in which the persona Iconoclasts appear, *Don Juan*, some of Churchill's poems, and the novels and essays of Mary McCarthy, for example. The oft-noted realism of satire and the willingness, even necessity, of its writers to dispense with or at least not feel closely bound by the conventional rules of plot form or structure are here again illustrated.

All of the Iconoclast characters share with their persona counterparts the status of outsiderhood stemming from convictions based on a belief in individualism or a sense of the rightness of their ideas, however much their ideas may set them apart from the common run of humanity. Goldsmith's Man in Black spent his early life in a "torpid state of simplicity" which made him beholden to all and a victim of life's vagaries. Finally resolving to pursue his self-interest, he gained respect and independence. By nature solitary and melancholic, his skeptical views of English life play off against the more benign attitude of Lien Chi Altengi, the Chinese

visitor for whom he acts as guide. They first meet in Westminster
Abbey (Letter 13) where Lien Chi's willingness to accept at face
value the greatness of those buried there contrasts with the view of
the Man in Black that money might have purchased such choice
burial spots. His views of English law (Letter 98), the theater
(Letter 21), and cuckolded men (Letter 19) are similarly skeptical.

Rica in the *Persian Letters* plays somewhat the same kind of role
as the Man in Black. Young, with no strong ties to his homeland,
integrated into French society without being involved, Rica carries
on commentary that is witty, irreverent, even sardonic. His letters
contain a gallery of vain and self-deluded people, an alchemist who
goes on a spending spree because he is convinced that he is rich
(Letter 45), elderly women who resent and fear growing old (Letter
52), two would-be wits who attempt to scenario their way to social
acclaim (Letter 54), and a judge who sold his law library as
superfluous (Letter 66). Fashion, genealogy, religion, and acade-
mia are all subjected to his ironic views. Rica's opinions contrast to
those of Usbek, his traveling companion, who is older, more
tolerant of French society and less liberated from Persian Society.

M. Bergeret, the central character of France's turn-of-the-
century exposé of French life, is a professor in a provincial town, an
ironic observer who spends much of his time on a bench on the
town mall or in the secondhand book corner of a local bookstore.
His critical mind sets him apart from all political and religious
factions, from colleagues and students at the university. His wife
sees him as an impractical dreamer and finally takes a lover. To the
surprise of all, M. Bergeret is promoted, divorces his wife, and is
invited to lecture at the Sorbonne. In Paris he embraces the Dreyfus
cause and socialism (as did Anatole France), further alienating
himself from the mainstream of French life. But through it all
M. Bergeret is a fountain of commentary on politics, religion,
monarchism, militarism, and the virulent anti-Semitism that ran
through much of French life, surfacing so dramatically in the
Dreyfus case. Like other Iconoclasts M. Bergeret combines an
ironic outlook with a lapidary style. "Work amuses our vanity," he
says in *The Amethyst Ring* (1899). "Work deceives our impotence
and gives us the hope of some good results. We flatter ourselves
that it helps us to control destiny. Not understanding the necessary
relations which bind our efforts to the mechanics of the universe, it
seems to us that this effort is directed in our favor against the rest

of the machine. Work gives us the illusion of will, strength and independence. It makes us divine in our own eyes." *M. Bergeret in Paris* (1901), the fourth novel in *Histoire Contemporaine,* contains his thoughts on the then-new socialism. He says, for example, "All property acquired by individual effort was created, and subsists, only by the cooperation of the whole community." He also declares, "No, I don't believe that men are naturally good. . . . But I also believe that men are least ferocious when they are least wretched, that in the long run the progress of industry will produce a certain softening of manners. A botanist has assured me that if a hawthorn be transplanted from a stony to a fruitful soil, its thorns will change into flowers."

Whereas M. Bergeret, Rica, and the Man in Black aim their ironic barbs at various aspects of their societies, Congreve's Mirabell and Wilde's dandies are much less conscious of or at least much less interested in life beyond the drawing room. They are nevertheless Iconoclasts, however limited their satiric range. Mirabell's superiority stems from his exemplifying a new social standard for men of his class. This isolates him from his social milieu, for he turns his back on the foppish and until-then-admired behavior of Witwould and Petulant. He becomes a satiric commentator (albeit a gentle one) on their "senseless ribaldry" as well as on the *beau monde*-ry of Fainall. Early in the first scene as they rise from the card table, Fainall remarks, "I'd no more play with a man that slighted his ill fortune, than I'd make love to a woman who undervalued the loss of her reputation." Mirabell responds, "You have a taste extremely delicate, and are for refining your pleasures." Fainall sees Mirabell's sarcasm only as a sign of being out of sorts, but it is the first indication that Mirabell is beginning to assert his independence from the "way of the world" for a new kind of liberty which he will share with Millimant (Gagen, 422–27; Roberts, 39–53). Even she is introduced satirically by Mirabell's famous, "Here she comes, i' faith, full sail, with her fan spread and streamers out, and a shoal of fools for tender." But Mirabell is perhaps more an early model Iconoclast, a suggestive neophyte, whose fate beyond the play can only be guessed at, a domesticated Byron-like outsider, at best misunderstood, at worst disliked or rejected, if his fate at the hands of critics is any indication.

Wilde's Iconoclasts have in fact undergone just such a fate, initial rejection, later a tentative and uneasy acceptance of them as representing a standard that rejects the commonplaces and clichés of the world. Lord Illington of *A Woman of No Importance* (1893) and Lord Goring of *An Ideal Husband* (1895) are two such Wildean creations, men whose callowness and cynicism are confused with but ultimately redeemed by their wit and "intellectual charm" (San Juan, 203). Both are voices for outrageous paradoxes perpetrated by Wilde: Illington points out that "moderation is a fatal thing; nothing succeeds like excess"; Goring claims that "fashion is what one wears oneself. What is unfashionable is what other people wear." Wilde's dandies carry on constant satire of social relations and decorum that militate against personal development and expression. They oppose romantic ideals, support ceremony and social manners, but desire such self-presence that they enjoy "the peculiar pleasure of astonishing and the proud satisfaction of never being astonished." This need to be a part of life but apart from it marks one source of trouble for the satiric Iconoclast, seeming thereby to want it both ways, needing life for his material but standing aside and seeming at times to reject it. This is also the risk that all satirists take—and finally lose, accounting in part for the fate that satirists suffer at the hands of society. The Iconoclast suffers even more because he or she is in one sense the satirist unabated, taking a position that emphasizes his or her superiority or isolation, unwilling to minimize the differences with society, unleashing ideas in scourging irony or invective.

The Iconoclast, whether as persona or as literary character, often seems unclearly or incompletely separated from his or her creator. The Ingenu, on the other hand, stands sharply as a literary creation, and no one confuses this character with its creator. The Eiron has its share of public personae, including Will Rogers, Mark Twain, and other nineteenth-century platform comedians, and a number of contemporary humorists, such as Woody Allen. But the role played by these humorists and satirists has rarely been seriously confused with the real person. But confusing the person with the persona of the Iconoclast may be in fact a feature of the character, a feature that is further complicated by figures in public life who have sometimes adopted the role, including political figures and entertainers. Personae as different as George Canning, Benjamin Disraeli, Gore Vidal, Clifton Webb, and Oscar Levant have been or are to some degree examples of the Iconoclast in life.

George Canning (1770–1827) in his younger days wrote for the conservative satiric magazine *Anti-Jacobin,* later served with great distinction in foreign affairs, twice as head of the Foreign Office, and became Prime Minister shortly before his death (Rolo). Despite a lifetime in public affairs, Canning was by taste and circumstances always something of an outsider, but ambitious, brilliant, principled and confident of his superiority. His humor, early evident in his satiric imitations of Robert Southey in the *Anti-Jacobin,* which opposed the French Revolution and its influence on English writers, especially Southey and other Romantics, was rich and ultimately dangerous, since his political opponents often found his humorous nicknames for them and his banter at their expense malicious even when no malice was intended. His sharp wit, his "omniscient authoritarian exactitude" as an administrator, and his inability to share the acquisitive and material desires of the aristocracy made him in some ways an anomaly in English political life of the late eighteenth and early nineteenth centuries, by inclination, talent, and circumstances a kind of public version of the Iconoclast.

Canning's willingness as a Tory to buck the more unenlightened wing of his party led Benjamin Disraeli (1804–81) to look upon Canning as his mentor, even though their beliefs were not particularly compatible (Canning, for example, supported slavery). Disraeli was by religious and ethnic background an outsider in English society, which he compounded in his early years by affecting foppish dress and manner and writing poetry and fiction. Disraeli wrote fiction, much of it political in nature, even after he entered politics in the 1830s, his last novel appearing shortly before his death. Several early works, *Ixion in Heaven, Popanilla,* and *Infernal Marriage,* all published in the 1820s, show Disraeli as a good-natured satirist of the fashions and foibles of English life. His style is marked by wit and epigram which, carried over into his political speeches, was seen at first as impudent and insolent but later as signs of boldness and high intellect. Disraeli's political career was long and distinguished, beginning as a leader of the Young England group against the Conservative party leadership, later serving as Chancellor of the Exchequer on several occasions, twice as Prime Minister, always as spokesman for enlightened conservatism (Froude; Meynell; Pearson, *Dizzy*).

Despite their successful careers as public figures, Canning and Disraeli exhibit some of the characteristics of the Iconoclast,

outsiders with exceptional senses of their superiority, a witty style
that was a mark of distinction, and a flirtation with satire during a
part of their careers. Disraeli's foppishness in his early life, the
carefully coiffed hair of his later life, and his mannered and
epigrammatic conversation suggest that more than Canning,
Disraeli consciously cultivated and eventually created an image,
much as that later dandy Oscar Wilde was to do (Wilde, in his late
twenties when Disraeli died, had already read Disraeli's novels well
enough to have their influence show up a decade later in *The Picture
of Dorian Gray*) (Pearson, *Life;* Shewan).

A latter-day version of the public figure as Iconoclast is Gore
Vidal, novelist, playwright, critic, screenwriter, essayist, Congressional candidate, and political gadfly. Vidal, who has published more than two dozen works, including twenty novels,
several collections of reviews and criticism, a volume of short
stories, and a handful of plays for stage and screen, is also a public
figure of sorts, having run for Congress in 1960, considered doing
so again in 1982, and for being an outspoken guest on television
talk shows. His fiction dismissed or ignored by most academic
critics and critics for the journals of opinion, he returns their lack of
regard with animosity reminiscent of Mencken's blasts at the
schoolmarms half a century ago (see "The Hacks of Academe" in
Matters of Fact and Fiction: Essays 1973–76). An interview with Vidal
in the *New York Times* (12 March 1981) captures not only the
public essence of Vidal but prototypically the spirit of many
Iconoclasts as well. The interviewer notes of Vidal:

- "He feels that he alone serves as the arbiter of truth."
- His novels "tend to be concerned with death, power,
  corruption and the willful throwing off of convention."
- His "satire has led to contempt and contempt to a
  misanthropy of sorts and willful isolation."
- "Mr. Vidal places himself outside and above most
  everything he observes."

In addition numerous direct quotes reveal Vidal's epigrammatic
turn of mind:

- "A narcissist is someone better looking than you are."
- "A crowd is a fool."
- "Christianity is a perfect religion for slaves."

- "I'm dedicated to the written culture. . . . It's like being one of the greatest living makers of stained glass windows and the age of faith has ended. I'm at the top of a very tiny heap."
- "Some writers take to drink, others, on the lecture circuit, take to audiences."

A watered-down version of the Iconoclast turns up in such popular entertainers as Clifton Webb (1891–1966) and Oscar Levant (1906–72). Webb's haughty demeanor and stylish clothes made him at home in Noel Coward comedies, although his greatest fame came when he was typecast in the 1940s and 1950s as a sharp-tongued, fussy bachelor, Mr. Belvedere, a kind of housebroken Hollywood Iconoclast. Levant portrayed a somewhat more sophisticated version in a number of films (in some of which he played himself), as a panelist on a radio quiz program, *Information Please,* and in three autobiographical books full of sardonic comments on the great and near-great of the entertainment world. Webb and Levant cultivated superciliousness and insolence for humor, fame, and fortune, using their wit to titillate rather than disturb or satirize. They were in effect distant cousins of the Iconoclast, de-fanged for popular consumption.

The Iconoclast in public life reminds us again of the connections between satire, ritual, and myth. Society allows the public Iconoclast to operate through the rituals of public life and the media, a tricky role that must be kept distinct from that of fool and of cynic, roles not permitted in the rituals of public life, at least not consciously. The public Iconoclast still trails behind him remnants of the old trickster figure, not the unbuttoned, hell-raising trickster, but the trickster who hobnobs ambivalently with those in power, whose trickiness with language earns him both fear and respect. Attenuated perhaps, vestigial even, the Iconoclast is yet a tangible expression of myth and ritual in satire in modern life.

9

Satire and Irony

When an ironic technique or device encompasses an entire work of satire, as with a beast fable or a dystopian fantasy or as in many satiric imitations, we can say that the irony and the satire are the same thing. The elements of the beast fable or dystopian allegory and the components of the satiric imitation create an interacting double structure necessary for irony as well as supply the essential contrast of values on which satire operates. But many of the devices and techniques discussed in chapters 7 and 8 are merely elements in an overall structure, say, a play or a novel, whose form may not be inherently ironic. (If the work assumes the satiric "plot" described by Kernan in which the plot builds on intensification of material rather than on change and development, unresolution instead of climax and denouement, there is inherent irony, although the extent to which this is a technique consciously used by satirists is not clear.) But consciously used techniques such as verbal irony, satiric imitations, ironic characters may be scattered rather than encompassing, cumulative rather than coessential with satire.

Karel Capek's *War with the Newts* contains an extensive collection of satiric imitations—manifestos, scientific articles, a movie scenario, news report, philosophical essays—but is not itself a satiric imitation but a dystopian fantasy. *Candide,* although it incorporates the stock characters and situations of the popular novel of Voltaire's time, is only incidentally concerned with satiric imitation. As the discussion on the use of animals in satire illustrates, such figures may generate irony in a variety of contexts without necessarily serving as an encompassing metaphor, but contributing names, occasional characters, and types of symbolism without supplying the all-embracing technique of the work. In what is generally called direct-attack satire, the diatribes of Philip Wylie, Mencken, and some formal verse satires of the Elizabethans and the ancients, irony is seemingly incidental, since the main targets are confronted apparently without guile. Yet when the satiric writer assumes a role, as he often does, and when the attack sparkles with various kinds of verbal irony, it is hard to say that irony is not inherent in satire. Irony then can be coessential with satire when the overall technique or structure is itself inherently ironic. It may on the other hand be merely pervasive or at least basic without being an exact overlay. In one case, it is impossible for satire to exist without producing irony, in the other, it is merely difficult. If the essays of Mencken or Wylie were shorn of irony, they could hardly be said to be satire. In their cases irony is the spice of a dish which if removed would result in a vastly different dish. Irony is essential to satire, but it clearly exists to different degrees and performs varying functions depending on the kind of satire.

Irony like satire is chameleon-like in that it takes on the coloration of the material out of which it emerges. To say that the irony of satire is satiric sounds tautological, but such is the case. Irony is obviously capable of functioning in many different ways, and cohabiting with satire is only one of them. The irony of Oedipus's prayer, the character of Sonya in *Crime and Punishment,* the outcome of Hawthorne's *Scarlet Letter,* the symbolism of the echo of the Marabar caves in *A Passage to India* illustrate various ways in which irony can work without the slightest hint of satire. Irony establishes a variety of relationships between material and audience in its conspiratorial way, creating what Wayne Booth calls "a tight bond," whereby the author "knows that we will know that he knows that we will assume—etc." (*Rhetoric,* 11). In effect, irony created by the author for audience participation is an illusion that the audience enjoys because it has been set up to discover what the author wanted it to in the first place. The discovery of the irony is part of a game between the author and the audience, thereby creating the "tight bond." Since irony involves contradictions, incongruities, "some kind of opposition," in Muecke's words, the audience is sometimes asked to make a choice, to side with the author for or against one element of the irony, the neglected and unrealized talents of Willy Loman in *Death of a Salesman* as opposed to his ineffective and dishonest career.

The ironist is not necessarily devoid of standards and values, nor is he reluctant to ask the audience to join him in celebrating them. The game clearly takes place at a level beyond the literal in which the writer asks the audience to transcend itself and join him in a realm that is at once more objective and more significant. According to Kenneth Burke, "The standpoint of the ironist is shifting—he cannot maintain a steady attack [as does the satirist]— by the standards of military morale he is treacherous. . . . The vigor of the pamphleteer is denied him. . . . The ironist is essentially *impure,* even in the chemical sense of purity, since he is divided" (102). Those ironists whose objectivity is highly refined are sometimes described as spectators, observers, outsiders, suggesting a detachment that may even, in some cases, be a kind of retreat or escape from reality. Sonya in *Crime and Punishment* is a sympathetic character even though she is a prostitute, since she is also innocent and pure in spirit. Oedipus's prayer-curse on his father's murderer is directed against himself although he doesn't at that point know it, but it is also an expression of a pride that must be tempered in order for his fate to run its course. In neither case is the audience forced into a clear-cut or simple reaction.

Irony, as these simple examples suggest, may establish a "bond" with the author, but the audience's relationship with the irony of the material may vary from detachment to involvement. The irony of satire rarely allows the audience this freedom of reaction. In the irony of satire, as in satire itself, there is always a target, a butt, a victim to be mocked, and generally the satirist does not allow, cannot afford to allow, the audience to doubt what he is about. In Northrop Frye's phrase, "Satire is militant irony." Moreover the "tight bond" claimed by Booth for irony in general may be subverted in satire when the audience itself is the target. The dual role of conspirator-victim may in fact be impossible, since the one creates a bond, the other alienates, which may account for why, as Swift noted in *Battle of the Books,* we tend to see others but not ourselves as the objects of satire. If, in fact, satire alienates an audience, and it is famous for doing so, has the satire failed in its bonding function?

Immersed in historical particulars and flaunting definite values or standards, satire makes demands on its audience quite different from those of other literary forms. Not only is the audience often expected to bring specific information and knowledge to the work, it is expected to choose certain values, or more often reject certain values or behavior that it may not wish or be able to change or abandon, or even reconsider. If a person in the mid-1960s found American foreign and military policy admirable, then the movie *Dr. Strangelove* (1963) was in all likelihood an abomination. If a person found the thirty-seventh president of the United States satisfactory, then Philip Roth's *Our Gang* (1971) was uncalled for. Television satire *That Was the Week That Was* (1964–65) demanded a viewer who was also an assiduous reader of newspapers and magazines, a demand that was not usually fulfilled, as its short life span indicates. The demands of satire and its irony for special knowledge and choosing among values gives satire a unique capacity for alienating an audience, quite apart from any individual irony blindness—inability to pay attention, lack of practice, incapacity for attaining the appropriate emotional state—as discussed by Booth in *A Rhetoric of Irony* (222–27).

George Orwell's *Animal Farm* was rejected by four publishers in England and a dozen in the United States before the public saw it in print (Crick; Lewis). Its attack on Communism during World War II when Russia was an ally of England and the United States made it unacceptable to many publishers, but T. S. Eliot, acting as a director for one publisher, objected to its totally negative attitude, while another publisher suggested that other animals than pigs be used to represent the Communists. But the book has been a publishing success because the story relates more than historical particulars, since these particulars fade in importance with the passing years. The depiction of the corrupting influence of power that brings about the defeat of idealism and hope is not confined to any age or place or set of events and thus has an appeal that transcends the circumstances that produced it. Orwell's lack of success in finding a publisher resulted from extraliterary considerations raised by the attack in the fable on certain values and behavior.

As the suggestion about the use of pigs indicates, the irony generated by the beast fable was for some objectionable as well. Eliot's reaction to the "negation" of *Animal Farm* turned on Orwell's failure to suggest a strong political alternative, an irrelevant expectation, since Orwell's point is that the working class or common people get it in the neck no matter who is in power, a negative but scarcely startling view of reality. This view is projected in the rich irony of the final scene when the animals cannot tell the difference between the pigs and the men who are playing cards together, indicating thereby that nothing has changed in the circumstances of the animals. The satiric irony of *Animal Farm* forced readers to take sides, and to reject its political ramifications. Such a reaction is by no means new or isolated, as reactions to works by Swift, Voltaire, Byron, and many others testify. Members of the audience will react depending on which side of the irony they find themselves. Those who are on the side of the author will enjoy the "tight bond"; those unable to cope with the author's ideas will rarely have a good word to say for anything in the work, let alone the irony (Theroux).

Some satirists encourage the "tight bond," creating personae who draw irony upon themselves, who adopt a confidential attitude or tone toward the audience, making clear that their targets can never be anyone in the audience—or can they? In many ways this is the pose that Horace adopts in his two books of satires. He admits that writing satire is not a particularly lofty literary act, being for him in fact a "minor vice," an activity that he carries on casually without any desire for an audience beyond a few friends. In Satire 1, 9 he shows himself put upon by a social climber who wishes Horace to use his influence with Horace's patron Maecenas to become a member of Maecenas's entourage. The bore patronizes Horace by suggesting that Horace's friendship is a matter of luck and that if he were a member of Maecenas's group he would work for Horace's interests. Unable to rid himself of this pushy person, Horace can only let him slowly reveal how socially inept he really is, putting in a dig now and then which the bore doesn't acknowledge probably because he is too involved with himself to understand:

> Then he started in,
> "If I know myself, you'll find me as good a friend
> As Varius or Viscus. What author writes *more,*
>   for example,
> Or *faster* than I do? What dancer is more suggestive?
> And sing? . . ."
> This was my chance to cut in, "And your poor mother,
> The relatives who care for you, won't they be worried
>   if . . .?"
> "I haven't a soul in the world! I've buried them all."
> "Lucky people," I sighed.

In Satire 2, 7 Horace even allows his slave Davus to reveal some of Horace's faults, pretending to lose his temper at Davus finally, all this part of the technique for maintaining Horace's special relationship with the audience. Horace's satires, however subtle the presentation and self-effacing the attitude, project a strong sense of social tact and moral discrimination without being self-righteous or dogmatic. Not wishing to alienate his audience, he appeals to good sense, self-interest, and reason. Hence his irony is hardly ever at the expense of the audience. Irony is turned against specific persons, himself included, or presented in the form of general behavior, as, for example, avarice or ingratitude. Horace satirizes fools and their inability to handle the subtleties and niceties of social relationships, and if the audience sees itself in such behavior, it is not Horace or his persona who have made the point. Such fools are outsiders with whom Horace's audience is not likely to identify. Yet the irony is unmistakable and militant, even though it is irony behind a smile rather than behind a snarl.

Irony at its most pervasive and most complex and startlingly different from that of Horace is the irony of Jonathan Swift, the master ironist of all satirists. For Swift irony was a technique for keeping the audience off-balance and for implicating it in the evils he is attacking. He achieves this by never allowing the audience to rest easily with the persona of the work, varying his own identification from complete opposition at one extreme to complete identification at the other, although the latter is the position least often taken. Gulliver, for example, is less often a spokesman for Swift than he is the spokesman for ideas and feelings that Swift is mocking. When Gulliver directly or indirectly attacks certain kinds of education, the courts, and lawyers, we can assume that he is speaking for Swift, but when he is uncritically patriotic, wants to live as long as the Struldbruggs, and finally to join the Houyhnhnms, Swift is having his way with Gulliver. The Projector of *A Modest Proposal* may voice Swift's humanitarian concern for the Irish and his practical advice for solving the problem, but the Projector's advocacy of cannibalism as the best solution hardly seems to have the support of Swift. As Robert Elliott remarks in his discussion of Swift's personae, "Most of the time [Swift's] persona is resolutely allied with the enemy" ("Swift's 'I,'" 385). Swift's practice of appropriating popular or familiar forms, travel books, the advice or how-to-do-it book, the report, and so on, casts an ironic glow over much of his work even before the persona clearly emerges. But the very texture of his prose is shot through with irony. From the diction of a single sentence, as the opening of *Argument against Abolishing Christianity* ("I am very sensible what a Weakness and Presumption it is, to reason against the general Humour and Disposition of the World") in which "reason" becomes something to apologize for, to the eleven different techniques of irony (of a possible nineteen) in *A Modest Proposal* compiled by D. C. Muecke, readers of Swift's works cannot ever be altogether sure that he isn't whisking an irony in front of them. The classical and biblical allusions of "A Description of a City Shower" ironically undercut the fallen and irredeemable London, but are themselves mocked as pretentious. Much of the scatological material of Swift's works is used for humor and irony, which serve as techniques for asserting the physical brotherhood of man. Swift's use of irony is so rich and complex that to discuss it adequately requires a virtual line-by-line or sentence-by-sentence analysis of particular selections. Swift's irony is his satire, and although he can be playful, humorous, witty, grotesque, scatological, and sardonic, specifically or in some combination, little or nothing he writes is far removed from the ironic. It is so pervasive and basic to his satire that irony is for him a kind of serious gamesmanship, a playfully grim-lipped technique and attitude that at once engages and disengages the audience, a deceitful imaginativeness that troubles as it beguiles.

Few if any satirists have used irony as extensively or as effectively as Swift, although Pope, Voltaire, Twain, Erasmus, Lucian, and Horace come to mind as successful practitioners. One may readily add Chaucer, Aristophanes, Byron, Thackeray, Waugh, and Anatole France, all accomplished ironists. But the point is not to nominate a Mr. Satire for a projected Hall of Fame at Paros, Greece, but to recognize that satire is inseparable from irony and that irony, whether it be playful or sardonic, is an essential technique that the satirist uses to force a judgment on the audience, whether the judgment is based on moral, ethical, political, social, religious, cultural, intellectual, or emotional values. The strategies and techniques for creating irony will vary in kind, in the number used, in the ways they are used, but they will be at the heart and core of the satire, a basic element in the humorous, gamy, critical aggression that is called satire.

Conclusion

No matter how societies and cultures are organized, how "complex" or "simple," how "advanced" or "primitive," satire in some of its numerous manifestations is there. In tribal and agrarian societies with common values, the folk satire of tales, poetry, and ritual may be strongly prescriptive but also playful and purgative. In nation-states of industrial or technological cultures with fragmented views of everything from social behavior to religious beliefs, with individual activities divided into work and leisure, in such societies rituals, popular and "high" art, and other manifestations of satire are divisive, tied to discrete social and historical events and groups rather than to nature and atemporal circumstances as tends to be the case in traditional societies (Turner, "Comments," 280–82). Satire in industrial societies seems to be more purgative and playful, less corrective and definitive. Its satire in ritual and communal contexts tends to be temporary, sometimes arbitrary, based more on commercial or aesthetic interests, less on common values and shared living patterns. Protean, amorphous, mercurial, diffuse, satire has survived under various conditions and even on occasion flourished. With the breakdown or disappearance of tribal and agrarian societies and the rise of other political and social arrangements came a change in the concept and function of art, a heritage of what is now called Western civilization. Whereas folk satire occurred mostly in ceremony and ritual, literary satire took its place, albeit a minor one, among the art of Western cultures.

Sometimes ignored or forgotten are the vestigial elements of ritual and ceremony in Aristophanes' plays, Horace's poems, Lucian's monologues, troubadour poetry, Chaucer's verse, Mark Twain's "lectures," and contemporary examples of satire performed in nightclubs and concert halls. Just as poetry moved from the court and tavern to the printed page, so satire became literary and "high," causing its ritual and oral characteristics to become recessive. Folk satire in tales, broadsheets, and songs was naturally outside the preserve of literature. Modern popular culture, in some ways a contemporary commercial version of folk art disseminated by the mass media, is still differentiated from "elite" or "high-brow" culture.

But satire has never rested comfortably in most literary or aesthetic theories of elite culture. If literature is thought of as the product of an individual struggling with his or her soul and that nothing matters but the creative act, satire becomes the expression of malcontents, neurotics, even madmen. But, as Kernan showed, in much satire the satirist and the satirist's messenger must often be separated. Moreover it is questionable psychology to attribute specifically to satirists personality traits that occur as frequently and intensively in other writers. Such a concept of the artist can treat of satire only partially since it ignores the social, political, and other cultural conditions outside the artist's psyche that trigger and focus his expression.

Literature as the history of literary forms and conventions that have a life of their own apart from individual talents, can go only so far with satire. When dealing with Scottish invective of the fifteenth and sixteenth century, Roman verse satire, or eighteenth-century English graphic satire, that is, a specific form or mode in a particular period, the literary or artistic tradition approach can be extremely useful. But since the forms and expressions of satire change from period to period, from society to society, there is no tradition of "satire," only of various types, some of which have had their day and then passed out of existence—*sotties,* "bur-lesque," formal verse satire, for example—while others persist but are adapted as satirists and the times require—"parody," apho-risms, for example. Literary satire has in fact created few forms or styles, operating mostly by usurping or appropriating documents, modes, and metaphors that already exist. Satire is therefore not autonomous, not the sum of its "style," manner, or metaphors, or the language of its individual selections. Satire, moreover, says what it means and only what it means. However rich, imaginative, or ironic, satire cannot succeed by ambiguity or ambivalence. What Edward Said has said of Swift's satire is true of satire in general: It "has no reserve capital: [satire] brings to the surface all [it] has to say" (87). If literature is a text without reference to the circumstances or events that shape it, then satire can scarcely be said to exist, since satire is above all else a reaction. The satirist needs a world of values and events to respond to judge. This dimension finds no place even in Northrop Frye's elaborate and sympathetic reading. Frye's theory, however brilliant, is ultimately "eccentric" (147), to use Edward Said's term, satire more in the service of theory than satire seen for itself in its unique context. In any judgmental act the satirist will attack the forces of change by stressing consensus and the shared assumptions of the time and place, or he or she will attack the groups or classes that thwart necessary or desirable change. Thus the assumptions, beliefs, habits, conflicts, and problems of the society in which the satirist exists are crucial to full understanding of the satirist and his or her work.

Any concept of satire that confines itself to "high" literary art, "the Matthew Arnold idea of culture," as Susan Sontag described it, will impoverish the concept. Satire is no respecter of literary or artistic categories, it cannot be confined to or defined by social class, political, or economic system, type of culture, educational background, academic discipline, or historical period. For example, there is the connection between the world upside down theme that was a staple of European broadsheets from the sixteenth to the nineteenth centuries (Kunzle; Curtius 94–98; Coupe) and its literary counterpart in Orwell's *Animal Farm* and other satiric beast fables. There is also a connection between the clowns of Javanese drama who portray the role of servants to princes in order to mock them, best them, and establish a relationship not unlike that of Falstaff and Prince Hal (Geertz, *Religion,* 277). The naif as a foil for satire is not confined to literature but appears in the comic strip characters Li'l Abner and Zonker Harris, types as different as night and day in some ways but brothers under the skin in their supernal innocence and therefore kin to Candide and Simplicissimus.

Exclusionary concepts that determine where satire may be found and what is worth considering assume a hierarchy of emotions and imply that some emotions are more worthy of literary expression than others. One of the thorniest problems in discussing satire has to do with what place to accord invective and other extreme emotional expressions. How can the expression of seemingly naked anger and indignation be afforded the aesthetic status of joy, gratitude, love, and even unhappiness? The fact is that ire and righteousness are strong emotions that have produced a rich literary reaction. Such emotions are universal and cultures have accommodated them in various ways. These responses with their verbal patterns and forms, their personae and other caricatures, plot structures, and the special relationship between satirist, audience, subject matter, and expression make up a recognizable body of material.

The essential elements of satire offered in this book make it possible to begin the task of setting up an agreed-upon group of works. At the edge of the territory direct verbal aggression will be recognized for providing a satirist with creative energy that finds or manufactures a form, that usurps the resources of language and exults in them just as any literary artist fashions a work. X. J. Kennedy confesses in the introduction to his anthology of poems of hate, anger, and invective, *Tygers of Wrath,* to occasionally being uncertain whether "the poet's object is to destroy an enemy, or to revel in hatred's aphrodisiac boost to the vocabulary" (13). Kennedy need not have been confused since these two objects may in fact reinforce each other rather than work at cross-purposes. In fact, the recourse to certain patterns of sound and meaning, to special forms and images, the inherent resources of a language give a quasi-ritual aura to such outbursts, even those that are most idiosyncratic. When invective becomes a distinguishing element of members of particular groups, for example, revolutionary blacks in the 1960s and 1970s in the United States, and Scottish poets since the sixteenth century, the communal element is intensified. Invective in effect provides an aesthetic medium for dealing with an enemy as perceived by that group.

Whenever and wherever there have been differences among persons and groups—personal, social, religious, philosophical, political—there have been strong emotions aroused that have expended themselves in verbal aggression. Kings, dictators, and presidents, wars and revolutions, racial antagonism, social move-ments—Socrates, Louis Phillipe, Richard Nixon, the Revolution of 1688, various phases of the women's movements of the nineteenth and twentieth centuries, the Reformation—whenever the social structure has been threatened or fragmented, various expressions of satire have erupted. The outbursts provoked by such events are usually deeply personal, sometimes malicious, sometimes playful, usually angry or indignant, often ephemeral. Vast numbers of such expressions fail to survive the events which spawned them, becoming the flotsam and jetsam left behind by changing circumstances, shifting alliances, transient emotions, eventually picked over by social and literary historians. The extent to which such outbursts are redeemed by the sieves of history indicates the value placed on them by society. Whether the ephemera of mass culture or the "classics" of literature courses, whether the expressions of idiosyncratic malice or universally felt indignation, no matter how society accommodates itself to such outbursts, they are always there.

NOTES

Chapter 1

1. See "The Definition of Satire" and article in *New Encyclopedia Britannica*. See also Spacks, Rosenheim, Sacks, and Guilhamet, 1–67, for attempts to corral the concept of satire.

2. Black surveys medical and psychological theories of laughter, and English uses a reader-response approach and nonliterary theories of humor to insinuate laughter into critical consideration again. See also Bristol, 125–39.

Chapter 2

1. The fullest coverage of writings on the trickster is Apte, *Humor and Laughter,* chap 7. Briefer accounts are in Teit, 4–10; Edmonson, 140–44; and Campbell, 269–81. Campbell calls the trickster a "super-shaman," neither god nor human but kin to both, not worshipped like a god but with powers and attributes not accorded humans, sometimes feared, sometimes respected, sometimes laughed at by both. See also Turner, "Myth," 580, and Basso.

2. La Pin makes clear the satiric function of Yoruban oral tales of the "wiley hero" Tortoise without mentioning satire. The nature of the Tortoise, his adventures, and the social function of the tales is a startling analogue for the role and status of the satirist in Western literature. Finnegan, 344–46, also notes the satiric nature of many trickster tales. Eliade, 157, cites Ricketts and sees the paradoxical behavior of the trickster reflecting a *mythology* of the human condition (Eliade's emphasis). See also Tekpetey; Evans-Pritchard, 22; Herskovits, 36.

3. Rooth, 190–92, argues that "it is the *associating mode of narration* and the *situation at the time of telling of the story* which creates *traditional humorous cycles* which are *attributed* to *person, an animal, a deity)*" (Rooth's emphasis). Toelkan presents a highly self-conscious and moral narrator, as well as noting the "presence both of humor and of those cultural references against which the morality of Coyote's actions may be judged" (228). Babcock-Abrahams emphasizes the marginality of the trickster drawing on ideas from Victor Turner, Mary Douglas, and others. Babcock-Abrahams also emphasizes the trickster's satiric role. Like other discussions of the trickster Babcock's ignores the role

of the teller and the social context in which the tales occur in favor of
finding a mythical function for the figure of the trickster, the
paradoxical role of enriching our perception of reality by implying the
opposite of what he is.

4. Wescott, 350–51, compares Hermes and the Yoruba Elegba; Kerenyi
   compares Hermes and Winnebago tricksters (in Radin).

Chapter 4

1. The following studies contributed to the discussion of "the dozens":
   Abrahams; Ayoub and Barnell; Chimizie; Dollard; Elton; Meyers; L.
   Miller; Simmons; Van Dam; Warner.

2. The following studies contributed to the discussion on drum
   matches: Balikci, 186–88; Greenway, 58–61; Huizinga, 85–86; Rink,
   34, 66–68; Thalbitzer, "Language," 164–69, 326–28, 354–55; Thalbitzer, *Ammasilik,* 615, 626; William Thomas, 544–47.

3. See the following studies for discussions of the calypso: Attaway;
   Castagne; Crowley, "Traditional"; Crowley, "Toward"; Elder;
   Hill; James, Jones; Kemlin.

4. On the hija see also Arberry, 44–45; Dunlop, 42–43; Geertz, *Local,*
   107–17; Nicholson, 72–75, 128–31.

5. On the varieties of *flyting* see: general: Gummere, 213, 287–88, 399;
   Irish: Mercier, 146–48; Italian: Jefferson Fletcher, 142; Wilkins, 161;
   French: Hueffer, 124–25.

6. More on flytings in Gill; Gray; W. MacKenzie; Shire, 15; George
   Stevenson; Wittig, 75–76, 123.

7. See the following on verbal dueling: Bricker, "Function"; Dundes et
   al.; Gossen; Lauria.

8. The distinction between Horatian and Juvenalian satire originally set
   forth by John Dryden is now a commonplace in satire criticism,
   although it has undergone some refinement. Although Horace and
   Juvenal are not different in some of the ways which Dryden noted,
   his concept is still valid. Each projects a different persona whose tone
   and relationship with his audience are different, which in turn
   determines the kinds of targets each attacks. Discussions of Dryden's
   ideas and considerations of the differences between the poets may be
   found in Kupersmith; Kernan, *Cankered Muse,* 149; Rudd; Weber.

9. The research on the joking relationship is extensive and unsettled. It
   is summarized in Apte, *Humor and Laughter,* 29–66. See also Burns;
   Hammond; Handeman and Kapfuer; Howell; F. Miller.

10. See the following on banter and raillery: Bullitt; Hayman; Knox;
    Loftis, 49; Hugh MacDonald; Probyn; David Sheehan, 189, et
    passim; J. H. Smith, 3; Steward, 196–98; Timpe; Wilkinson, 62–64;
    Wilson, 28, 74–80.

11. See Elkin, 15–19, in which he discusses raillery as "one of the key

words of the Augustan age," which preferred the spirit of Horace to that of Juvenal; the latter was convicted of railling, that is, a sharp, biting attack as opposed to Horace's playful, laughing, delicate faulting by raillery. This is not to say that some joking relationships do not involve insults and abuse, just as some of Horace's satires are not always urbane and witty. See Sharman, 114–15, for a comment on the varied tones of joking relationships. Horace's Satire II, 5, is closer to Juvenal in spirit than to Horace's usual tone. See also McKnight.

Chapter 5

1. *Maledicta, The International Journal of Verbal Aggression* tends to emphasize discussions of scatological terms, epithets, and other minutiae of verbal aggression rather than literary expression and the nature of the beast. Averill, 197–98, notes that "verbal aggression occurs in about 80–100% of angry episodes" and that it is more "fundamental" than physical aggression. Baron discusses experiments conducted in the subject, which is more than Fromm, Lorenz, and Montagu do.
2. Prior to the 1960s there was Kingsmill (1929), Herzberg (1941), and Harding (1953). Since the early 1960s, see Safian, Rosner, Kronenberger, Wannan, Bufe, McPhee, Kennedy, Winokur, Norman, John Baker, and Conniff.
3. No similar collection exists for writers, but see Mordell, E. Stevenson, Haney, Rigg, Muir, Land, Henderson, Redhead and McLeish.
4. Since the lampoon distorts, exaggerates, and simplifies in the manner of the caricature, lampoon and caricature are sometimes confused and the words used interchangeably. But lampoon is usually applied to actual persons, rarely to fictional characters. Caricature clearly applies to fictional characters, but it is sometimes loosely applied to actual persons as well.
5. Kenneth Burke in *Counter-Statement* sets forth in a much more formal way a similar concept. Art, he argues, is the use of "eloquence, ceremony, ritual" to endow a revelation with significance. By creating a verbal equivalent or pattern for dealing with and presenting an emotional experience and the adjustment to it, the writer [read here satirist] enables an audience to deal with similar feelings, experiences and situations. Humor enables us to deal with a situation by "belittling it"; a satire "enables us to admit the situation by permitting us to feel aloof from it." See "Patterns of Experience" and "Ritual" in "Lexicon Rhetoricae," especially 154–55 and 168, in Kenneth Burke's *Counter-Statement*.

Chapter 6

1. The literature on the play element has exploded in the last twenty years and may be best approached through James A. G. Marino's

208-item annotated bibliography in the *Canadian Review of Comparative Literature* 12 (1985). Peter Hutchinson's *Games Authors Play* is a general introduction to the subject. Part II of Hutchinson's book classifies literary games according to literary techniques and other devices but does not include satire. The number of works and authors discussed by the play element approach grows more extensive by the day. It may be time for an academic journal on the subject. See also Gombrick for a discussion of how Huizinga's book "changes from a book about man and play to a meditation about man and God" (1089). Callois's discussion of *Homo Ludens* appears in "Play and the Sacred" in *Man and the Sacred*, 152–63.

2. Mikhail Bakhtin's view of the medieval Carnival as a time of freedom and "new, purely human relations," a merging of the "utopian ideal and the realistic" (10) fails to square with the account of Carnival in Anthony Caputi, *Buffo*, chap. 2.

3. A study of children's storytelling and television-program watching reveals that modern equivalents of tricksters (for example, Bugs Bunny) mock figures of authority and break rules of society. As expressions of humorous play such stories and programs seem to contribute to the social and psychological adjustment of children five to eleven. See Abrams & Sutton-Smith; Geltrick-Ludgate.

Chapter 7

1. Other discussions of the devices of verbal attack include Muecke, 67–83; Feinberg, *Introduction*, 101–42, 143–76; Worcester, 77–90; Eden.

2. Punning in English finds appreciative advocates in Fadiman and Redfern. Nash classifies the main types of puns.

3. The freedom to appropriate the styles of others accords with Johnson's definition of parody in his *Dictionary*: "A kind of writing, in which the words of an author or his thoughts are taken, and by a slight change adapted to some new purpose." See Chambers for a contemporary working out of Johnson's definition. Critical writing on parody in modern and postmodern fiction is extensive. An excellent discussion is by Hutcheon. See also Patricia Waugh.

4. See Weisstein; Markiewicz; Riewald; Rose, esp. chaps. 1 and 2. Dane emphasizes the role of the reader in the perception of parody, as does the system advanced in this study, but Dane argues that because satire is concerned with content and parody with expression, they must be read in different ways and their "relation is accidental," even though they can support and reinforce each other. Traditional satiric parody is thoroughly discussed in Bakhtin, *Dialogic*, 51–83. The *Southern Review* (Australia) 13 (1980) is devoted to parody.

5. Thackeray's *Novels from Eminent Hands* (1847, originally *Punch's Prize*

Novelists) and the brothers James and Horace Smith's *Rejected Addresses* (1812), both popular in their day, are other efforts at sustained prose satiric imitations. *Probationary Odes for the Laureateship* (1784–85) and National Lampoon's *This Side of Parodies* (1974) are collections by various hands. Collections by Kaplan and Wells are surveys.

Chapter 8

1. All allegorical satires do not present parallel worlds. Swift's *Tale of a Tub* and Erasmus's *The Praise of Folly* are allegories of a different type. Dryden's *Absalom and Achitophel* is different, closer in some ways to what was described in chapter 6 as "irony of disparate elements." But these allegories and others like them are few compared to the allegories of parallel worlds.

2. Anthony Brandt notes that a treatise in physiognomy attributed to Aristotle elaborates on the folk belief that persons who resemble certain animals will have the "psychic qualities" of those animals, a belief that persisted for two thousand years. A classic statement of that belief is made by Lady Philosophy to Boethius in *The Consolation of Philosophy,* trans. S. J. Tester (Cambridge: Harvard University Press, 1973), p. 335. "To give oneself to evil," she says, "is to lose one's human nature." She then supplies a catalogue of analogies between human weakness and their animal counterpart. Le Brun's studies have recently been made available in *Resemblances: Amazing Faces,* with an introduction by graphic artist Edward Sorel.

3. Brief comments on the Ingenu appear in Feinberg, 239–41; Worcester, 102–8; Muecke, 91–92; Hodgart, 124–25.

4. Kuckuck (*cuckoo* in German), his theory of existence, and their role in the novel must remain open given the novel's unfinished condition. Felix believes that Kuckuck's revelation is prompted by Felix's being a Marquis, which is as exhilarating as his exposure to such a cosmical description, and ultimately as ironic. But without a completed novel, the meaning of this section of the novel must remain ambiguous. George Steiner, 278–79, and Riley, 256–60, discuss the matter.

5. The literature on the concept of the personae is extensive going back over more than three decades. Maynard Mack's "The Muse of Satire" encouraged critics to separate the statement of the poet from his person and to see that statement as the expression of an objectified character. Patrick Cruttwell in "Makers and Persons" refined the concept, but Irwin Ehrenpreis objected to the practice in his "Personae." The *Satire Newsletter* 3 (1966) brought together inconclusively the statements of a number of critics reacting to Ehrenpreis's argument. Since then the work of Erving Goffman has been used to bolster the concept as well as Robert Elliott's subtle investigation of Swift's persona.

WORKS CITED

Abrahams, Roger D. "Playing the Dozens." *Journal of American Folklore* 75 (1962): 209–20.

Abrams, David M., and Brian Sutton-Smith. "The Development of the Trickster in Children's Narrative." *Journal of American Folklore* 90 (1977): 29–47.

Adams, Robert M. *Bad Mouth: Fugitive Papers on the Dark Side.* Berkeley: University of California Press, 1977.

Adler, Renata. "The Current Cinema: Dangling Satire." *New Yorker* (13 August 1966): 96–98.

Alden, Whitman. "Stephen Potter, Satirist, Dead." *New York Times* (3 December 1969): 55.

Alexander, Sidney. *Lions and Foxes.* New York: Macmillan, 1974.

Alford, Finnegan. "Who Are You Kidding? Joking Relationships in American Society." Convention of Popular Culture Association. Cincinnati, 27 March 1981.

Alter, Robert. *Rogue's Progress.* Cambridge: Harvard University Press, 1964.

Anderson, W. S. "The Roman Socrates: Horace and His Satires." *Satire: Critical Essays in Roman Literature.* Edited by J. P. Sullivan. Bloomington: Indiana University Press, 1963.

Apte, Mahadev L. *Humor and Laughter: An Anthropological Approach.* Ithaca: Cornell University Press, 1985.

———. "Humor Research, Methodology, and Theory in Anthropology." *Handbook of Humor Research.* Edited by Paul E. McGhee and Jeffrey H. Goldstein. Vol. 1. New York: Springer-Verlag, 1983.

Apter, T. E. *Thomas Mann: The Devil's Advocate.* New York: New York University Press, 1979.

Arberry, A. J. *Arabic Poetry: A Primer for Students.* Cambridge: Cambridge University Press, 1965.

Arden, Heather. *Fools' Plays: A Study of the Satire in the "Sottie."* Cambridge: Cambridge University Press, 1980.

Armin, Robert. *Nest of Ninnies.* London: Shakespeare Society, 1842.

Atlas, James. Review of *Frederick Rolfe: Baron Corvo,* by Miriam J. Benkovitz. *New York Times Book Review* (17 July 1977): 1, 25.

Attaway, William. *Calypso Song Book.* New York: McGraw-Hill, 1957.

Auden, W. H. "The Life of a That-There Poet." *New Yorker* (26 April 1958): 133–50.

———. "Notes on the Comic." *Thought* 27:2 (1952): 66. Reprinted in *The Dyer's Hand and Other Essays*. New York: Random House, 1962.

Averill, James. *Anger and Aggression: An Essay in Emotion*. New York: Spring-Verlag, 1982.

Ayoub, Millicent R., and Stephen A. Barnell. "Ritualized Verbal Insults in White High School Culture." *Journal of American Folklore* 78 (1965): 337–44.

Babcock, Barbara A. "Arrange Me into Disorder: Fragments and Reflections on Ritual Clowning." *Rite, Drama, Festival, Spectacle: Rehearsals Toward a Theory of Cultural Performance*. Edited by John J. MacAloon. Philadelphia: Institute for the Study of Human Issues, 1984.

Babcock-Abrahams, Barbara. " 'A Tolerated Margin of Mess': The Trickster and His Tales Reconsidered." *Folklore Institute Journal* 11 (1975): 147–86.

Bainton, George, ed. *The Art of Authorship*. New York, 1890.

Baker, John F. "Erma Bombeck." *Bookviews* (March 1978): 7, 9–10.

Baker, Kenneth. *I Have No Gun But I Can Spit: An Anthology of Satirical and Abusive Verse*. London: Eyre Methuen, 1980.

Baker, Russell. "Observer: The Decline of the Insult." *New York Times* (3 December 1968): 46.

Bakhtin, Mikhail. *The Dialogic Imagination: Four Essays*. Translated by Caryl Emerson and Michael Holquist. Austin: University of Texas Press, 1981.

———. *Rabelais and His World*. Cambridge: Harvard University Press, 1968.

Baldwin, Barry. *Studies in Lucian*. Toronto: Toronto University Press, 1973.

Bales, Jack. "Herbert R. Mayes and Horatio Alger, Jr.: Or the Story of a Unique Literary Hoax." *Journal of Popular Culture* 8 (1974): 317–19.

Balikci, Asen. *The Netsilik Eskimo*. Garden City, N.Y.: Natural History Press, 1970.

Ball, Allan P., ed. *The Satire of Seneca on the Apotheosis of Claudius*. New York: Columbia University Press, 1902.

Bandelier, Adolf F. *The Delight Makers*. New York: Dodd, Mead, 1890.

Barclay, Lillian Elizabeth. "The Coyote: Animal and Folk Character." *Coyote Wisdom*. Edited by J. Frank Dobie, et al. Dallas: Southern Methodist University Press, 1938.

Baron, Robert A. *Human Aggression*. New York: Plenum, 1977.

Barton, Anne. *Byron and the Mythology of Fact*. Nottingham: University of Nottingham Press, 1968.

Basso, Ellen B. *In Favor of Deceit: A Study of Tricksters in an Amazonian Society.* Tucson: University of Arizona Press, 1987.

Basso, Keith. *Portraits of "The Whiteman."* Cambridge: Cambridge University Press, 1979.

Beerbohm, Max. "Two Pantomime." *Saturday Review* (London, 31 December 1898).

Bellamy, Joe David. *Superfiction, or The American Short Story Transformed.* New York: Vintage, 1975.

Bellinger, Alfred R. "Lucian's Dramatic Technique." *Yale Classical Studies* 1 (1928): 3–29.

Bentley, Joseph. "Semantic Gravitation: An Essay on Satiric Reduction." *Modern Language Quarterly* 30 (1969): 3–19.

Bergson, Henri. *Laughter.* Translated by Cloudesley Brereton and Fred Rothwell. New York: Macmillan, 1911.

Besterman, Theodore. *Voltaire.* New York: Harcourt, 1969.

Bezucha, Robert J. "Masks of Revolution: A Study of Popular Culture During the Second French Republic." In *Revolution and Reaction: 1848 and the Second French Republic,* edited by Roger Price, 236–53. London: Helm, 1975.

Billington, Sandra. *A Social History of the Fool.* New York: St. Martin's, 1984.

Bjornson, Richard. *The Picaresque Hero in European Fiction.* Madison: University of Wisconsin Press, 1977.

Black, Donald W. "Laughter." *Journal of American Medical Association* 252 (7 December 1984): 2995–98.

Bleznick, Donald W. *Quevedo.* New York: Twayne, 1972.

Bloom, Edward A. "*Sacramentum Militiae*: The Dynamics of Religious Satire." *Studies in the Literary Imagination* 5 (1972): 119–42.

Boas, Franz. *Race, Language and Culture.* New York: Macmillan, 1940.

Bogel, Frederic V. "Dulness Unbound: Rhetoric and Pope's *Dunciad.*" *PMLA* 97 (October 1982): 844–55.

Bond, Richmond. *English Burlesque Poetry, 1700–1750.* Cambridge: Harvard University Press, 1932.

Bonner, Anthony, ed. and trans. *Songs of the Troubadour.* New York: Schocken, 1972.

Booth, Wayne. "The Empire of Irony." *Georgia Review* 37 (1983): 719–37.

———. "The Pleasures and Pitfalls of Irony: or, Why Don't You Say What You Mean?" In *Rhetoric, Philosophy and Literature: An Exploration,* edited by Don M. Burks. West Lafayette, Ind.: Purdue University Press, 1978.

———. *A Rhetoric of Irony.* Chicago: University of Chicago Press, 1974.

Boughner, Daniel. *The Braggart in Renaissance Comedy.* 1954. Westport, Conn.: Greenwood, 1970.

Bourke, John G. *Scatologic Rites of All Nations.* 1891. New York: Johnson, 1968.

Bowerman, Robert. "Horatio Alger, Jr., or Adrift in the Myth of Rags to Riches." *Journal of American Culture* 2 (1979): 83–112.

Brandt, Anthony. "Face Reading: The Persistence of Physiognomy." *Psychology Today* (December 1980): 90–96.

Brayman, Harold. *The President Speaks Off the Record.* Princeton: Dow Jones, 1976.

Brenneis, Don, and Ram Padarath. " 'About Those Scoundrels I'll Let Everyone Know': Challenge Dueling in a Fiji Indian Community." *Journal of American Folklore* 88 (1975): 283–91.

Bricker, Victoria Reifler. "The Function of Humor in Zinacantan." *Journal of Anthropological Research* 36 (1980): 411–18.

————. *Ritual Humor in Highland Chiapas.* Austin: University of Texas Press, 1973.

Bristol, Michael D. *Carnival and Theater: Plebeian Culture and the Structure of Authority in Renaissance England.* London: Methuen, 1985.

Brown, Norman O. *Hermes the Thief: The Evolution of a Myth.* 1947. New York: Vintage, 1969.

Bryan, Robert A. "John Donne's Use of the Anathema." *Journal of English and Germanic Philology* 61 (1962): 305–12.

Bufe, Charles, ed. *The Heretics Handbook of Quotations.* San Francisco: See Sharp Press, 1988.

Bullitt, John M. "Swift's 'Rules of Raillery.' " In *Veins of Humor,* edited by Harry Levin, 93–108. Harvard English Studies 3. Cambridge: Harvard University Press, 1972.

Burke, Kenneth. *Counter-Statement.* 1953. 2d ed. Berkeley: University of California Press, 1968.

Burke, Peter. *Popular Culture in Early Modern Europe.* New York: New York University Press, 1978.

Burland, C. A. *Myths of Life and Death.* New York: Crown, 1974.

Burns, Tom. "Friends, Enemies, and the Polite Fiction." *American Sociological Review* 18 (1953): 654–62.

Busby, Mary Olive. *Studies in the Development of the Fool in Elizabethan Drama.* Oxford: Oxford University Press, 1923.

Buxton, L. H. Dudley, and Strickland Gibson. *Oxford University Ceremonies.* Oxford: Oxford University Press, 1935.

Bynum, David E. *The Daemon in the Woods: A Study of Oral Narrative Patterns.* Cambridge: Harvard University Press, 1978.

Caillois, Roger. *Man and the Sacred.* Translated by Meyer Barash. Glencoe, Ill.: Free Press, 1959.

————. *Man, Play and Games.* Translated by Meyer Barash. New York: Free Press, 1961.

Cairns, Francis. *Generic Composition in Greek and Roman Poetry*. Edinburgh: Edinburgh University Press, 1972.

Campbell, Joseph. *The Masks of God: Primitive Mythology*. New York: Viking, 1959.

Caputi, Anthony. *Buffo*. Detroit: Wayne State University Press, 1978.

Carroll, Linda L. "Carnival Rites as Vehicles of Protest in Renaissance Venice." *Sixteenth Century Journal* 16 (1985): 487–501.

Carson, Katharine Whitman. "Aspects of Contemporary Society in *Gil Blas*." *Studies in Voltaire and the Eighteenth Century*. Vol. 110. Edited by Theodore Besterman. Banbury: The Voltaire Foundation, 1973.

Castagne, Patrick S. "This Is Calypso." *Music Journal* 16 (1958): 32–33, 88–89.

Chambers, E. K. *The Medieval Stage*. Vol. 2. London: Oxford University Press, 1903.

Chambers, Robert. "Parodic Perspective—A Theory of Parody." Ph.D. diss. Indiana University, 1974.

Chesterton, G. K. *The Uses of Diversity*. New York: Dodd, Mead, 1921.

Chimizie, Amuzie. "The Dozens: An African-Heritage Theory." *Journal of Black Studies* 6 (1976): 401–19.

Churchill, Charles. *Poetical Works*. Edited by Douglas Grant. Oxford: Clarendon, 1956.

Clark, John R. "Anti-climax in Satire." *Seventeenth Century News* 33 (1975): 22–26.

Clark, John R., and Anna Motto, eds. *Satire—That Blasted Art*. New York: Putnams, 1973.

Clarke, Robin. *The Science of War and Peace*. New York: McGraw-Hill, 1972.

Cleugh, James. *The Divine Aretino*. New York: Stein & Day, 1966.

Cobb, Richard. "Sous les torts d'aberys-twyth." *Times Literary Supplement* (4 March 1977): 242.

Coleridge, Samuel Taylor. *The Table Talk and Omniand*. London: Bell & Sons, 1888.

Collins, Glenn. "An Expert on the Roles People Play in Life." *New York Times* (23 February 1981): B6.

Colson, Elizabeth. *The Makah Indians: A Study of an Indian Tribe in Modern American Society*. Manchester: Manchester University Press, 1953.

Conniff, Richard. *A Devil's Book of Verse, Masters of the Poison Pen from Ancient Times to the Present Day*. New York: Dodd, Mead & Co., 1983.

Coupe, William. *The Topsy-Turvy World*. Amsterdam: Goethe-Institut, 1985.

Crick, Bernard. "How the ('Freedom of the Press') Essay Came to Be Written." *Times Literary Supplement* (15 September 1972): 1039–40.

Crowley, Daniel J. "The Traditional Masques of Carnival." *Caribbean Quarterly* 4 (1956): 194–223.

———. "Toward a Definition of Calypso: I." *Ethnomusicology* 3 (1959): 57–124.

Cruttwell, Patrick. "Makers and Persons." *Hudson Review* 12 (1959–60): 487–507.

Curtius, Ernst Robert. *European Literature and the Latin Middle Ages.* Translated by Willard R. Trask. 1953. Harper Torchbook, 1963.

Dane, Joseph A. "Parody and Satire: A Theoretical Model." *Genre* 13 (1980): 145–59.

Davidson, H. R. Ellis. *Gods and Myths of Northern Europe.* Baltimore: Johns Hopkins University Press, 1946.

———. "Loki and Saxo's Hamlet." In *The Fool and the Trickster,* edited by Paul V. A. Williams. Cambridge: Brewer, 1979.

Davis, Natalie Zemon. "Charivari, Honor, and Community in Seventeenth-Century Lyon and Geneva." In *Rite, Drama, Festival, Spectacle: Rehearsals Toward a Theory of Cultural Performance,* edited by John J. MacAloon. Philadelphia: Institute for the Study of Human Issues, 1984.

———. "The Reasons of Misrule: Youth Groups and Charivari in Sixteenth-Century France." *Past and Present* 50 (1971): 41–75.

Deacon, Mary R. *The Clover Club of Philadelphia.* Philadelphia, 1897.

Deas, Malcolm. Review of *Ombras Completas,* by Jose Maria Vargas Villa. *Times Literary Supplement* (6 August 1976): 989–90.

de Vries, Jan. *The Problem of Loki.* Helsinki: Suomalainen Tiedeakatemia, Societas Scientiarum Fennica, 1933.

DeLoria, Vine, Jr. *Custer Died For Your Sins.* New York: Macmillan, 1969.

Dirks, Robert. *The Black Saturnalia: Conflict and Its Ritual Expression on British West Indian Slave Plantations.* Gainesville: University of Florida Press, 1987.

Disraeli, Isaac. "Pasquin and Marforio: Jocular Preachers." *Curiosities of Literature.* London, 1864.

Dollard, John. "The Dozens: The Dialect of Insult." *American Imago* 7 (1936): 4–20.

Donaldson, E. Talbot. "Chaucer the Pilgrim." In *Chaucer Criticism: The Canterbury Tales,* edited by Richard Schoeck and Jerome Taylor. Notre Dame: University of Notre Dame Press, 1960.

Dover, K. J. *Aristophanic Comedy.* Berkeley: University of California Press, 1972.

DuBruck, Edelgard. "*Homo ludens—homo cogitans:* Images of Fifteenth-Century Man in German Carnival Plays." *Fifteenth-Century Studies* 4 (1981): 61–72.

Du Chaillu, Paul. *Explorations and Adventures in Equatorial Africa.* London, 1861.

Dundes, Alan, et al. "The Strategy of Turkish Boys' Verbal Dueling Rhymes." *Journal of American Folklore* 83 (1970): 325–49.

Dundes, Alan, and Carl R. Pragter. *Urban Folklore from the Paperwork Empire.* Austin: University of Texas Press, 1975.

Dunlop, D. M. *Arab Civilization to A.D. 1500.* New York: Praeger, 1971.

Dyson, A. E. *The Crazy Fabric: Essays in Irony.* New York: St. Martin's, 1965.

Eden, Rick. "Master Tropes in Satire." *Style* 21 (1987): 589–606.

Eder, Richard. "Stage: Two-Way Hamlet Parody." *New York Times* (6 July 1977): 3, 17.

Edmonson, Munro. *Lore: An Introduction to the Science of Folklore and Literature.* New York: Holt, 1971.

Edwards, Jay D. *The Afro-American Trickster Tale: A Structural Analysis.* 4. Bloomington: Folklore Institute of Indiana, 1978.

Ehrenpreis, Irwin. "Personae." In *Restoration and Eighteenth-Century Literature: Essays in Honor of Alan Dugald McKillop,* edited by Carroll Camden, 25–37. Chicago: University of Chicago Press, 1963.

Ehrmann, Jacques. "Homo Ludens Revisited." *Yale French Studies* 41 (1968): 31–57.

Elder, J. D. "Calypso: A Living Tradition in the West Indies." *Sing Out!* 14 (1964): 38–42.

Eliade, Mircea. *The Quest: History and Meaning.* Chicago: University of Chicago Press, 1969.

Elkin, P. K. *The Augustan Defence of Satire.* Oxford: Oxford University Press, 1973.

Elliott, Robert C. "The Definition of Satire: A Note on Method." *Yearbook on Comparative and General Literature* 11 (1962): 19–23.

———. "Jonathan Swift: The Presentation of Self in Doggerel Rhyme." *The Poetry of Jonathan Swift.* Clark Memorial Library Seminar, 1979. Los Angeles: University of California Press, 1981.

———. *The Power of Satire: Magic, Ritual, Art.* Princeton, N.J.: Princeton University Press, 1960.

———. "Satire." *New Encyclopedia Britannica.* 1979 ed.

———. *The Shape of Utopia: Studies in a Literary Genre.* Chicago: University of Chicago Press, 1970.

———. "Swift's 'I.' " *Yale Review* 62 (1972–73): 372–91.

Elton, William. "Playing the Dozens." *American Speech* 25 (1950): 148–49; 230–33.

English, James F. "The Laughing Reader: A New Direction for Studies of the Comic." *Genre* 19 (1986): 129–54.

Enright, D. J. *The Alluring Problem: An Essay on Irony.* London: Oxford University Press, 1987.

Erasmus. *The Praise of Folly.* Translated by Betty Radice. London: Folio Society, 1974.

Esslin, Martin. "Pataphysical Saint." *New Statesman* (25 October 1968): 548–50.

Evans-Pritchard, E. E. *Nuer Religion.* Oxford: Oxford University Press, 1956.

———. *Zande Trickster.* Oxford: Oxford University Press, 1967.

Fadiman, Clifton. "Small Excellencies: A Dissertation on Puns." *Any Number Can Play.* Cleveland: World, 1957.

Farb, Peter. *Man's Rise to Civilization: The Cultural Ascent of the Indians of North America.* Rev. 2d ed. New York: Dutton, 1978.

Farrell, James. "Dr. Mencken: Criticus Americanus." *Reflections at Fifty and Other Essays.* New York: Vanguard, 1954.

Feiffer, Jules. Lecture. Chilmark, Mass. 12 August 1982.

Feinberg, Leonard. *Introduction to Satire.* Ames: University of Iowa Press, 1967.

———. "Satire: The Inadequacy of Recent Definitions." *Genre* 1 (1968): 31–37.

Findlater, Richard. *Joe Grimaldi: His Life and Art.* Cambridge: Cambridge University Press, 1978.

Fink, Eugene. "The Oasis of Happiness: Toward an Ontology of Play." *Yale French Studies* 41 (1968): 19–30.

Finnegan, Mary. *Oral Literature in Africa.* Oxford: Oxford University Press, 1970.

Fletcher, Angus. *Allegory: The Theory of Symbolic Mode.* Ithaca: Cornell University Press, 1964.

Fletcher, Jefferson Butler. *Literature of the Italian Renaissance.* New York: Macmillan, 1934.

Fletcher, John. "Wit Without Money." In *Works of Beaumont and Fletcher,* vol. 2. Cambridge: Cambridge University Press, 1905–12.

Fowler, Alastair. *Kinds of Literature: An Introduction to the Theory of Genres and Modes.* Cambridge: Harvard University Press, 1982.

Fraenkel, Eduard. *Horace.* Oxford: Oxford University Press, 1957.

Fromm, Erich. *The Anatomy of Human Destructiveness.* New York: Rinehart, 1973.

Froude, J. A. *Lord Beaconsfield.* London, 1890.

Gagen, Jean. "Congreve's Mirabell and the Ideal of the Gentleman." *PMLA* 79 (1954): 422–27.

Ganz, Arthur. "The Divided Self in the Society Comedies of Oscar Wilde." *Modern Drama* 3 (1960): 16–23.

Geertz, Clifford. *Local Knowledge: Further Essays in Interpretive Anthropology*. New York: Basic Books, 1983.

———. *Religion in Java*. Glencoe: Free Press, 1960.

Geltrick-Ludgate, Brigitta. "Pointed Funnybones: Dyadic Verbalization of Play Territories: Satirical Expressions by Children." *The Language of Humor, The Humor of Language*. Proceedings of the 1982 WHIM Conference, Arizona State University, Tempe, 365–66.

Gill, R. B. "The Structures of Self-Assertion in Sixteenth-Century Flytings." *Renaissance Papers* (1983): 31–41.

Gilmore, David D. *Aggression and Community: Paradoxes in Andalusian Culture*. New Haven: Yale University Press, 1987.

Girard, René. *Violence and the Sacred*. Translated by Patrick Gregory. Baltimore: Johns Hopkins University Press, 1977.

Gluckman, Max. *Politics, Law and Ritual in Tribal Society*. Chicago: University of Chicago Press, 1965.

Godfrey, Sima. "The Dandy as Ironic Figure." *Sub-Stance* 36 (1982): 21–33.

Goffman, Erving. *Frame Analysis: An Essay on the Organization of Experience*. Cambridge: Harvard University Press, 1974.

———. *Strategic Interaction*. Philadelphia: University of Pennsylvania Press, 1969.

———. *The Presentation of Self in Everyday Life*. Garden City: Doubleday, 1959.

Goldman, Albert. *Ladies and Gentlemen - Lenny Bruce!!* New York: Random House, 1974.

Gombrick, E. H. "Huizinga and 'Homo Ludens.'" *Times Literary Supplement* (4 October 1974): 1083–89.

Goodman, Walter. "Insult as Entertainment: Cultural Evil or Fad?" *New York Times* (20 May 1984): H1, 19.

Goonatilleka, M. H. "Mime, Mask and Satire in Kolam of Ceylon." *Folklore* 81 (1970): 161–73.

Gossen, Gary H. "Verbal Dueling in Chamula." In *Speech Play: Research and Resources for Studying Linguistic Creativity,* edited by Barbara Kirshenblatt-Gimblett. Philadelphia: University of Pennsylvania Press, 1976.

Gray, Douglas. "Rough Music: Some Early Invectives and Flytings." In *English Satire and the Satiric Tradition,* edited by Claude Rawson, 21–43. London: Blackwell, 1984.

Greenway, John. *Literature among the Primitives*. Hatboro, Penn.: Folklore Association, 1964.

Grigson, Geoffrey. Introduction to *Faber Book of Nonsense Verse*. London: Faber & Faber, 1979.

Grumbach, Doris. *The Company She Keeps*. New York: Coward-McCann, 1967.

Guilhamet, Leon. *Satire and the Transformation of Genre*. Philadelphia: University of Pennsylvania Press, 1987.

Gummere, Francis B. *The Beginnings of Poetry*. New York: Macmillan, 1908.

Haight, M. R. "Nonsense." *British Journal of Aesthetics* 11 (1971): 247–56.

Haile, H. G. "Luther and Literacy." *PMLA* 91 (1976): 816–28.

Haitch, Richard. "Ostracizing Crime." *New York Times* (26 June 1977): 31.

Halliwell, Stephen. "Aristophanic Satire." In *English Satire and the Satiric Tradition,* edited by Claude Rawson, 6–20. London: Blackwell, 1984.

Hammond, Peter B. "Mossi Joking." *Ethnology* 3 (1964): 359–67.

Handeman, Don, and Bruce Kapfuer. "Forms of Joking Activity: A Comparative Approach." *American Anthropologist* 74 (1972): 484–517.

Haney, John Louis. *Early Reviews of English Poets*. 1904. Folcroft, Penn.: Folcroft, 1969.

Harding, Gilbert. *Treasury of Insult*. London: Weidenfeld, 1953.

Harris, Leon. *The Fine Art of Political Wit*. New York: Dutton, 1964.

Harvey, Howard Graham. *The Theatre of the Basoche*. Cambridge: Harvard University Press, 1941.

Hayman, John. "Raillery in Restoration Satire." *Huntington Library Quarterly* 31 (1968): 107–22.

Henahan, Donal. "Are There Any Good Jokes in 'Musical Humor'?" *New York Times* (13 January 1980): D17.

Henderson, Bill, ed. *Rotten Reviews: A Literary Companion* I. Stamford, Conn.: Pushcart, 1986.

Hendra, Tony. *Going Too Far*. New York: Doubleday, 1987.

Herskovits, Frances S. *Dahomean Narratives*. Evanston: Northwestern University Press, 1958.

Herskovits, Melville J. *Life in a Haitian Village*. New York: Knopf, 1937.

Herzberg, Max, ed. *Insults, a Practical Anthology of Scathing Remarks and Acid Portraits*. New York: Greystone, 1941.

Hess, Robert L. *Ethiopia: The Modernization of Autocracy*. Cornell University Press, 1970.

Highet, Gilbert. *The Anatomy of Satire*. 1962. Princeton: Princeton University Press, 1972.

Highsmith, James Milton. "The Forms of Burlesque in *The Devil's Dictionary.*" *Satire Newsletter* 7 (1970): 115–27.

Hill, Errol. "On the Origin of the Term Calypso." *Ethnomusicology* 2 (1967): 359–67.

Hodgart, Matthew. *Satire*. London: Weidenfeld & Nicolson, 1969.

Holden, Stephen. "Comedy's Bad Boys Screech into the Spotlight." *New York Times* (28 February 1988): sec. 2, pp. 1, 38.

Howell, Richard W. "Teasing Relationships." *Addison-Wesley Module in Anthropology* 46 (1973).

Hueffer, Francis. *The Troubadours: A History of Provençal Life and Literature in the Middle Ages*. London, 1878.

Huizinga, Johan. *Homo Ludens: A Study of the Play Element in Culture*. Translated by R. F. C. Hull. London: Routledge, 1950.

Humphreys, S. C. *Anthropology and the Greeks*. London: Routledge & Paul, 1978.

Hunter, Marjorie. "House Curbs 'Gas' in School Busing." *New York Times* (14 December 1973): 1, 18.

Hutcheon, Linda. *A Theory of Parody: The Teachings of Twentieth-Century Art Forms*. London: Routledge, 1985.

Hutchinson, Peter. *Games Authors Play*. London: Methuen, 1983.

Ingram, Martin. "Ridings, Rough Music and Mocking Rhymes in Early Modern England." In *Popular Culture in Seventeenth-Century England*, edited by Barry Reay, 166–97. London: Croom Helm, 1985.

Jemielity, Thomas. "Divine Derision and Scorn: The Hebrew Prophets as Satirists." *Cithara* 25 (1985): 47–68.

Jenkins, Roy. "Two-Way Mirrors," *Parabola* 6:3 (1981): 17–21.

Johnson, Edgar, ed. *A Treasury of Satire*. New York: Simon & Schuster, 1945.

Jones, G. I. "Masked Plays of Southeastern Nigeria." *Geographical Magazine* 18 (1945): 190–99.

Jones, James M., and Hollis V. Liverpool. "Calypso Humor in Trinidad." In *Humor and Laughter: Theory, Research and Applications*, edited by Tony Chapman and Hugh Foot. New York: Wiley, 1976.

Jorgensen, Marilyn. "Anti-School Parodies as Speech Play and Social Protest." In *The World of Play*, edited by Frank E. Manning, 91–102. Proceedings of the 7th Annual Meeting of the Association of the Anthropological Study of Play. West Point: Leisure, 1983.

Jump, John D. *Burlesque*. London: Methuen, 1972.

Jung, C. G. "On the Psychology of the Trickster." In *The Trickster: A Study in American Indian Mythology*, edited by Paul Radin, 195–211. New York: Schocken, 1972.

Kael, Pauline. "Spoofing and Schtik." *Atlantic* (December 1965): 84–85.

Kakutani, Michiko. "Drama Critic in Role of Enthusiast." Review of *Profiles*, by Kenneth Tynan. *New York Times* (6 November 1990): C18.

———. "Satirist with a Camera." *New York Times*. (2 March 1982): 30B.

Kaplan, Charles, ed. *The Overwrought Urn: A Potpourri of Parodies of Critics Who Triumphantly Present the Meaning of Authors from Jane Austen to J. D. Salinger*. New York: Pegasus, 1969.

Kay, W. David. "Erasmus' Learned Joking: The Ironic Use of Classical

Wisdom in *The Praise of Folly.*" *Texas Studies in Language and Literature* 19 (1971): 247–67.

Kehl, D. G. "Roman Hands Gave Us the Verbal Finger: Graffiti and Literary Form." *Maledicta* 1 (1977): 285–86.

Kemlin, Laurence. "Trinidad English—The Origin of 'Mamaguy' and 'Picong.' " *Caribbean Quarterly* 17 (1971): 36–39.

Kennedy, X. J. *Tygers of Wrath: Poems of Hate, Anger, and Invective.* Athens: University of Georgia Press, 1981.

Kerenyi, Karl. *Dionysos: Archetypal Image of Indestructible Life.* Translated by Ralph Manheim. Princeton: Princeton University Press, 1976.

———. "The Trickster in Relation to Greek Mythology." Translated by R. F. C. Hull. In *The Trickster: A Study in American Indian Mythology,* edited by Paul Radin, 173–91. New York: Schocken, 1972.

Kernan, Alvin B. "Aggression and Satire: Art Considered as a Form of Biological Adaptation." In *Literary Theory and Structure,* edited by Frank Brady, John Palmer, and Martin Price. New Haven: Yale University Press, 1973.

———. *The Cankered Muse: Satire of the English Renaissance.* New Haven: Yale University Press, 1959.

King, Florence. *He: An Irreverent Look at the American Male.* New York: Stein & Day, 1978.

Kingsmill, Hugh. *An Anthology of Invective and Abuse.* New York: Dial, 1929.

Kinsley, William. "From Aesop to Buchwald: A Review Essay." *Genre* 4 (1971): 349–59.

———. " 'Malicious World' and the Meaning of Satire." *Genre* 3 (1970): 137–55.

Kirshenblatt-Gimblett, Barbara, ed. *Speech Play: Research and Resources for Studying Linguistic Creativity.* Philadelphia: University of Pennsylvania Press, 1976.

Kleiman, Dena. "Fifth-Graders Go to Jail for a Short Harsh Lesson in Life." *New York Times* (15 April 1979): 30.

Klingender, Francis. *Animals in Art and Thought to the Middle Ages.* Cambridge: Harvard University Press, 1971.

Knox, Norman. *The Word Irony and Its Context: 1500–1700.* Durham: Duke University Press, 1961.

Kramer, Samuel Noel. *The Sumerians.* Chicago: University of Chicago Press, 1963.

Kraus, Karl. *Half-Truths and One-and-a-Half Truths: Selected Aphorisms.* Edited by Harry Zohn. Montreal: Engendra, 1976.

Kronenberger, Louis. *The Cutting Edge.* Garden City: Doubleday, 1970.

———. *The Polished Surface: Essays in the Literature of Worldliness.* New York: Knopf, 1969.

Kunzle, David. "World Upside Down: The Iconography of a European Broadsheet Type." *The Reversible World:* Symbolic Inversion in Art and Society. Ed. and Intro. Barbara A. Babcock. Ithaca: Cornell University Press, 1978.

Kupersmith, William. "Vice and Folly in Neo-Classical Satire." *Genre* 11 (1978): 45–62.

Ladurie, Emmanuel Le Roy. *Carnival in Romans.* Translated by Mary Feeney. New York: Braziller, 1979.

Land, Myrick. *The Fine Art of Literary Mayhem: A Lively Account of Famous Writers and Their Feuds.* New York: Holt, 1963.

Lander, Walter Savage. *Selections.* Edited by Sidney Colvin. London: MacMillan, 1885.

Lanson, Gustave. *Voltaire.* Translated by Robert A. Wagoner. New York: Wiley, 1966.

La Pin, Deirdre. "Tale and Trickster in Yoruba Verbal Art." *Research in African Literature* 11 (1980): 327–41.

La Rochefoucauld, François. *Oeuvres Complètes.* Paris: Gallimard, 1957.

Lauria, Anthony, Jr. " 'Respeto,' 'Relajo,' and Interpersonal Relations in Puerto Rico." *Anthropological Quarterly* 36 (1964): 53–73.

Le Brun, Charles. *Resemblances: Amazing Faces.* Introduction by Edward Sorel. New York: Harlin Quist, 1980.

Levine, Donald N. *Wax and Gold: Tradition and Innovation in Ethiopian Culture.* Chicago: University of Chicago Press, 1965.

Levine, Jacob. "Humor." In *International Encyclopedia of the Social Sciences,* edited by David L. Sills. New York: Macmillan, 1968.

Levine, Lawrence W. " 'Some Go Up, and Some Go Down': The Meaning of the Slave Trickster." In *The Hofstadter Aegis: A Memorial,* edited by Stanley Elkins and Eric McKitrick. New York: Random House, 1974.

Lewis, Anthony. "T. S. Eliot and *Animal Farm.*" *New York Times Book Review* (26 January 1969): 14, 16.

Leyburn, Ellen Douglass. *Satiric Allegory: Mirror of Man.* New Haven: Yale University Press, 1956.

Lockwood, Thomas. *Post-Augustan Satire.* Seattle: University of Washington Press, 1979.

Loftis, John. *Comedy and Society from Congreve to Fielding.* Palo Alto: Stanford University Press, 1959.

Lorenz, Konrad. *On Aggression.* Translated by Marjorie Kerr Wilson. New York: Harcourt, 1966.

McCarthy, Mary. *Memories of a Catholic Girlhood.* New York: Harcourt, 1957.

McCormack, Jerusha. "Masks Without Faces: The Personalities of Oscar Wilde." *English Literature in Transition* 22 (1979): 253–69.

MacDonald, Dwight. *Parodies: An Anthology from Chaucer to Beerbohm— and After*. New York: Random House, 1960.

MacDonald, Hugh. "Banter in English Controversial Prose After the Restoration." *Essays and Criticism* 32 (1946): 21–39.

Mack, Maynard. "The Muse of Satire." *Yale Review* 41 (Autumn 1951): 80–92.

McKenzie, Barbara. *Mary McCarthy*. New York: Twayne, 1966.

MacKenzie, W. MacKay, ed. *The Poems of William Dunbar*. Edinburgh: Porpoise Press, 1932.

McKnight, Phillip S. " 'Sudden Glory': Some Preliminary Notes on the Assailant, the Victim and the Collaborator in 'Type J' Satire." Symposium on Satire and Irony at the 1984 University of Kentucky Foreign Language Conference. *Colloquial Germanica* 18 (1985): 193–201.

McPhee, Nancy. *The Book of Insults, Ancient and Modern*. New York: Penguin, 1980.

———. *The Second Book of Insults*. New York: St. Martin's, 1982.

McWilliams, Carey. *Ambrose Bierce: A Biography*. Hamden, Conn.: Archon, 1967.

Makarius, Laura. "Ritual Clowns and Symbolic Behavior." *Diogenes* 69 (1970): 44–73.

Malone, Kemp. "Meaningful Fictive Names in English Literature." *Names* 5 (1957): 10–13.

Mandel, Morris. *Affronts, Insults and Indignities*. Middle Village, N.Y.: Jonathan David, 1975.

Marchand, Leslie. "Narrator and Narration in *Don Juan*." *Keats-Shelley Journal* 25 (1976): 26–42.

Marcovitz, Eli. "Aggression: An Overview." *Psychoanalytic Inquiry* 2 (1982): 11–20.

"Marginalia." *Chronicle of Higher Education*. 12 May 1980: 2.

Markiewicz, Henryk. "On the Definition of Literary Parody." In *To Honor Roman Jackson: Essays on the Occasion of His Seventieth Birthday, 11 October 1966*, 126–72. The Hague: Mouton, 1967.

Marriott, McKim. "The Feast of Love." In *Krishna: Myths, Rites and Attitudes*, edited by Milton Singer, 200–12. Honolulu: East-West Center Press, 1966.

Marvell, Andrew. *Complete Works*. Edited by Alexander B. Grosart. 1873. Reprinted in four volumes. New York: AMS Press, 1960.

Mencken, H. L. "Ambrose Bierce." *H. L. Mencken: The American Scene, a Reader*. Ed. Huntington Cairns. New York: Knopf, 1965.

———. *The American Language*. One-Volume Abridged Edition. Edited by Raven I. McDavid, Jr. New York: Knopf, 1963.

————. *The Bathtub Hoax and Other Blasts and Bravos From the Chicago Tribune*. Edited by Robert McHugh. New York: Knopf, 1958.

————. *Prejudices. Third Series*. New York, Knopf, 1922.

Mencken, H. L., and George Jean Nathan. "Clinical Notes." *American Mercury* 1 (January 1924): 75–78.

————. "Hero of the Open Spaces." *American Mercury* 4 (May 1926): 125–27.

Menninger, Karl. *Whatever Became of Sin?* New York: Hawthorne, 1973.

Mercier, Vivian. *The Irish Comic Tradition*. Oxford: Oxford University Press, 1962.

Merrill, Norman Williams. "Cicero and Early Roman Invective." Ph.D. diss., University of Cincinnati, 1975.

Messing, S. D. "Ethiopian Folktales Ascribed to the Late Nineteenth-Century Wit, Aläga Gäbre-Hanna." *Journal of American Folklore* 70 (1957): 69–72.

Meyer, Adolf. *Voltaire: Man of Justice*. New York: Howell, Soskin, 1945.

Meyers, Mary Ann. "Cool Bill." *Pennsylvania Gazette* 72 (December 1973): 18–21.

Meynell, Wilfred. *Benjamin Disraeli: An Unconventional Biography*. New York: Appleton, 1903.

Miller, Frank. "Humor in a Chippewa Tribal Council." *Ethnology* 6 (1967): 263–71.

Miller, Linda. " 'Playing the Dozens' Among High School Students." *Ohio Folklore Society Journal* 2 (1943): 21–29.

Mimker, Dona F. "That Paultry Burlesque Stile: Seventeenth-Century Poetry and Augustan 'Low Seriousness.' " *Seventeenth-Century News* 33 (1975): 14, 16–21.

Montagu, Ashley. *The Anatomy of Swearing*. 1967. New York: Collier Books, 1973.

————, ed. *Man and Aggression*. 2d ed. London: Oxford University Press, 1973.

————. *The Nature of Human Aggression*. New York: Oxford University Press, 1976.

Montiero, George. "Parodies of Scripture, Prayer and Hymns." *Journal of American Folklore* 77 (1964): 45–52.

Moore, W. G. *La Rochefoucauld: His Mind and Art*. Oxford: Oxford University Press, 1969.

Mordell, Albert, ed. *Notorious Literary Attacks*. 1926. Freeport, N.Y.: Books for Libraries Press, 1969.

Muecke, D. C. *The Compass of Irony*. London: Methuen, 1969.

Muir, Frank. *An Irreverent and Thoroughly Incomplete Social History of Almost Everything*. New York: Stein & Day, 1976.

Murphy, Cullen. "Watching the Russians." *Atlantic* 21 (February 1983): 33–52.

Murray, Oswyn. "The Greek Symposium in History." *Times Literary Supplement* (6 November 1981): 1307–8.

Nash, Walter. *The Language of Humor: Style and Technique in Comic Discourse.* Foreword by Randolph Quirk. English Lanugage Series No. 16. London: Longman, 1985.

New, Melvyn. "Ad Nauseum: A Satiric Device in Huxley, Orwell, and Waugh." *Satire Newsletter* 8 (1970): 24–28.

Nichols, James W. *Insinuation.* The Hague: Mouton, 1971.

Nicholson, Reynold. *A Literary History of the Arabs.* 1907. Cambridge: Cambridge University Press, 1956.

Norman, Philip. *Pieces of Hate: A Treasury of Invective and Abuse.* London: Elm Tree Books, 1987.

Norton, Charles Eliot. "Pasquin and Pasquinades." *Atlantic Monthly* 6 (October 1860): 395–405.

Norwood, Gilbert. *Greek Comedy.* New York: Hill & Wang, 1963.

"Notebooks." *Psychology Today* 15 (February 1981): 65.

O'Connor, John J. "TV: 'Scared Straight,' Documentary." *New York Times* (8 March 1979): C20.

Oldham, John. *Complete Works.* 4 vols. Edited by H. F. Brooks. Oxford: Oxford University Press, 1940.

———. *Poems.* Introduction by Bonamy Dobree. London: Centaur Press, 1960.

Onwuckekwa, Jemie. "Signifying, Dozens, and Toasts: A Selection." *Alcheringa* 1 (1976): 27–40.

Opie, Iona, and Peter Opie. *The Lore and Language of School Children.* Oxford: Oxford University Press, 1959.

Partridge, Colin J. "Some Functions of Ideological Satire." *Literary Half-Yearly* 12 (1971): 4–37.

Patterson, Anne E. "Descartes' Animal-Machine and Neoclassical Satire: Animal Imagery in Selected Works of LaFontaine and Swift." DAI 34 (1974): 6601A. University of Wisconsin.

Paulson, Ronald. *The Fictions of Satire.* Baltimore: Johns Hopkins University Press, 1967.

———, ed. *Satire: Modern Essays in Criticism.* Englewood Cliffs: Prentice-Hall, 1971.

Peake, Charles. *Jonathan Swift and the Art of Raillery.* Princess Grace Irish Library Lecture 3. Gerrards Cross, England: Colin Smythe, 1986.

Pearson, Hesketh. *Dizzy: The Life and Personality of Benjamin Disraeli, Earl of Beaconsfield.* New York: Harper, 1951.

———. *The Life of Oscar Wilde.* 1954. London: Methuen, 1966.

Pederson, Lee A. "Terms of Abuse for Some Chicago Social Groups." *Publication of the American Dialect Society* 42 (1964): 26–48.

Pelton, Robert D. *The Trickster in West Africa: A Study in Mythic Irony and Sacred Delight.* Berkeley: University of California Press, 1980.

Pierson, William D. "Puttin' Down Ole Massa: African Satire in the New World." *Research in African Literature* 7 (1976): 166–80.

Pinkus, Philip. "Satire and St. George." *Queen's Quarterly* 80 (1963): 30–49.

Probyn, Clive T. "Pope's Bestiary: The Iconograpy of Deviance." In *The Art of Alexander Pope,* edited by Howard Erskine-Hill and Anne Smith. London: Vision, 1979.

———. "Realism and Raillery: Augustan Conversation and the Poetry of Swift." *Durham University Journal* 70ns (1977): 1–14.

Puttenham, George. *The Art of English Poesie.* Edited by Gladys Doidge Willcock and Alice Walker. Cambridge: Cambridge University Press, 1936.

Quinlan, Maurice J. "Swift's Use of Literalization as a Rhetorical Device." *PMLA* 82 (1967): 516–21.

Radcliffe-Brown, A. R. "On Joking Relationships." *Africa* 13 (1940): 195–210.

Radin, Paul. "The Literature of Primitive People." In *Identity and Anxiety: The Survival of the Person in Mass Society,* edited by Maurice Stein, et al. Glencoe: Free Press, 1960.

———, ed. *The Trickster: A Study in American Indian Mythology.* 1956. New York: Schocken, 1972.

Raitt, A. W. *Prosper Mérimée.* New York: Scribner, 1970.

Randall, Lillian M. C. "The Snail in Gothic Marginal Warfare." *Speculum* 37 (1962): 358–67.

Rattray, R. S. *Akan-Ashanti Folk Tales.* 1930. Oxford: Oxford University Press, 1969.

———. *Ashanti.* Oxford: Oxford University Press, 1923.

Rawson, Claude, ed. *English Satire and the Satiric Tradition.* London: Blackwell, 1984.

Read, Walter Allen. *Lexical Evidence from Folk Epigraphy in Western America.* Paris, 1935. Reprinted under the title *Classical American Graffiti.* Waukesha, Wisc.: Maledicta Press, 1977.

Redhead, Brian, and Kenneth McLeish, eds. *The Anti-Booklist.* London: Hodder and Stoughton, 1981.

Redfern, Walter. *Puns.* London: Blackwell, 1985.

Reeves, James. *A Vein of Mockery: Twentieth-Century Verse Satire.* London: Heinemann, 1973.

Reichard, Gladys A. *Navaho Religion: A Study in Symbolism.* 2d ed. New York: Bollingen, Pantheon, 1963.

Reinach, Salamon. *Cults, Myths and Religion.* Translated by Elizabeth Frost. London: D. Nutt, 1912.

Reisner, Robert. *Graffiti: Two Thousand Years of Wall Writing.* New York: Cowles, 1971.

"Remarks on *Don Juan.*" *Blackwood's* (August 1819).

Renfield, Leonora Cohen. *From Beast-Machine to Man-Machine: Animal Soul in French Letters from Descartes to La Mettre.* Oxford: Oxford University Press, 1941.

Ricketts, Mac Linscott. "The North American Indian Trickster." *History of Religion* 5 (1965–66): 327–50.

Riewald, J. G. "Parody as Criticism." *Neophilologus* 50 (1968): 125–48.

Rigg, Diana. *No Turn Unstoned.* Garden City: Doubleday, 1983.

Riley, Anthony W. " 'Humor Plus Morality': As Aspect of Thomas Mann's Felix Krull." *Humanities Association Bulletin* 27 (1976): 256–60.

Rink, Henry. *Tales and Traditions of the Eskimo, With a Sketch of Their Habits, Religion, Language and Other Peculiarities.* 1875. New York: AMS Press, 1975.

Roberts, Philip. "Mirabell and Restoration Comedy." In *William Congreve,* edited by Brian Morris, 39–53. London: Benn, 1972.

Rolo, P. J. V. *George Canning: Three Biographical Studies.* London: Macmillan, 1965.

Rooth, Anna Birgetta. *Loki in Scandinavian Mythology.* Lund: Gleerup, 1961.

Rose, Margaret A. *Parody/Meta-Fiction: An Analysis of Parody as a Critical Mirror to the Writing and Reception of Fiction.* London: Croom Helm, 1979.

Rosenheim, Edward. *Swift and the Satirist's Art.* Chicago: University of Chicago Press, 1963.

Rosner, Joseph. *The Hater's Handbook.* New York: Delacorte, 1965.

Ross, Joan Belcourt. "Mark Twain and the Hoax." Ph.D. diss., Purdue, 1973.

Rowland, Beryl. *Animals with Human Faces: A Guide to Animal Symbolism.* Knoxville, University of Tennessee Press, 1973.

Rudd, Niall. "Dryden on Horace and Juvenal." *University of Toronto Quarterly* 32 (1963): 159–69.

Ruddick, W. "Don Juan in Search of Freedom: Byron's Emergence as a Satirist." In *Byron: A Symposium,* edited by John D. Jump. New York: Barnes & Noble, 1975.

Rudwin, Maximilian. "The Origin of the German Carnival Comedy." *Journal of English and Germanic Philology* 18 (1919): 402–54.

Russell, Frances T. *Satire in the Victorian Novel.* 1920. New York: Russell & Russell, 1964.

Sacks, Sheldon. *Fiction and the Shape of Belief: A Study of Henry Fielding with Glances at Swift, Johnson and Richardson.* Berkeley: University of California Press, 1964.

Safian, Louis A. *2000 Insults for All Occasions.* New York: Citadel, 1965.

Safire, William. "Banned Words." *New York Times Magazine* (28 October 1984): 12, 14.

Said, Edward. "Swift as Intellectual." *The World, The Text, and The Critic.* Cambridge: Harvard University Press, 1983.

Saintsbury, George. *The Earlier Renaissance.* New York: Scribner, 1901.

Sand, George. *Impressions et Souvenirs.* Paris, 1873.

San Juan, Epifano, Jr. *The Art of Oscar Wilde.* Princeton: Princeton University Press, 1967.

Santayana, George. *Soliloquies in England and Later Soliloquies.* Ann Arbor: University of Michigan Press, 1967.

Schecter, Joel. *Durov's Pig: Clowns, Politics and Theatre.* New York: Theatre Communications Group, 1985.

Scholes, Robert. "Towards a Poetic of Fiction: An Approach Through Genre." *Novel* 2: 2 (Winter 1969): 101–11.

Sexson, Lynda. "Craftsman of Chaos." *Parabola* 4 (1969): 25–33.

Shai, Donna. "Public Cursing and Social Control in a Traditional Jewish Community." *Western Folklore* 37 (1978): 39–46.

Sharman, Anne. " 'Joking' in Padhola: Categorical Relationships, Choice and Social Control." *Man* 4 (1969): 103–17.

Sheehan, David. *Chiapas.* Austin: University of Texas Press, 1973.

Sheehan, David. "Swift, Voiture, and the Spectrum of Raillery." *Papers in Language and Literature* 14 (1978): 171–88.

Shewan, Rodney. *Oscar Wilde: Art and Egotism.* New York: Barnes & Noble, 1977.

Shipley, Joseph T. *Dictionary of World Literary Terms.* Rev. and enl. ed. Boston: Writer, 1970.

Shire, Helen M. Introduction to *Alexander Montgomerie: A Selection from His Songs and Poems,* edited by Shire. Edinburgh: Oliver & Boyd, 1960.

Sider, Gerald. "Christmas Mumming and the New Year in Outport Newfoundland." *Past and Present* 71 (1976): 102–25.

Silenzi, Fernando, and Renato Silenzi. *Pasquino: Quattro Secoli di Satira Romano.* Rome: Vallechi, 1968.

Simmons, Donald C. "Possible West African Sources for the American Negro 'Dozens.' " *Journal of American Folklore* 76 (1963): 339–40.

Slonimsky, Nicolas. *Lexicon of Musical Invective.* 2d ed. Seattle: University of Washington Press, 1969.

Smith, Bromley, and Douglas Ethninger. "The Terrafilial Disputations at Oxford." *Quarterly Journal of Speech* 36 (1950): 333–39.

Smith, Edwin W., and Andrew Murray Dale. *The Ila-Speaking Peoples of Northern Rhodesia.* 1920. New Hyde Park, University Books, 1968.

Smith, Henry Nash. " 'That Hideous Mistake of Poor Clemens.' " *Harvard Library Bulletin* 9 (1955): 145–80.

Smith, John Harrington. *The Gay Couple in Restoration Comedy.* 1948. Cambridge: Harvard University Press, 1971.

Smith, Preserved. *Erasmus: A Study of His Life, Ideals and Place in History.* New York: Harper, 1923.

Smith, Raymond J. *Charles Churchill.* Boston: Twayne, 1977.

Smith, William Jay. *The Spectra Hoax.* Middletown: Wesleyan University Press, 1961.

Sonstroem, David. "An Animadversion upon Spoof." *Midwest Quarterly* 8 (1967): 239–46.

Southern Review (Australia) 13 (1980): Parody Issue.

Spacks, Patricia Meyer. "Some Reflections on Satire." *Genre* 1 (1968): 13–30.

Speiser, E. A. "The Case of the Obliging Servant." *Journal of Cuneiform Studies* 8 (1954): 98–105.

Stanton, Donna. *The Aristocrat as Art: A Study of the "Honnête Homme" and the "Dandy" in Seventeenth- and Nineteenth-Century French Literature.* New York: Columbia University Press, 1980.

Steiner, George. *Language and Silence: Essays on Language, Literature, and the Inhuman.* New York: Atheneum, 1967.

Stendhal. *Rome, Naples and Florence.* Translated by R. N. Coe. New York: Braziller, 1959.

Stenerson, Douglas C. *H. L. Mencken: Iconoclast From Baltimore.* Chicago: University of Chicago Press, 1971.

Stevenson, E. *Early Reviews of Great Writers, 1786–1832.* London, 1890.

Stevenson, George, ed. *Poems of Alexander Montgomerie.* Edinburgh: Scottish Text Society, 1910.

Steward, Julian. "The Ceremonial Buffoon of the American Indian." *Papers of the Michigan Academy of Science, Art and Letters.* 14 (1931): 188–207.

Suetonius. *The Twelve Caesars.* Trans. Robert Graves. London: Cassell, 1962.

Sutton-Smith, Brian, and Diana Kelly-Byrne. "The Idealization of Play." In *Play in Animals and Humans,* edited by Peter K. Smith. New York: Blackwell, 1984.

Swain, Barbara. *Fools and Folly During the Middle Ages and the Renaissance.* New York: Columbia University Press, 1932.

Synge, J. M. *Poems and Plays.* Edited by T. R. Henn. London: Methuen, 1963.

Szwed, John F. "The Mask of Friendship." In *Christmas Mumming in Newfoundland,* edited by Herbert Halpert and George Story. Toronto: University of Toronto Press, 1969: 112–18.

Taeuber, Conrad. "Fastnacht in the Black Forest." *Journal of American Folklore* 46 (1933): 69–76.

Taft, William Howard. "Personal Aspects of the Presidency." *Saturday Evening Post* (28 February 1914): 6–7, 32.

Teit, James. Introduction. "Traditions of the Thompson River Indians." *Memoirs of the Folklore Society* 6 (1898): 1–10.

Tekpetey, Kwawisi. "The Trickster in Akan-Asante Oral Literature." *Asemka* 5 (1979): 78–82.

Test, George A. "The Club of Wits." *Thalia* 1 (1978): 71–75.

———. "The Roast: American Ritual Satire and Humor." In *Rituals and Ceremonies in Popular Culture,* edited by Ray B. Browne. Bowling Green: Bowling Green University Press, 1980.

Thalbitzer, William. *The Ammasilik Eskimo.* Copenhagen: Reitzel, 1923.

———. "Language and Folklore." *The Ammasilik Eskimo: Contributions to the Ethnology of East Greenland Natives.* Vol. 40: 166 ff. Copenhagen: B. Luno, 1923.

Theroux, Alexander. "Do Not Print This Letter: Hating My Hate Mail." *Harpers* 276 (January 1988): 170–73.

Thomas, Keith. *Man and the Natural World: A History of Modern Sensibility.* New York: Pantheon, 1983.

Thomas, William I. *Primitive Behavior: An Introduction to the Social Sciences.* New York: McGraw-Hill, 1937.

Thompson, Hunter. *Fear and Loathing: On the Campaign Trail '72.* San Francisco: Straight Arrow, 1973.

Tilton, John W. *Cosmic Satire in the Contemporary Novel.* Lewisburg: Bucknell University Press, 1977.

Timms, Edward. *Karl Kraus, Apocalyptic Satirist: Culture and Catastrophe in Hapsburg Vienna.* New Haven: Yale University Press, 1986.

Timpe, Eugene F. "Swift as Railleur." *Journal of English and Germanic Philology* 69 (1970): 41–49.

Toelkan, J. Barre. "The 'Pretty Language' of Yellowman: Genre, Mode, and Texture in Coyote Narrative." *Genre* 2 (1969): 211–35.

Topliss, Patricia. *The Rhetoric of Pascal: A Study of His Art of Persuasion in the "Provinciales" and the "Pensees."* Leicester: Leicester University Press, 1966.

Torrance, Robert M. *The Comic Hero.* Cambridge: Harvard University Press, 1978.

Triandis, Harry C., and William W. Lambert. "A Restatement and Test of Schlosberg's Theory of Emotion with Two Kinds of Subjects from Greece." *Journal of Abnormal and Social Psychology* 56 (1958): 321–28.

Trouard, Dawn. "Mary McCarthy's Dilemma: The Double Bind of Satiric Elitism." *Perspectives on Contemporary Literature* 7 (1981): 98–109.

Tucker, Samuel M. *Verse Satire in England.* 1908. New York: AMS Press, 1966.

Turner, Victor. "Comments and Conclusions." In *The Reversible World: Symbolic Inversion in Art and Society,* edited by Barbara A. Babcock. Ithaca: Cornell University Press, 1978.

———. "Myth and Symbol." In *International Encyclopedia of the Social Sciences,* edited by David L. Sills. New York: MacMillan & Free Press, 1968.

———. *The Ritual Process.* Chicago: University of Chicago Press, 1969.

———. "Variations on a Theme of Liminality." *Secular Ritual.* Papers originally presented at a conference entitled "Secular Rituals Considered," . . . 1974 at Burg Wartenstein, Austria. Edited by Sally F. Moore and Barbara G. Myerhoff. Assen: Van Gorcum, 1977.

Twain, Mark. "How to Tell a Story." *The Writings of Mark Twain.* Vol. 22. New York, 1898.

Tylor, Edward B. *Primitive Religion.* 1871. Reprinted as *Religion in Primitive Culture.* Introduction by Paul Radin. New York: Harper Torchbook, 1958.

Tyrrell, R. Emmett, Jr. *The Liberal Crack-up.* New York: Simon & Schuster, 1984.

United States. *Abusive and Harassing Telephone Calls, Hearings Before the Subcommittee on Communications of the Committee on Commerce.* U.S. Senate, 89th Congress, 1966, on S. 2825 and S. 3072.

Vailland, Roger. *The Law.* Translated by Peter Wiles. New York: Knopf, 1958.

Van Dam, Theodore. "The Influence of the West African Songs of Derision in the New World." *African Music* 7 (1954): 53–56.

Walsh, William S. *Curiosities of Popular Customs.* London, 1897.

Wannan, Bill. *With Malice Aforethought: Australian Insults, Invective, Ridicule and Abuse.* Melbourne: Lansdowne, 1973.

Warner, Maureen. "Some Yoruba Descendants in Trinidad." *African Studies Association of the West Indies* 3 (1970): 18–30.

Wasserman, George R. *Samuel "Hudibras" Butler.* Boston: Twayne, 1976.

Watt, Hugh. "Humanists." *Encyclopedia of Religion and Ethics.* Edited by James Hastings. New York: Scribner's, 1962.

Waugh, Evelyn. Interview. *Paris Review.* No. 30 (1963): 72–85.

Waugh, Patricia. *Metafiction: The Theory and Practice of Self-Conscious Fiction.* London: Methuen, 1984.

Weber, Harold. "'The Jester and the Orator': A Re-Examination of the Comic and the Tragic Satirist." *Genre* 13 (1980): 171–85.

Weisstein. Ulrich. "Parody, Travesty, and Burlesque: Imitation with a Vengeance." *Proceedings of the Fourth Congress of the International Literature Association.* Fribourg, 1964: 802–11.

Weitenkampf, Frank. "The Literary Hoax." *Boston Public Library Quarterly* 3 (1951): 202–9.

Wells, Carolyn. *A Parody Anthology*. 1904. New York: Dover, 1967.

Welsford, Enid. *The Fool: His Social and Literary History*. 1935. London: Faber, 1968.

Wertmuller, Lina. *The Screenplays of Lina Wertmuller*. Translated by Steven Wagner. New York: Quadrangle, 1977.

Wescott, Joan. "The Sculpture and Myths of Eshu-Elegha, The Yoruban Trickster." *Africa* 32 (1962): 336–54.

Wilhelm, J. J. *Seven Troubadours*. University Park: Penn State University Press, 1970.

Wilkins, Ernest Hatch. *A History of Italian Literature*. Cambridge: Harvard University Press, 1954.

Wilkinson, P. R. M. *The Comedy of Habit: An Essay on the Use of Courtesy Literature in a Study of Restoration Comic Drama*. Leiden: Universitaire Pers, 1964.

Willeford, William. *The Fool and His Sceptor*. Evanston: Northwestern University Press, 1969.

Wilson, John Harold. *Court Wits of the Restoration*. Princeton: Princeton University Press, 1948.

Windt, Theodore Otto. "The Diatribe: Last Resort of Protest." *Quarterly Journal of Speech* 58 (1972): 1–14.

Winokur, Jon. *The Portable Curmudgeon*. New York: New American Library, 1981.

Wittig, Kurt. *The Scottish Tradition in Literature*. Edinburgh: Oliver & Boyd, 1958.

Wolfenstein, Martha. *Children's Humor*. Glencoe: Free Press, 1954.

Worcester, David. *The Art of Satire*. Cambridge: Harvard University Press, 1940.

Yates, Norris. *The American Humorist: Conscience of the Twentieth Century*. Ames: University of Iowa Press, 1964.

Yunck, John. "The Two Faces of Parody." *Iowa English Yearbook* 8 (1963): 29–36.

Zijderveld, Anton C. *Reality in a Looking-Glass: Rationality through an Analysis of Traditional Folly*. London: Routledge, 1982.

Zohn, Harry. *Karl Kraus*. New York: Twayne, 1971.

INDEX